124 MWF 1000
Shurill

Study Guide To Accompay

WEST'S BUSINESS LAW TEXT & CASES

Prepared by
Barbara E. Behr
Department of Business
Bloomsburg State College

KENNETH W. CLARKSON
ROGER LeROY MILLER
BONNIE BLAIRE

WEST PUBLISHING CO.
St. Paul • New York • Los Angeles • San Francisco

Contents

Preface

The function of this Resource and Study Guide is to assist you in your efforts to grasp the fundamental principles of law developed in *West's Business Law: Text and Cases* by K. W. Clarkson, R. L. Miller and B. E. Blaire.

Students approaching the subject of business law tend to be overwhelmed because of the unfamiliar terms used and the apparently countless number of legal rules which they are expected to understand. This Resource and Study Guide highlights important concepts and terminology and provides a framework for structuring your studying. It is hoped that this structured approach will reduce anxiety and eliminate confusion. With this in mind, the materials in the Study Guide have been developed in order to give you a variety of learning tools so that you can do your studying in an organized fashion. It is assumed, of course, that you will be reading, studying and referring to the text and relevant appendixes while using these supplementary materials.

Included in the Resource and Study Guide you will find the following:

1. **Unit Summaries**—Brief overviews of the areas of law covered in each of the nine units.

2. **Chapter Introductions**—Short summaries of the topics covered in each of the 55 chapters. The introductions preview and tie together the concepts presented in more detail both in the text and the chapter outlines provided in this Study Guide.

3. **Things to Keep in Mind**—Reminders of important principles. A difficult concept may be clarified or reiterated; relevant principles, developed in earlier chapters, may be recalled; explanations may be given for terminology or items, the significance of which may have been overlooked.

4. **Chapter Outlines**—Detailed systematic reviews of legal principles presented in the text.

5. **Fill-In Questions**—The function of these questions is to enable you to determine whether or not you have become familiar with major and/or difficult concepts and important terminology. Answers to these questions are provided at the end of the book.

6. **Multiple Choice Questions**—Suitable for self-testing. The degrees of difficulty of the questions vary. Answers to the questions may be found at the end of the book.

I am indebted to Leon E. Behr, Esq., for his encouragement and his thorough and critical reading of the entire draft of the book.

Barbara E. Behr

UNIT I

The Legal Environment of Business

The purpose of the chapters in this unit is to furnish you with a foundation for your continued study of business law and to introduce you to what have become traditional topics for students in such courses, such as contracts (covered in Unit II) and commercial transactions (covered in Unit IV).

The first chapter is devoted to material dealing with philosophies and approaches to the law, sources and classifications of law. The second chapter gives an overview of the legal and court systems in the United States. The remaining chapters deal with particular areas of substantive law of importance to most people, including business-persons, those of torts and criminal law.

Introduction
to the Law

This introductory chapter will give you some insight into various approaches and philosophies concerning the concept of the law. It provides background, dealing with sources and origins of law in the United States, and contains explanations of some frequently used classifications of law.

THINGS TO KEEP IN MIND

Business law is a category of law, which includes a number of areas of substantive, private, civil law, dealing with relationships among parties engaging in commercial transactions.

An important function of law is that it provides certainty. Knowledge of legal principles is an aid in business decision making for, with such knowledge of existing rules of conduct, one can predict how others will behave in the future.

OUTLINE

I.   What is "The Law"?

   A. Traditional approach—Body of principles and rules that courts apply in deciding disputes. Emphasis is on the function of law to provide stability and certainty.

   B. Environmental approach—System of social control, which is part of the total environment of society. Emphasis is on the function of law to provide orderly process for social change and adaptability.

II. Schools of legal, or jurisprudential thought—Custom, history, logic and ideals have influenced the development of legal thought and decision making.

A. Natural law school—Moral ideal of what is right and wrong is source of law.

B. Historical school—Law develops from evolution of customs, which become accepted by society.

C. Analytical school—Laws are derived logically from general principles.

D. Legal realists school—Law is a means of serving desirable social needs.

III. Sources of American law.

A. Historical sources.

1. Much of law in the United States is derived from the English common law system, rules developed by judges, based on general principles established in previously decided cases.

2. Doctrine of *stare decisis*—To stand by or adhere to decisions in previously determined cases.

   a. Courts will use past decisions as precedents in adjudicating cases before them if they are based on similar fact situations.

   b. Results in stability and predictability.

   c. Occasionally, a previous decision will not be adhered to by a court.
      1) Legislation changed the prior rule.
      2) Changes in technology, business practices, society's attitudes, etc.
      3) Error made in prior case.
      4) Conflicting precedents.

B. Present sources of the law.

1. Constitutions.

   a. Federal Constitution.
      1) Supreme law of the land. Any statutory or common law that is contrary to the Constitution will not be enforced.
      2) Defines the powers and limitations of the federal government and the rights of the states and people.

   b. State constitutions—Are supreme within the jurisdiction of the state, if not in conflict with U.S. Constitution.

2. Statutes and ordinances—Enacted by legislative bodies.

3. Administrative agency regulations—Rulings, issued by state and federal commissions, boards, etc., having legislative, executive and/or judicial power.

4. Common law—Case law, which includes interpretation of constitutions and

legislation, in addition to decisions in disputes, in which there is no relevant codified law.

IV. The Uniform Commercial Code—A statute that has been adopted, at least in part, by all the states in the United States; a major source of law relating to business.

   A. The Law Merchant—Rules, based on commercial customs, developed before common law in England and incorporated into both common law and codified law in the United States.

   B. Codification of commercial law.

      1. National Conference of Commissioners on Uniform State Laws drafts proposals for uniform laws, which the state legislative bodies may adopt.

      2. Uniform Commercial Code—Does not change basic principles, but provides an internally consistent, modern body of clearly stated uniform rules relating to business transactions.

V. Classifications of law.

   A. Substantive versus procedural law.

      1. Substantive law—Defines legal relationships, rights and obligations.

      2. Procedural law—Method and means of enforcing substantive, legal rights.

      3. May be further classified, according to subject matter, for example, substantive law may be divided into agency, commerical paper, contracts, etc.

   B. Public versus private law.

      1. Public law—Law that affects relationships between individuals and their government and affects the interests of society.

         a. Constitutional law.

         B. Criminal law.

         c. Administrative law.

      2. Private law—Involves legal relationships among individuals.

   C. Civil versus criminal law.

      1. Civil law—Rules dealing with rights and duties between individuals.

      2. Criminal law—Wrongs committed against the public as a whole and proscribed by statute.

   D. Remedies in law versus remedies in equity.

1. Legal remedies provided historically by courts of law.

    a. Possession of land.

    b. Possession of items of value.

    c. Money as compensation.

2. Equitable relief when remedy at law was inadequate, unavailable or would result in hardship.

    a. Specific performance—A decree ordering a party to perform a particular act.

    b. Injunction—An order requiring a party to refrain from doing something.

FILL-IN QUESTIONS

1. Common law refers to rules of law that have been developed over time by _____
    _____ .

2. The body of law, which pertains to the relationship between individuals in an organized society, is termed *Private Law* ; the body of law, which pertains to the relationship between individuals and the government, is termed *Public Law*   .

3. Today, in the United States, sources of law would include _____
    _____ .

MULTIPLE CHOICE QUESTIONS

1. Generally speaking, precedents are rules of law established by:
    a. federal and state constitutions.
    b. legislatures.
    c. courts, in deciding cases arising in common law subjects.
    d. legislatures and courts.

2. A basic characteristic of case law is:
    a. statutes are derived from it.
    b. it establishes precedents for other courts to follow when a similar controversy is litigated.
    c. it eliminates the need to apply antiquated doctrines, such as *stare decisis*.
    d. all case law is codified.

3. The classification "private law" includes:
    a. criminal law
    b. administrative law.
    c. constitutional law.
    d. contract law.

4. A source of law in the legal system of the United States would include:
    a. the federal Constitution.
    b. state statutes.
    c. town ordinances.
    d. court decisions.
    e. all of the above.

5. Current principles of business law:
    a. are derived from the Law Merchant.
    b. are codified in the Uniform Commercial Code.
    c. have been developed in cases decided by state courts.
    d. all of the above.

6. Public law as contrasted with private law:
    a. involves legal relationships between individuals.
    b. involves legal relationships between society and individuals.
    c. includes only criminal law.
    d. includes procedural law and agency law.

7. Private law includes:
    a. constitutional and administrative law.
    b. contracts and property law.
    c. criminal and civil law.
    d. criminal and tort law.

8. In regard to actions in equity:
    a. the remedy that will be given may be an injunction.
    b. the remedy that will be given will be compensatory money damages.
    c. the distinction between law and equity has no relevance today.
    d. the court will not apply the doctrine of *stare decisis*.

Courts
and Procedures

As indicated in the previous chapter, an important source of law in the United States is case law—the rules of conduct, determined by judges, deciding cases that have been brought before them by parties involved in controversies. How cases get to appropriate courts so that the disputes can be adjudicated is the subject matter of this chapter. Usually the legal principles, which become part of the body of law with which business-persons will be concerned, have been established by appellate courts. Material in the chapter deals with the federal and state court systems, requirements for jurisdiction and judicial procedure.

THINGS TO KEEP IN MIND

Most issues between parties never reach the courts, many because parties recognize and perform their legal obligations. In addition, should a controversy arise between parties, it is often settled or solved without recourse to the courts.

OUTLINE

I. Jurisdiction—Power of a court to decide a case. A court must have jurisdiction over the subject matter and the person and/or property involved in the dispute. In addition, the controversy must have arisen within the territory, over which the court has jurisdiction and/or the parties to the litigation are available within that geographic area.

    A. General and special jurisdiction over the subject matter.

        1. General jurisdiction—A court with general jurisdiction has the power to hear all kinds of controversies.

        2. Special or limited jurisdiction—A court is limited in the types of cases it may hear and decide.

B. Jurisdiction over the person or the property.

    1. *In personam* jurisdiction over the parties involved in the lawsuit.

        a. The plaintiff submits to the court's jurisdiction by commencing his or her lawsuit.

        b. The court has jurisdiction over the defendant if he or she can be served within the territorial jurisdiction of the court, is a resident of the state or, if a corporation, is incorporated in, has an office or does business within the boundaries of the court's jurisdiction.

    2. *In rem* jurisdiction over property, which is the subject matter of the lawsuit.

C. Venue—A particular court has power to hear and decide a case only within a specified geographic area.

D. Original and appellate jurisdiction.

    1. Appellate jurisdiction—Court has power to review decisions rendered in other courts, based on the record.

    2. Original jurisdiction—Court has power to hear controversy when it is first brought for adjudication. (Trial court)

II. Hypothetical state court system.

A. Inferior trial courts with original, specialized, limited subject matter jurisdiction in either criminal or civil cases.

B. Trial courts of general jurisdiction.

C. Appellate courts with jurisdiction to review decisions of inferior courts, based on the record of the case only.

    1. Intermediate appellate courts.

    2. Courts of final appeal.

III. The federal court system.

A. Specialized courts with limited jurisdiction, created by Congress in accordance with power granted in the United States Constitution, such as Court of Claims (which hears cases brought against the United States), Tax Court, etc.

B. District Courts with general trial court jurisdiction.

C. Circuit Courts of Appeal with intermediate general appellate jurisdiction to review cases decided in District Courts and some inferior courts and administrative agencies.

D. Supreme Court has mainly only limited appellate jurisdiction, as provided by the United States Constitution.

IV. Jurisdiction of federal courts.

A. Established by Article III of the United States Constitution.

B. Controversies involving federal questions.

1. Federal courts may have exclusive jurisdiction as provided in the Constitution—Federal crimes, admiralty, bankruptcy, patents, copyrights, trademarks, etc.

2. Federal courts may have concurrent jurisdiction with state courts in civil suits.

a. Amount in controversy exceeds $10,000.

b. There is diversity of citizenship. For example, one or more of the parties are individuals, residing in different states, or corporations, incorporated or having their principal offices in a state different than that of another party to the controversy.

C. Cases which reach the Supreme Court.

1. Those in which a party has an absolute right to appeal. (For example, a case involving the constitutionality of a statute.)

2. Those which the Supreme Court determines it will hear following granting of *writ of certiorari.*

V. Judicial procedures: following a case through the courts.

A. Adversary nature of proceedings.

B. Parties—Litigants.

1. Plaintiff—Initiates proceedings.

2. Defendant—Party against whom action is brought.

C. Pleadings.

1. Complaint.

a. States facts upon which plaintiff bases his or her cause of action and the remedy sought.

b. Filed with clerk of court and served on defendant.

2. Answer—Filed by defendant.

    a. Defendant admits, denies or otherwise challenges the legal validity of the plaintiff's claim.

    b. Defendant may:
       1) Counterclaim—Set forth his or her own claim and cause of action.
       2) Raise affirmative defense—Give reason why plaintiff's action should be dismissed.

  3. Reply—Plaintiff may respond to issues raised in answer.

D. Pretrial procedures.

  1. Motion to dismiss (demurrer)—Defendant claims, as a matter of law, that the plaintiff has not stated a claim upon which relief can be granted.

  2. Motion for judgment on the pleadings—Either plaintiff or defendant claims that, based upon the pleadings, there is no issue requiring a trial.

  3. Motion for summary judgment—May be made by either party. No issue exists regarding the facts and the issue of law should, therefore, be decided by the judge.

  4. Discovery—Procedural devices to obtain information.

    a. Depositions—Sworn testimony given before and recorded by court official.

    b. Interrogatories—Answers to questions submitted in writing by one party, involved in the litigation, to the other party.

  5. Requests for admissions (written requests for admissions by one party to the other relating to matters involved in the case), documents, objects, etc.

  6. Physical and mental examinations—Subject to individual's right of privacy.

  7. Pretrial hearing or conference may be initiated by a party or the court.

E. Right to jury.

  1. Jurors are triers of facts; judge is trier of law.

  2. One's right to have a jury is limited.

    a. Case which is not based upon an equitable cause of action.

    b. States may limit right to jury.

  3. Jury may be waived.

F. The trial.

1. Opening statements by attorneys or parties.

2. Examination of witnesses. Direct, cross, redirect and recross.

3. Motion for directed verdict—judge is requested to enter verdict.

4. Charges to jury—Judge instructs jury on matters of law.

5. Judgment notwithstanding the verdict may be entered following motion made by party if decision is contrary to evidence.

G. Appeal.

1. Either or both parties may file notice of appeal with trial court and copies of pleadings, transcript, rulings on motions, arguments of attorneys, charge to jury, verdict, judgment and brief with appellate court.

2. Appellant—Party initiating appeal.

3. Appellee—Other party.

4. Reviewing court bases its decision on the record and the arguments of the party. It may affirm the lower court's decision, reverse it or remand the case, by returning it to the trial court for a new trial.

FILL-IN QUESTIONS

1. The power of a court to hear and decide a case is termed *Jurisdiction*.

2. Courts, which have power to hear most kinds of controversies, without regard to the subject matter, have _____ jurisdiction. A federal court, having such jurisdiction is _____. A federal court, such as _____, has limited or _____ jurisdiction, because it may hear only cases dealing with particular subject matters.

3. A court, having the power to review decisions rendered by other courts that have original jurisdiction, has _____ jurisdiction. A federal court, having such power is _____. In the federal court system, the _____ is a court with original, general jurisdiction.

4. The party initiating a legal proceeding is called the _____. He or she commences the action by _____.

5. In order to limit the issues of a case and to save time, the parties in a case may use pretrial procedures. For example, the defendant, who claims that the plaintiff has not stated a cause of action, upon which relief can be granted, will make a motion _____. Either party, desiring to preserve the testimony of a witness, who will be unable to appear in court, may request that _____.

MULTIPLE CHOICE QUESTIONS

1. A court, having original jurisdiction, would be the appropriate court in which to commence an action involving:
    a. the commission of a crime.
    b. a contract.
    c. a corporation.
    d. all of the above.

2. A court, having appellate jurisdiction, would be the appropriate court in which to commence an action involving:
    a. the commission of a crime.
    b. a contract.
    c. both of the above.
    d. none of the above.

3. A case, involving a resident of Pennsylvania and a resident of New York, may be commenced in:
    a. an appropriate Pennsylvania or New York court and then appealed as of right to the U.S. Circuit Court of Appeals.
    b. a federal district court, since there is diversity of citizenship.
    c. a federal district court if the amount in controversy exceeds $10,000.
    d. a federal Court of Appeals if the amount in controversy exceeds $10,000.

4. The United States Court of Claims is:
    a. a general trial court.
    b. a specialized court having limited jurisdiction.
    c. a court having jurisdiction over bankruptcy matters.
    d. an appellate court.

5. A litigant has a right to appeal from a decision rendered by a trial court:
    a. to a court having original jurisdiction.
    b. and on appeal he may cross examine witnesses.
    c. when an error as to a fact has been made.
    d. when an error as to law has been made.

6. In connection with a controversy brought to court, the term, "legal pleadings," refers to:
    a. the complaint filed by the plaintiff and the answer filed by the defendant.
    b. the reply filed by the defendant and complaint filed by the plaintiff.
    c. the trial of a case in a court, with or without a jury.
    d. the procedure required in order to appeal a case after a trial.

Torts

Torts are civil wrongs committed against the person or property of another. All torts involve a breach of duty, owed by the defendant to the plaintiff, which is the proximate cause of an injury incurred by the plaintiff. Conduct may be tortious because of an intentional act or because of a failure to exercise reasonable care. In some instances, strict tort liability is imposed without regard to fault.

THINGS TO KEEP IN MIND

If a plaintiff is alleging that a defendant was negligent, it is not necessary to show that the defendant's conduct was intentional. If liability is imposed because of strict liability, it is not necessary to establish the intent or negligence of the defendant.

OUTLINE

I. The scope of tort law.

    A. Unreasonable, wrongful conduct by one individual, resulting in injury to the person or property of another, for which the wrongdoer (tortfeasor) should compensate the injured party.

    B. Elements of a tort—As a result of the defendant's breach of a duty not to harm the plaintiff, the plaintiff is injured.

        1. Breach of duty.

            a. Duty owed by defendant.
               1) Private obligation, other than an obligation arising out of contract.

          2) Defendant owed duty of not unreasonably causing harm to the person or property of the plaintiff.
          3) Plaintiff has a reciprocal right not to be wrongfully injured.

    b. Breach of duty—Defendant violated the duty owed to plaintiff because of some act or omission, which was intentional or careless or abnormally dangerous.

  2. Injury to plaintiff.

    a. Plaintiff incurred some loss, harm, wrong to or invasion of a protected interest.

    b. It is not necessary that plaintiff be financially or physically harmed.

  3. Proximate causation—Plaintiff's injury was caused by defendant's breach of duty.

    a. Factual cause.
          1) Injury would not have occurred without the defendant's wrongful act of omission.
          2) Defendant's conduct was a substantial factor in causing the injury.

    b. Proximate or legal cause—Defendant's conduct was the immediate, forseeable, direct, rather than remote cause of plaintiff's injury.

II.   Intentional torts—Defendant intended to commit the tortious act.

  A. Wrongs against the person.

    1. Battery.

      a. Intentional act which brings about harmful or offensive contact.

      b. Defenses.
         1) Privilege or consent.
         2) Reasonable force to defend oneself or one's property.

    2. Assault.

      a. Threat by defendant to inflict immediate bodily harm to plaintiff, which creates a reasonable apprehension of harmful or offensive contact.

      b. Defenses—Privilege, self defense and defense of property.

    3. False imprisonment (false arrest).

      a. Intentional confinement of plaintiff.

      b. Present interference with freedom to move without restraint.

c. Merchant protection statutes permit reasonable detention of suspected shoplifter, if there is justified cause for suspicion.

d. Injury may be harm to reputation and mental distress.

4. Infliction of mental distress—Extreme, outrageous conduct, resulting in severe emotional stress.

5. Defamation—Harm to reputation and good name.

a. Publication of statement to or within hearing of others, which holds plaintiff up to contempt, ridicule or hatred.

b. Slander—False oral statement.

c. Libel—False written statement.

d. Defenses—Truth or privilege.

6. Invasion of right to privacy.

a. Use of plaintiff's name or picture without permission for commercial purposes.

b. Intrusion upon plaintiff's affairs or seclusion.

c. Public disclosure of private facts about plaintiff or information placing plaintiff in false light.

7. Fraud (and deceit).

a. False representation of fact.

b. Representation made by the defendant with knowledge of its falsity or reckless disregard of truth.

c. Defendant intended to induce plaintiff to change his or her position.

d. Plaintiff reasonably relied on the representation.

e. As a result of the misrepresentation, the plaintiff was damaged.

B. Wrongs against property.

1. Trespass to land—Wrongful interference with another's real property rights, even though there is no actual harm to the land.

2. Trespass to personal property—Defendant unlawfully injures or interferes with plaintiff's right to exclusive possession and enjoyment of personal property.

     3. Conversion—A wrongful taking and keeping of personal property to which one has no right.

     4. Nuisance—Improper use by defendant of his or her property so as to unreasonably interfere with the health, safety, comfort or right of another to enjoy his or her own property.

C. Business torts—Usually intentional torts.

     1. Slander of title and disparagement of goods—Publication of false statements concerning another's product, business or title to property.

     2. Defamation by computer—Erroneous information, relating to plaintiff's credit standing or business reputation, provided to third persons.

     3. Infringement of patents, copyrights, trademarks, etc.

     4. Unfair competition.

        a. Malicious injury to business—Defendant's use of abusive business practice, not for the purpose of making a profit or a fair legitimate business interest, but to interfere with or injure plaintiff's business relations.

        b. Combinations to divert trade—May also constitute violation of antitrust statutes.

     5. Interference with contractual relationships by inducing another to breach a contract that he or she has entered with someone else.

III. Negligence.

A. Unintentional failure to exercise reasonable care under the circumstances, so that a forseeable risk to another person is created, resulting in an injury to plaintiff.

B. Defenses.

     1. Supervening or intervening unforseen force was the cause of plaintiff's injury.

        a. Intervening force breaks the causal connection between defendant's carelessness and plaintiff's injury.

        b. A defendant is not relieved of liability if an intervening occurrence is foreseeable. It is considered to be forseeable that:
          1) One, who is tortiously personally injured, may develop a reaction or subsequent illness or accident or receive improper medical care.
          2) One, whose property is endangered, may be injured in an attempt to protect the property.

3) One, who is personally endangered, may take defensive action.

4) Rescuers may attempt to aid an imperiled victim and be harmed.

2. Assumption of the risk—Plaintiff, expressly or impliedly, knowingly and voluntarily places himself or herself in a situation involving risk.

3. Contributory and comparative negligence—Plaintiff's own negligence contributed to his or her own injury.

   a. Common law doctrine of contributory negligence—Plaintiff cannot recover from defendant at all.

   b. Comparative negligence doctrine has been adopted in about half the states. The amount of damages is apportioned between the plaintiff and defendant, based upon the relative fault of each of the parties.

IV. Strict liability—Liability without fault and without regard to defendant's intent or exercise of reasonable care.

A. Abnormally dangerous activities.

   1. The activity involves a high degree of risk, which cannot be completely guarded against even with the exercise of reasonable or extraordinary care.

   2. The risk is one of serious harm.

   3. The activity is one that is not commonly performed in the geographic area.

B. Employers are strictly liable to their employees for injuries sustained in the ordinary course of their employment under the workmen's compensation statutes. See Chapter 35.

C. Employers and principals are strictly liable for torts committed by employees and agents, acting within the ordinary course of their employment. See Chapter 35.

D. Manufacturers of product are held strictly liable for damages caused by their products in many states. See Chapter 21.

FILL-IN QUESTIONS

1. In order to recover in an action based on tort, a plaintiff must establish that the elements of a tort were present. In other words, plaintiff must show that _____ _____.

2. Some torts are intentional torts because the defendant intended to commit a particular act. Intentional torts, such as defamation and battery are wrongs against the _____; others, such as trespass and conversion are wrongs against _____.

3. Business torts are usually intentional torts and include disparagement of goods, which means _____ and unfair competition, such as _____ .

4. A person is liable for the tort of negligence, if he or she causes an injury to the person or property of another because of a failure to exercise the care that a reasonable person would exercise. There are, however, defenses, which can be raised by a defendant in an action based on negligence. Such defenses include

    _____ .

MULTIPLE CHOICE QUESTIONS

1. A tort action may be based upon:
    a. negligence.
    b. an intentionally caused injury.
    c. strict liability.
    d. all of the above.

2. The following is a tort:
    a. a breach of duty owed by one person to another, which produces an injury when the one who breaches the duty did not actually know that he or she owed a duty.
    b. a breach of duty owed by one person to another, which was provided for by a contract so that he or she knew that a duty was owed to the other party.
    c. a crime that results in no injury to another party, such as "running a stop sign" when no other car or person is in the vicinity.
    d. all of the above.

3. If John punches Tim without provocation, John has committed:
    a. an assault.
    b. an assault and a battery.
    c. a nuisance.
    d. negligence.

4. Mr. House's home was destroyed by a fire that had been caused by Pyro when he knocked over a kerosene heater that House had placed in front of the entrance to his home.
    a. Pyro can successfully raise the defense of contributory or comparative negligence if he is sued for negligence.
    b. Pyro can successfully raise the defense of assumption of the risk if he is sued for an intentional tort.
    c. Pyro is strictly liable for the tort of arson.
    d. Pyro is not liable for the tort of trespass if House invited him into his home and House did not incur a personal injury.

Questions 5 and 6 are based on the following fact situation: Donna was driving in an erratic manner on an interstate highway at a speed of 76 miles per hour when observed by State policemen, who put on their siren and sped after her. Donna became flustered when she realized that the police were trying to stop her. She carelessly put pressure on the accelerator, rather than the brake, causing her car to collide with that of

Victoria. As a result, Victoria's property was damaged and Victoria suffered personal injuries.

5. Victoria may successfully sue:
   a. the policemen, who are strictly liable for the personal injuries suffered by Victoria.
   b. both the policemen and Donna for false imprisonment because Victoria was unable to extricate herself from the wreckage for ten minutes.
   c. Donna, who as a result of her failure to exercise reasonable care, caused both property damage and personal injuries.
   d. Donna, who as a result of her failure to exercise reasonable care, is liable for the property damage but not personal injuries.

6. If Victoria sues Donna, Donna may:
   a. successfully raise the defense of comparative negligence (or contributory negligence) if Victoria was also speeding and driving in an erratic manner.
   b. successfully raise the defense of supervening cause because it was forseeable that if she was speeding, she would be apprehended by the police.
   c. successfully raise the defense of assumption of the risk because one who drives on an interstate highway assumes the risk of injury.
   d. not raise any defenses because her conduct was the basis for Victoria's suit based on an intentional tort.

7. Sterling, in order to induce Luton to lend him $1,000, which he promised to repay, told Luton that he was the owner of a money making machine but needed funds to purchase paper. Luton has not been repaid and brings a lawsuit against Sterling based on tort.
   a. Luton's contributory negligence will prevent him from recovery for an intentional tort.
   b. Luton will not be able to recover for the tort of fraud because his reliance on the representation made by Sterling was unreasonable.
   c. Luton will not be able to recover for the tort of fraud because Sterling's representation did not result in any injury to Luton.
   d. Luton will be able to recover for the tort of interference with a contractual relationship.

Criminal Law

Crimes are wrongful acts committed against society and prosecuted by the government. The elements of each specific crime are defined by statute. Usually, a crime consists of an act, or omission, in conjunction with criminal intent. In some instances, a person, having a valid defense, may be excused from or relieved of criminal responsibility. Under our system of laws too, one accused of a crime is afforded certain safeguards by the federal and state constitutions.

THINGS TO KEEP IN MIND

One act may be both criminally and civilly wrongful. The state is a party in the criminal prosecution; the injured party is the plaintiff in the civil action based on tort. If the accused is found guilty of the crime beyond a reasonable doubt, he or she will be punished. If a defendant is found, by a preponderance of evidence, to have committed a tort, he or she will be required to compensate the plaintiff, who was injured by the tortious conduct.

OUTLINE

I. Nature of crime.

    A. Crimes are public wrongs that are defined by statute and prosecuted by the government on behalf of society. Those, who are found guilty of committing crimes, are punished normally by imprisonment and/or a fine, in accordance with the criminal statutes.

    B. Classification of crimes based upon their seriousness.

       1. Treason.

      2. Felonies—Punishable by death or imprisonment for more than one year.

      3. Misdemeanors—Punishable by imprisonment for less than one year and/or a fine.

      4. Offenses—Punishable by a fine and possibly brief imprisonment.

II. Essentials of criminal liability—Most crimes consist of a combination of a prohibited act and a specific criminal intent.

    A. Prohibited act—The particular criminal behavior for each crime is defined by statute. It may be an act or omission.

    B. State of mind—Criminal intent or state of mind is required for most crimes. It may be based on purpose, knowledge and awareness, recklessness or negligence or inferred for one is presumed to intend the proximate and natural consequences of his or her own acts.

III. Defenses to criminal liability—Conditions that relieve a defendant of liability may exist. A criminal defendant may show that he or she did not commit the crime of which he or she has been accused because he or she did not commit the specific act or did not have the requisite intent. Some other defenses are:

    A. Infancy—Most states have statutes providing that certain minors are treated as lacking the necessary moral sense to be capable of knowing right from wrong. There is, however, great variety among the states.

    B. Intoxication.

      1. Involuntary intoxication is a defense to a crime, if the perpetrator was unable to understand that the act committed was wrong.

      2. Voluntary intoxication is a defense only if it prevented the perpetrator from having the necessary intent.

    C. Insanity—Different standards are applied among the states.

      1. Perpetrator lacked capacity to "appreciate the wrongfulness" of his or her conduct or to conform his or her "conduct to the requirements of the law."

      2. The person accused of a crime did not appreciate the nature of the act or know that it was wrong.

      3. The person committed the criminal act because of an "irresistible impulse."

    D. Mistake—Generally ignorance or mistake of law is no excuse.

    E. Consent.

      1. If the presence of consent cancels the harm that is intended to be prevented, consent is a defense.

2. Some crimes are forbidden without regard to a victim's consent, in which case, consent is not a defense.

F. Duress—Threat of imminent serious bodily harm, which is greater than the harm committed by the person accused of a crime.

G. Justifiable use of reasonably necessary force.

1. Self defense.

2. Defense of dwelling or other property.

H. Entrapment—Law enforcement officer encourages or induces criminal acts in order to apprehend criminal.

I. Statute of limitations—Statutes restrict prosecution after expiration of a stated period of time.

J. Immunity or agreement to prosecute for a less serious offense may be given by the state in exchange for information.

IV. Criminal procedure.

A. Constitutional safeguards—Most of the guarantees, found in Amendments to the United States Constitution, apply to the states as well as the federal government by virtue of the Fourteenth Amendment. State constitutions contain similar provisions.

1. Fourth Amendment—Protection against unreasonable searches and seizures and prohibition against issuance of warrants without probable cause.

2. Fifth Amendment—Prohibits self incrimination and double jeopardy; guarantees due process.

3. Sixth Amendment—Guarantees speedy, public trail by jury, right to be informed of charges, confront the accused, subpoena witnesses and assistance of an attorney.

4. Eighth Amendment—Prohibits excessive bail and fine and cruel and unusual punishment.

B. Criminal process.

1. Arrest—A warrant, based upon a showing of probable cause that the accused committed the crime, is required unless probable cause reasonably justifies an immediate arrest.

2. Indictment—Issued by a grand jury or an information issued by a magistrate. The effect is to formally charge a defendant with a specified crime or crimes.

3. Trial—The state must prove guilt beyond a reasonable doubt.

V. Crimes involving and affecting business.

A. Forgery—Fraudulent making or material alteration of an instrument so as to change the liability of another.

B. Robbery—Unlawful taking of property with force.

C. Burglary—Breaking and entering with intent to commit a felony.

D. Larceny—Unlawful taking without force.

E. Embezzlement—Fraudulent conversion of property or money.

F. Arson—Willful, malicious burning of a building (and in some states, personal property) of another.

G. Obtaining goods by false pretenses.

H. Receiving stolen goods.

I. Use of mails to defraud—Federal crime.

J. Corporate criminal liability—A corporation is liable for crime if the penalty provided by statute is a fine and intent is not an element of the crime or intent may be inferred.

FILL-IN QUESTIONS

1. A crime is a public ___wrong___, which is defined by statute and prosecuted by ___state___.

2. In order to be found guilty of a specific crime, one must have ___comitted specified act or act of Omission___ with the requisite specified criminal state of mind or intent. Criminal intent may be based upon ___purpose Knowledge + awareness___.

3. If an accused person can show that he or she committed a criminal act while insane or because of duress, he or she has a valid ___defense___, which relieves him or her of criminal responsibility.

4. An accused person is protected against ___unreasonable search + seizure___ by the Fourth Amendment and against ___Excessive Bail + cruel unusual punishment___ by the Eighth Amendment of the United States Constitution.

5. Prohibitions against the issuance of a warrant without probable cause are provided by the Fourth Amendment and prohibitions against ___self incrimination___ by the Fifth.

6. The Sixth Amendment guarantees one accused of a crime ___Speedy trial, trial by jury, confront accusers, assistance of attorney___.

MULTIPLE CHOICE QUESTIONS

1. A crime is considered to be a felony if it is:
    a. a federal offense.
    b. punishable by death or imprisonment for more than a year.
    c. punishable by a fine or imprisonment for less than a year.
    d. so stated by the grand jury in its indictment.

2. Least serious crimes are referred to as:
    a. felonies.
    b. misdemeanors.
    c. civil wrongs.
    d. torts.

3. One act may be the basis for more than one crime. For example, if C breaks into V's home, while V is away, and steals a television set, C may be found guilty of the crimes of:
    a. burglary and robbery.
    b. arson and misrepresentation.
    c. burglary and larceny.
    d. arson and larceny.

4. One act may be the basis for a criminal prosecution by the state and a civil lawsuit by the victim. For example, if an employee takes $600 from his employer's cash register, without the knowledge or permission of his employer, he may be sued by the employer for the tort of:
    a. conversion and prosecuted for the crime of embezzlement.
    b. conversion and prosecuted for the crime of robbery.
    c. larceny and prosecuted for the crime of burglary.
    d. fraud and prosecuted for the crime of deceit.

5. Jones shot and wounded Smith. Jones may:
    a. be charged with homicide or murder if her mental state was such that she premeditatedly intended to kill Smith.
    b. be charged with a crime but not sued civilly by Smith.
    c. not be found guilty if she establishes that she had reasonable justification.
    d. not be found guilty if she establishes that Smith consented to be shot.

6. A policeman stopped a college student, who was running down the street with a smoking revolver in his hand, searched and arrested him without first having obtained a warrant:
    a. The absolute right to be free from a search and seizure has been violated.
    b. The right to be free from an unreasonable search and seizure has been violated if an indictment had not been previously issued by a grand jury or an information issued by a magistrate.
    c. The right to be free from an unreasonable search and seizure has been violated.
    d. The right to be free from an unreasonable search and seizure has not been violated even if a warrant had not been previously obtained from a court.

UNIT II

Contracts

The objective of Unit II is to help you understand concepts of contract law, which is the foundation upon which other areas of law relating to business are superimposed. The law of contracts deals with promises that have been made by parties who voluntarily have entered into private agreements, or contracts. Contracts create expectations that the parties to them will act in an agreed manner. Contract law provides the framework for assuring that those expectations will be realized or remedies provided if they are not.

In the chapters in this unit you will be learning about the rules that have been adopted relating to the rights and duties of the parties to such agreements, how contracts are formed and discharged and what happens when parties fail to carry out the promises that they have made.

Nature, Form and Terminology

Rights and duties of parties to agreements are created when the parties make promises in contracts. Usually contractual promises are executed by the parties so that recourse to the courts is not necessary. Contract law is the body of legal rules that relate to the formation, discharge and breach of legally enforceable promises. In order to understand contract law, it is important that you become familiar with some basic concepts and terminology.

THINGS TO KEEP IN MIND

1. Not all promises that are made will be enforced by the courts.
2. Contracts may be oral, written or inferred from conduct.

OUTLINE

I. Basic concepts underlying contract law.

    A. Freedom of contract and freedom from contract—In general, one may freely enter into any contract unless it is contrary to law or public policy.

    B. Elements of contracts—In order to have a contract certain requisites must be present.

        1. Agreement.

        2. Consideration.

        3. Contractual capacity.

        4. Legality.

5. Genuineness (or reality) of assent.

6. Form.

II. Nature and types of contracts.

A. Definition of a contract—An agreement made by two or more parties, containing a promise or set of promises to perform or refrain from performing some act or acts, which will be enforced by a court.

B. Types of contracts.

1. Express and implied-in-fact contracts.

    a. Express contract—The terms of the agreement are stated in words used by the parties.

    b. Implied-in-fact contract—The terms of the agreement are inferred from the conduct of the parties.

    c. The parties must objectively have the intention of entering a contract.

2. Bilateral and unilateral contracts.

    a. Bilateral contract—Reciprocal promises exchanged by parties, i.e., the promise of one party is exchanged for the promise of the other.

    b. Unilateral contract—Promise exchanged for actual performance, i.e., the promise of one party is exchanged for the other party's actually performing or refraining from performing some act (forbearance).

3. Executed and executory contracts.

    a. Executed contract—Contract that has been completely performed.

    b. Executory contract—Contract that has not been fully performed by one or more of the parties.

4. Valid, void, voidable and unenforceable contracts.

    a. Valid contract—All elements of a contract are present.

    b. Void contract—Agreement has no legal effect. (It is really not a contract.)

    c. Voidable contract—One of the parties has the option of avoiding his or her contractual obligations.

    d. Unenforceable contract—Contract that cannot be proven in the manner required by law.

5. Formal and informal contracts.

   a. Formal contract—Some formality is prescribed for its creation.
      1) Contract under seal.
      2) Recognizance.
      3) Negotiable instrument or letter of credit.

   b. Informal contract—Simple contract, for which no special form is required.

6. Quasi contracts—Contracts implied-in-law—Equity imposes a duty to pay reasonable value for a benefit received in order to avoid unjust enrichment. It is not really a contract but an equitable principle.

FILL-IN QUESTIONS

1. A contract is a legal relationship created when *2 or More* competent, consenting parties agree to perform or refrain from performing a legal act.

2. The elements of a contract are *Agreement By Two or More Competent Parties whose apparent Assent to Same terms is Real + Genuine supported By valid legal Consideration in The form Required By law + having a legal purpose and subject matter*.

3. When words are used to create and define the terms of a contract, the parties have formed *Express* contract; when the parties have used conduct, rather than words, they have entered into *Implied in fact* contract.

4. A *Bilateral* contract consists of reciprocal promises; a unilateral contract consists of an exchange of a promise for *Performance of forbearance*.

5. Contracts under seal, recognizances and negotiable instruments are characterized as *formal* contracts. Other contracts are referred to as simple or *informal* contracts. Most contracts are *informal*.

MULTIPLE CHOICE QUESTIONS

1. An implied-in-fact contract can be defined as one:
   a. which lacks one or more elements of a true contract, but which may nevertheless be enforced by the courts if it is in the best interests of the parties to do so.
   b. which is formed entirely without the use of words.
   c. in which the intentions of the contracting parties are inferred by the courts in large part from their conduct and surrounding circumstances.
   d. in which the intentions of the contracting parties are expressed with the use of words.

2. A unilateral contract:
    a. is a promise to perform an act.
    b. consists of mutual promises to act.
    c. consists of a promise to act exchanged for performance of an act.
    d. is one that is binding on one of the parties only.

3. A bilateral contract exists if:
    a. a promise to perform is exchanged for performance.
    b. a promise to forbear is exchanged for performance.
    c. a promise to perform is exchanged for a promise to forbear.
    d. performance is exchanged for forbearance.

4. A says to B, "I will pay you $10 if you change the flat tire on my car." B changes the flat tire.
    a. A unilateral contract is created so that A must pay B $10.
    b. A bilateral contract is created so that A must pay B $10.
    c. A formal contract is created so that A must pay B $10.
    d. No enforceable contract results.

5. G says to H, "If you promise to paint my car, I promise to pay you $100." H says, "It's a deal; I promise to paint the car." This creates:
    a. an express unilateral contract.
    b. an express bilateral contract.
    c. an implied-in-fact unilateral contract.
    d. an implied-in-fact bilateral contract.

6. An executed contract:
    a. involves more than two parties.
    b. will be enforced unless one of the parties elects to disaffirm it.
    c. is yet to be completely performed.
    d. has been completely performed.

7. An executory contract:
    a. has been completely performed.
    b. is yet to be completely performed.
    c. will not be recognized as enforceable by the courts.
    d. is illegal and will not be enforced by the courts.

8. An agreement to commit arson by burning down a building is an example of a:
    a. valid, enforceable contract.
    b. voidable express contract.
    c. voidable implied-in-law contract.
    d. void, unenforceable contract.

9. V requests and accepts the services of A, an accountant, without agreeing to pay a specified fee therefor. As to the compensation which A is to receive, there is:
    a. a formal contract.
    b. an express contract.
    c. an implied-in-fact contract.
    d. an implied-in-law contract.

10. An implied-in-law contract can be defined as one:
    a. that is the same as an implied-in-fact contract.
    b. in which one of the parties would be unjustly enriched even though he or she had not consented to the conferring of a benefit.
    c. in which the intentions of one or all of the parties is inferred from their conduct and surrounding circumstances rather than words.
    d. which has been fully performed by all of the parties.

6

Agreement

In order to have a contract there must be an agreement. The parties, the offeror and the offeree, must indicate their present, objective willingness and intention to assent to the same terms regarding their respective rights and duties. Their assent is evidenced by the process of offer and acceptance. An offer must have been made by the offeror and an acceptance given by the offeree.

THINGS TO KEEP IN MIND

The parties may contemplate either:

1. A unilateral contract—Actual performance of an act or actual forbearance exchanged for a promise to act or refrain from acting; OR

2. A bilateral contract—A promise to act or a promise to refrain from acting in exchange for a promise to act or forbear.

OUTLINE

I. Manifestation of apparent mutual assent by parties to agreement.

    A. Objective assent—Law recognizes only present, objective intent of the parties, which they have manifested by such words or conduct as would indicate to a reasonable person an intention to be bound.

    B. Terms.

        1. Material, essential terms—Identification of parties, the subject matter and price.

        2. Incidental terms.

II. The offer—The offeror shows his or her assent when he or she communicates a proposal, the offer, to the offeree, setting forth with reasonable clarity, definiteness and certainty the material terms to which he is presently, objectively agreeing and intending to be bound.

A. Objective intent manifested by offeror.

    1. The words and/or conduct used by the offeror must be such that a reasonable person would be warranted, under the circumstances, in believing that a real agreement was intended by the offeror.

    2. It is necessary to distinguish offers from:

        a. Expressions of opinion.

        b. Preliminary negotiations and invitations soliciting offers.

        c. Statements of intention.

        d. Advertisements, catalogues, circulars, price lists.

        e. Other non-offer situations.
           1) Requests for bids, auctions.
           2) Social invitations.
           3) Agreements to agree.
           4) Sham transactions.

B. Material terms clear, definite and certain—All of the material, essential terms must be stated in the offer with clarity, definiteness and certainty or a method stated by which the terms will be made certain.

    1. The offeror may provide that one or more of the terms will be made more definite by reference to an outside standard or third person.

    2. Material terms.

        a. The subject matter.
           1) Property to be sold.
           2) Services to be performed.
           3) Sum of money to be borrowed.

        b. The price.
           1) Reasonable price if price not fixed but a party fully performs.
           2) Refer to outside standard or appraiser.
           3) Open price terms (U.C.C. Sec. 2-305).

        c. The quantity.
           1) Requirements and output contracts (U.C.C. Sec. 2-306).
           2) Exclusive dealings contracts.

C. Communication of offer—The terms of the offer must be received by the offeree.

1. Offeree must have knowledge of all the material terms of the offer.

2. Offer to specific offeree.

3. Public offers.

D. Termination of offer.

    1. By operation of law.

        a. Lapse of time.
          1) Duration stated in offer.
          2) No duration specified in offer.

        b. Destruction of the subject matter.

        c. Death or adjudication of insanity of a party.

        d. Supervening illegality.

    2. By action of the parties.

        a. Revocation by offeror.
          1) Revocation must be communicated to offeree. (It must, therefore, be received by the offeree.)
          2) Offer to specific offeree.
          3) Public offers.
          4) Irrevocable offers.
             a) Common law option contracts—Consideration must be given to offeror by offeree.
             b) Statutory "firm offers"—A writing signed by the offeror is necessary.
             c) Distinguish from provisions in offer that acceptance is to be given prior to a specified date.
          5) Offers to unilateral contracts.

        b. Rejection by offeree.
          1) Rejection must be communicated to offeror.
          2) Counter-offer constitutes a rejection.
          3) Inquiry by offeree distinguished from rejection.

III. Acceptance—The offeree accepts the offer when he unequivocally manifests his assent to the terms of the offer.

A. Requisites.

    1. Offeree has knowledge of the terms of the offer.

    2. Offeree's overt conduct manifests willingness and intention to be bound.

    3. Offeree complies with conditions, if any, stated in offer. (Acceptance must be in the proper manner, at the proper place and at the proper time.)

4. Acceptance must be by the party to whom the offer was directed.

5. Acceptance must positively, unequivocally accord to the terms of the offer.

B. Manner of acceptance.

1. If bilateral contract contemplated, offeree makes a promise.

2. If unilateral contract contemplated, offeree performs required act or forbears from acting.

3. Silence generally will not be considered to be an acceptance unless:

a. There was a similar prior course of dealings, or

b. The offeree accepted the benefits, or

c. The offeree exercised dominion over the subject matter.

C. Effective moment of acceptance.

1. If unilateral contract contemplated, acceptance is effective when performance or forbearance is completed.

2. If bilateral contract contemplated, acceptance is effective when offeree gives the requisite promise. (Usually this is when the acceptance is sent so that it is out of the offeree's control, even if the acceptance is not received by the offeror.)

a. If the manner of acceptance is specified by the offeror:
    1) Acceptance is effective when sent in the manner authorized by the offeror.
    2) Acceptance is not effective until received by the offeror if the acceptance is sent in an unauthorized manner.

b. If the manner of acceptance is not specified by the offeror, acceptance is effective when sent, if it is sent by the same means of communication as was used for communicating the offer or any customary or reasonable means of communicating.

3. Offeror may include a condition in the offer that acceptance will not be effective until it is received by the offeror.

4. A contract is created at the moment that the acceptance is effective.

FILL-IN QUESTIONS

1. An essential element of a contract is mutual assent of the parties to the same terms of the agreement, which is evidenced when the offeror communicates a _proposal_ to the offeree, who _accepts_ the offeror's terms.

2. Material terms, which must be clearly stated in an offer, include *subject*, *price + quantity.*

3. If an offeror has the power to terminate an offer before it has been accepted, one may say that the offeror has the power of *communication*.

4. A communication from the offeree to the offeror, setting forth different terms than those contained in the original offer, is considered to be a *counter offer*.

5. An offer is terminated by operation of law if *lapse of time, destruction of property, death or adjudication, supervening illegality* or *no duration specified in offer*.

MULTIPLE CHOICE QUESTIONS

1. The following advertisement appeared in a newspaper:

    "Brand new bicycles. Worth up to $100. Our price $25. Limited number available."

    This would be considered to be:
    a. an invitation to make an offer.
    b. an offer to a unilateral contract.
    c. an offer to a bilateral contract.
    d. an offer in the alternative.

2. B and S have evidenced an agreement by signing a paper containing the terms of the agreement. It provides that S will sell and B will buy all of the corn grown on S's farm in the coming year at a price to be agreed upon by B and S.
    a. As the quantity is not stated, this is not a contract.
    b. As the price and quantity are not stated, this is not a contract.
    c. If the parties do not agree to the price for the corn before it is delivered and S delivers the corn, B will have to pay the reasonable price for the corn on the date of delivery.
    d. If the parties do not agree to the price for the corn before it is delivered, there is no contract.

3. The ABC Auto Sales Co. sent the following telegram to Ford Motor Company:

    "We need ten automobiles as soon as possible. Ship to ABC Auto Sales Co."

    a. The telegram contains an offer.
    b. Acceptance by Ford Motor Company will not take place until receipt of the automobiles by ABC Auto Sales Co.
    c. The telegram is too indefinite and uncertain to constitute an offer.
    d. The telegram creates a contract.

4. When goods are placed on sale at an ordinary auction, a contract is formed at the moment that:
    a. the auctioneer shows the goods.
    b. the highest bid is made.
    c. the auctioneer brings down his hammer.
    d. the highest bidder pays for the goods.

5. A communication by the offeree setting forth different terms than those contained in the original offer is considered to:
    a. be a rejection.
    b. result in a binding contract.
    c. keep the original offer open.
    d. create a unilateral contract.

6. An outstanding offer to sell a tract of real property is terminated at the time the:
    a. buyer mails a rejection of the offer if the original offer was sent by mail.
    b. buyer learns of the sale of the property to a third person.
    c. buyer learns of the seller's death.
    d. seller mails a revocation of the original offer if the offer was sent by mail.

7. John writes a letter to Bill in which he offers to sell his motorcycle to Bill for $1,000. John may revoke his offer:
    a. after the expiration of one week.
    b. at any time before Bill sends an acceptance.
    c. at any time before John receives an acceptance from Bill.
    d. at no time because the offer is in writing.

8. If no time is specified by the offeror as to when an offer will terminate, the offer lapses after the expiration of a reasonable period of time, which depends on:
    a. the nature of the subject matter.
    b. the period of time within which the offeror's purpose can be effected.
    c. the prior course of dealings of the parties.
    d. all of the above.

9. An offer is terminated:
    a. by the expiration of a reasonable period of time although a specified period of duration is stated in the offer.
    b. by the expiration of a reasonable period of time when no specified period of duration is stated in the offer.
    c. when it is not rejected by the offeree.
    d. within a reasonable period of time after the offeror and offeree separate if the offer had been oral.

10. In order to be effective, if the United States mails are used:
    a. an offer must be received by an offeree and a rejection sent by an offeree.
    b. an offer must be received by an offeree and a revocation received by an offeror.
    c. an acceptance must be received by an offeror and a revocation received by an offeree.
    d. an acceptance must be sent by an offeree and a revocation received by an offeree.

Consideration

In order for a contractual promise to be legally enforceable, it must be supported by sufficient legal consideration so that there is a bargained for exchange. In general, the party making the promise, the promisor, must be receiving a legal benefit (something which he or she does not already have a right to receive) or the promisee, the party to whom the promise is made, must be incurring a legal detriment (giving up something which he or she has a legal right to keep) or both.

THINGS TO KEEP IN MIND

The issue of lack of consideration arises when a promisee sues a promisor, who has failed to carry out a promise and who raises the defense that the promise was unenforceable because he or she received nothing in exchange for the promise.

OUTLINE

I. The concept of consideration.

    A. Parties to a contract.

        1. Promisor—The party who makes a promise to do or refrain from doing something.

        2. Promisee—The party who receives a promise.

        3. If, as in the diagram below, a unilateral contract is contemplated, only one party (A) is the promisor. The other party (B) is the promisee.

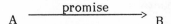

$$A \xrightarrow{\text{promise}} B$$

43

4. If, as in the diagram below, a bilateral contract is contemplated, promises are exchanged by the parties. Each party is, therefore, a promisor as to the promise he makes and a promisee as to the promise he receives. Each promise must be supported by consideration.

$$A \xrightarrow[\text{promise made by B}]{\text{promise made by A}} B$$

B. There must be a presently bargained for exchange between the parties. Consideration may be thought of as the "price" paid by the promisee for a promise so that mutual obligations are present.

$$A \xrightarrow[\text{bargained for "price" = consideration}]{\text{promise}} B$$

C. Legally sufficient consideration exists when either the promisee incurs a legal detriment or the promisor receives a legal benefit or both.

1. Legal detriment to promisee—The promisee must:

a. Actually give up something he or she has a legal right to keep (unilateral contract), as in the diagram below, or

$$A \xrightarrow[\text{actual performance = consideration}]{\text{promise}} B$$

b. Actually refrain or forbear from doing something he or she has a legal right to do (unilateral contract), as in the diagram below, or

$$A \xrightarrow[\text{actual forbearance = consideration}]{\text{promise}} B$$

c. Promise to surrender something he or she has a legal right to retain (bilateral contract), as in the diagram below, or

$$A \xrightarrow[\text{promise to perform = consideration}]{\text{promise}} B$$

d. Promise to forbear from doing something he or she has a right to do (bilateral contract) as in the diagram below.

$$A \xrightarrow[\text{promise to forbear = consideration}]{\text{promise}} B$$

2. Legal benefit to promisor—The promisor receives something to which he or she is not entitled, but for the contract.

3. It is not necessary that an economic or material loss be incurred by the promisee or benefit received by the promisor. All that is necessary is a surrender or receipt of a legal right.

II.   Adequacy of consideration—Because of the doctrine of freedom of contract, the relative value of consideration given by contracting parties is not examined by courts unless:

A. It is evidence that assent of one party was not genuine.

B. The consideration received by one party was grossly inadequate (equitable principle).

C. No consideration was given.

1. Past or moral consideration, "love and affection."

2. Performance of a pre-existing duty imposed by law or owed because of an existing contract.

3. Performance of an illegal act.

4. Illusory promise—A promise that appears to be a promise but is not really an undertaking to do anything.

III. Special situations involving consideration.

A. Settlement of debts.

1. A promise to pay or actual payment of part of a mature, liquidated, undisputed debt is not consideration for creditor's release of balance.

2. Parties may settle if:

a. Debt is disputed.

b. Obligation to pay is not yet due.

c. Amount owed is not liquidated (a sum certain).

d. Other or additional consideration is given.

e. Creditor's promise to release debtor is in a signed writing.
1) U.C.C. Sec. 1-107.
2) Model Written Obligations Act.

B. Construction contracts—A promise to pay additional compensation for construction is sometimes enforceable if unknown, unanticipated, unforeseen difficulties arise which greatly increase the burden of performance.

C. Output and requirements contracts.

D. Exclusive dealings contracts.

IV. Promises enforceable without consideration.

A. In past, consideration was not necessary if instrument was under seal.

B. Doctrine of Promissory Estoppel—Promisor, in some states only, will not be able to plead lack of consideration if:

1. A promise is made to induce a promisee to act in a particular way,

2. The promisor can foresee that the promisee will justifiably rely upon the promise,

3. The promisee substantially changes his or her position and incurs damage because of reasonable reliance on the promise, and

4. It is grossly unfair not to enforce the promise.

C. Charitable subscriptions.

D. Uniform Commercial Code provisions.

1. Signed, written firm offer by merchant (Sec. 2-205).

2. Signed, written waiver or renunciation of a claim (Sec. 1-107).

3. Commercial paper (Art. 3).

4. Modifications of existing contract for sale of goods (Sec. 2-209).

E. Model Written Obligations Act and other state statutes.

F. New promise to pay debt barred by the Statute of Limitations.

G. New promise to pay debt discharged in bankruptcy.

FILL-IN QUESTIONS

1. Sufficient legal consideration exists if the promisor receives a legal _benefit_ or the promisee incurs a legal _detriment_ in exchange for a contractual promise.

2. At common law, the payment of a lesser sum of money could not be consideration for a promise of a creditor to release the balance of a _mature_, _liquidated_, _undisputed_ debt in a greater sum.

3. A promise to buy all the widgets one wishes in exchange for a promise to sell all such widgets is _illusory_ and not supported by legal _consideration_; a

promise to buy all the widgets one may require or need in exchange for a promise to sell all such widgets is supported by legal *consideration* and is termed a *requirements* contract.

4. In general, past consideration is not sufficient consideration to support a present promise. There are, however, exceptions to this rule. For example, _____ _____ _____ _____.

MULTIPLE CHOICE QUESTIONS

1. The common law doctrine of consideration:
   a. recognizes that forbearance from a legal right constituted consideration.
   b. requires a roughly equal exchange of value by the parties to a contract.
   c. requires only that the promisee receive something of value.
   d. has been completely abrogated by statutes in a majority of states.

2. Consideration for a promise must be either a detriment to the:
   a. offeror or a legal benefit to the offeree.
   b. offeree or a legal benefit to the offeror.
   c. promisee or a legal benefit to the promisor.
   d. promisor or a legal benefit to the promisee.

3. The following is an example of a binding promise:
   a. An agreement by a manufacturer to agree to make a contract in the future with a retailer.
   b. A promise by a grandparent to give a grandchild a $10,000 bequest in his/her will.
   c. A promise to obtain free tickets for a friend for a rock concert.
   d. None of the above.

4. Aunt told Nephew, "If you go to Europe and spend the summer there, I will reimburse you for all the expenses that you incur." Nephew went to Europe for the summer but Aunt refused to reimburse him for his expenses. If Nephew sues Aunt, the court will probably hold that Nephew may:
   a. recover because Aunt made a promise to make a gift.
   b. recover because Nephew incurred a legal detriment.
   c. not recover because Aunt received no legal benefit.
   d. not recover because Nephew received a legal benefit.

5. As a general rule, when a creditor accepts a payment of money from a debtor and promises to release the debtor from any further liability, the creditor is legally bound by his/her promise to release the debtor:
   a. only if the debtor can clearly prove that the promise was made (regardless of other circumstances).
   b. only if the original debt was a mature, liquidated, undisputed debt.
   c. only if the original debt was neither mature, liquidated nor undisputed.
   d. as long as the statute of limitations had not run before the payment was made (regardless of other circumstances).

6. The doctrine of promissory estoppel:
    a. requires legal consideration in order to be effective.
    b. results in an irrevocable offer.
    c. applies to the sale of goods when one of the parties is a merchant.
    d. allows enforcement of a promise in the absence of consideration.

7. A promise to buy such quantity of goods as one may wish is:
    a. an illusory promise.
    b. a valid contract.
    c. sufficient consideration for a promise to sell such quantity.
    d. sufficient consideration because the promisee is incurring a detriment.

8. Which of the following agreements is not enforceable?
    a. An agreement between a seller of goods and a buyer to alter the place of delivery prior to performance of the contract.
    b. An agreement by a seller to supply to a buyer all the flour the buyer needs to run his bakery for one year at a set price per pound although the total amount is not precisely established at the time the agreement is entered.
    c. An agreement between a buyer and seller for delivery of specified goods in six months which gives the buyer the right to cancel at any time within the six months.
    d. None of the above.

9. Best Buy Sneaker Co. has entered into a contract to purchase all of the shoe laces it may require at a price of 25¢ each for six months from the Last Lace Corp.; and Last Lace Corp. has agreed to sell all of the shoe laces that Best Buy might require during that time at 25¢. The contract is:
    a. void because of illegality.
    b. valid and enforceable.
    c. voidable because no place of delivery is stated.
    d. enforceable by Last Lace Corp. only.

10. Two armed men robbed the First National Bank of Metropolis. A reward of $10,000 was offered by the bank to anyone who gave information leading to the arrest and conviction of the perpetrators of the robbery. Based on information furnished by a bank employee, a local policeman and a bank customer, the robbers were apprehended and convicted. The employee, policeman and customer applied for the reward. The reward should be given to:
    a. the bank employee.
    b. the local policeman.
    c. the bank customer.
    d. the bank employee, the local policeman and the bank customer.

11. Today in most states, although no consideration is given, a written promise will be enforceable when:
    a. the promise is to pay a debt that is mature and for an undisputed, stated amount.
    b. the promise is to pay a debt that is barred by the statute of limitations.
    c. the promise is to pay a debt that is barred by a discharge in bankruptcy.
    d. all of the above.

12. Cochran purchased a television set from the Acme Appliance Store. One of the terms of sale was that the Acme Appliance Store would service the television set without charge within 24 hours after Cochran advised it that there was improper functioning of the set during the first year following the purchase. Two months after the sale there was a loss of sound. Cochran called the store promptly but was advised that a service man could not be sent to Cochran's home for a week. Cochran promised to pay $25 if a service man were sent the next day because he desperately wanted to watch the world series. A service man was sent and the difficulty was corrected. Acme Appliance Store sent Cochran a bill for $25.
   a. Cochran will not have to pay the bill because the store was obligated to send the service man.
   b. Cochran will not have to pay the bill but will have to pay the reasonable value for the services rendered.
   c. Cochran will have to pay the bill because the store can show that the cost of sending the service man was $25.
   d. Cochran will have to pay the bill because it was the fifth time Cochran called the store in order to request service.

Contractual Capacity

People are presumed to be sufficiently competent to enter contracts unless they are considered to be at a disadvantage when dealing with others because of minority, insanity, intoxication or other disability recognized by law.

THINGS TO KEEP IN MIND

Contracts made by one lacking capacity are generally voidable. As a result the one lacking in capacity has the option of enforcing them or disaffirming them by:

1. suing for rescission (cancellation of the contract), or

2. raising the defense of lack of capacity when sued on the contract by the other party.

OUTLINE

I. Minors.

    A. Statutes prescribe the age of majority. In most states it is 18.

    B. Minors' rights to disaffirm.

        1. Words or conduct may be used.

        2. Minors may disaffirm contracts during minority and for a reasonable period of time after attaining age of majority.

3. Minors may not disaffirm if a contract has been approved by a court or, in some states because of statute, if contract is for:

    a. Life or medical insurance.

    b. Educational loan.

    c. Medical care.

    d. Marriage.

    e. Enlistment in armed forces.

    f. Transportation by common carrier.

4. Conveyances of real property cannot be disaffirmed until minor reaches age of majority.

5. Contract is voidable by minor but not by adult. If minor disaffirms, each party must make restitution by returning consideration received from other party.

6. Executory contracts.

    a. Minor may disaffirm contract—As the minor received nothing from the other party, there is no need to make restitution.

    b. Majority rule—Continued silence after reaching majority is treated as disaffirmance of executory contract.

7. Executed contracts.

    a. Minor may disaffirm contract.
        1) The adult with whom a minor has contracted must make restitution (return any consideration received from minor).
        2) If personal property was sold by minor to an adult, who resold it to an innocent good faith purchaser, the purchaser will not be required to return the property to the minor.
        3) The minor must return consideration received from adult.
            a) The majority rule is that he or she must make restitution only if he or she is able to do so.
            b) In some states:
                (1) By statute, a deduction is made for deterioration, depreciation and damage.
                (2) Minor must pay reasonable value for benefit conferred.

8. Contracts for necessaries.

    a. Necessaries include food, clothing, shelter and services rendered for minor's protection.

      b. Minor may disaffirm contract for necessaries, not provided by parent or guardian, but is liable in quasi contract for reasonable value.

C. Ratification.

    1. Contract will be enforceable if minor indicates an intention to be bound (ratification) after reaching age of majority.

    2. Express ratification.

    3. Implied ratification by conduct indicating satisfaction with contract, such as retaining consideration or accepting benefits.

D. Tort liability of minors.

    1. Minors are liable for all torts unless:

      a. Very young, or

      b. Enforcement of tort liability has indirect effect of also enforcing a contract, which minor has disaffirmed.

    2. In most states, if minor has misrepresented his or her age in order to induce another to enter a contract, the minor may still disaffirm the contract.

      a. Other party may also disaffirm contract.

      b. Other states.
        1) Contract is not voidable by minor because of statutes.
        2) Contract is voidable but minor must pay reasonable value for benefits conferred.
        3) Minor will be estopped from showing lack of capacity.

II. Intoxicated persons.

A. Contracts made by one, who is so intoxicated that his or her judgment is impaired so that he or she does not comprehend the legal consequences of entering into a contract, are voidable.

B. Contracts may be disaffirmed while intoxicated or within a reasonable time after becoming sober.

    1. Restitution must be made.

    2. Cannot disaffirm if a third person would be injured.

    3. Must pay reasonable value for necessaries furnished.

III. Insane persons.

A. One is considered insane or incompetent if his or her judgment is impaired because he or she cannot understand or comprehend the nature and effect of a particular transaction.

B. If judicially declared incompetent, contracts are void.

C. If not adjudicated incompetent, contracts are voidable by insane party, when insane or within a reasonable time after regaining sanity, or by guardian or other representative.

D. Contracts for necessaries may be disaffirmed, but insane party is liable for reasonable value of necessaries furnished.

IV. Others who may be treated as lacking capacity.

A. Convicts—In some states, those who have been convicted of major felonies do not have full capacity to make contracts.

B. Aliens.

1. Citizens of other countries, who are legally in the United States, generally have contractual capacity and their contracts are valid.

2. Enemy aliens and illegal aliens have limited contractual capacity.

C. Women—Today most of the common law restrictions, limiting the contractual capacity of women, have been abolished.

FILL-IN QUESTIONS

1. If a minor or insane person or intoxicated person makes a contract with another person, who does not have a contractual disability, the contract is _____. The one who lacks capacity may _____ the contract, but the other party may not do so.

2. During minority, a minor may _____ a contract to which he was a party.

3. A minor, who has been furnished with necessaries, such as _____ _____, must make restitution if he or she is rescinding the contract, by paying _____ for the benefits received.

4. A minor may not ratify a contract he has entered until he attains the age of _____ or a reasonable period of time thereafter.

5. A person who is insane because _____ _____ may disaffirm his or her contract. If an insane person is adjudicated to be incompetent, his contracts are _____.

MULTIPLE CHOICE QUESTIONS

1. The following best describes a contract entered into by a minor:
   a. Illegal.
   b. Void.
   c. Voidable.
   d. Unenforceable.

2. A contract between a minor and an adult may be disaffirmed by:
   a. the minor only.
   b. the adult only.
   c. the minor's parent or guardian only.
   d. either party.

3. When she was 17 years of age, Mary purchased an automobile for $5,000, to be paid for in 36 monthly installments, from AAA Car Sales. Two years later the car was totally demolished in an accident and Mary failed to make the last 11 payments. AAA Car Sales sued to recover these 11 payments. In a state in which the age of majority is 18, a court will probably hold for:
   a. Mary because Mary was a minor at the time of the purchase and may disaffirm contracts made when she was a minor.
   b. Mary because the contract was nullified when the automobile was demolished.
   c. AAA Car Sales because Mary ratified the contract by making several payments after turning 18.
   d. AAA Car Sales but recovery will be limited because the automobile was demolished.

4. An item which would be considered to be a necessary if purchased by a minor is:
   a. a winter jacket.
   b. a pizzaburger.
   c. a filling in a tooth.
   d. all of the above.

5. A minor may disaffirm a contract entered into with an adult:
   a. for the furnishing of goods other than necessaries.
   b. for the furnishing of goods even if they are necessaries.
   c. before the minor reaches the age of 18 because, as a result of a federal statute, the age of majority has been established at 18 years of age.
   d. before he has reached the age of majority as may the adult with whom he has contracted even if the goods, which are the subject matter of the contract, are necessaries.

6. Courts of equity may deny relief to a minor, who is a party to a contract, if the minor has:
   a. disaffirmed the contract.
   b. purchased necessaries.
   c. misrepresented his/her age.
   d. all of the above.

7. Civil liability arising out of a tort committed by a minor:
    a. may be disaffirmed much like contractual liability because of common law principles.
    b. may be disaffirmed much like contractual liability because of statutory law.
    c. may be disaffirmed under common law principles, but only if the wrongful act (the tort) was not a crime.
    d. may not, as a general rule, be disaffirmed at all.

8. The Uniform Commercial Code:
    a. does not alter the law with regard to minor's contracts.
    b. does not allow a minor to avoid a contract for the purchase of necessaries.
    c. permits a minor to recover goods originally sold by the minor to an adult if the adult has sold the goods to a good faith purchaser.
    d. prevents a minor from recovering goods originally sold by the minor to an adult if the adult has sold the goods to a good faith purchaser.

9. The contracts of one who is in fact insane, but not adjudicated insane, may be ratified by:
    a. the insane person while sane.
    b. the insane person while sane or insane.
    c. the other party to the contract so as to bind the insane party.
    d. the insane party only if the contract is for the furnishing of necessaries.

10. If a person is adjudicated insane and subsequently agrees to purchase a CB radio from the Radio Palace for $600, the contract of sale is:
    a. enforceable.
    b. void.
    c. voidable.
    d. illegal.

Legality

If an act to be performed or the purpose of an agreement is criminal, tortious or contrary to public policy, the agreement is void.

THINGS TO KEEP IN MIND

1. Illegal bargains are usually considered to be void and, therefore, really not contracts. In general, courts will neither enforce illegal bargains nor give remedies for their breach.

2. Public morality and ideas, as to what is considered to be wrongful conduct, are reflected in statutes and policies and vary over time and from place to place.

OUTLINE

I. Contracts contrary to statutes.

    A. Usury.

        1. Statutes fix the maximum lawful rate of interest that can be charged for a loan of money.

        2. Exceptions.

            a. Prohibitions against usury do not apply if the borrower is a corporation.

            b. Statutes often allow higher rates of interest for small loans.

     c. Usury laws generally do not apply to sales of goods of credit but other statutes restrict the amount of interest that can be charged for such transactions.

   3. If more than the statutory maximum rate is charged, the effect varies from state to state.

     a. Transaction is void as to excess interest only.

     b. Transaction is void as to interest but not as to principal.

     c. Entire transaction is tainted by usury and void as to principal and interest.

B. Gambling.

   1. Gambling or wagering involves creation of risk and distribution of property by chance among persons who have given consideration in order to participate.

   2. Distinguish.

     a. Contracts for property and life insurance which provide for shifting an existing risk.

     b. Futures contracts, contracts for future purchase or sale of commodities, purchase of stock on margin.

     c. Games of skill.

C. Sunday laws.

   1. The nature of statutes, restricting contracting on Sunday, varies as does their enforcement.

   2. If a statute prohibits formation or performance of a contract on a Sunday, contracts made or performable on Sunday are illegal, void and unenforceable.

   3. In some states, contracts may be entered into on Sunday but performance is prohibited except for labor of charity or necessity.

   4. Sunday laws have been held to be unconstitutional in a number of states.

D. Licensing statutes.

   1. Statutes require that licenses be obtained in order to engage in certain trades, professions or businesses.

   2. Enforceability of contracts made by unlicensed persons.

    a. Some statutes expressly provide that contracts made by unlicensed persons are void and unenforceable.

    b. If the object of a statute is regulatory (to protect the public from unauthorized practitioners), contracts are void and unenforceable.

    c. If the purpose of a statute is merely to raise revenue, contracts are enforceable.

II. Contracts contrary to public policy.

A. Contracts, which injure an established interest of or which have a negative impact on society, will not be enforced.

B. Restraints of trade.

  1. Agreements not to compete.

    a. An agreement, the sole purpose of which is not to compete, is contrary to public policy and not enforceable.

    b. An ancillary (subsidiary) promise or covenant not to compete will be enforced if it is reasonable (no more extensive than necessary, under the circumstances, to protect a property or other valuable interest of the promisee).
      1) Sale of business—Reasonableness determined by nature of business, period of duration and geographic area covered.
      2) Employment contracts—Enforceable if not excessive in scope or duration.

  2. Resale price maintenance—Today a promise by a dealer not to sell a manufactured product at a price below some established minimum will not be enforced.

C. Unconscionable contracts.

  1. Agreements that are unreasonably oppressive or excessive will not be enforced.

  2. Exculpatory clauses—Promises to relieve another from potential liability based on tort, without regard to fault, will be strictly construed and often found to be violations of public policy.

  3. Contracts may be unconscionable if a party, receiving an unusually greater benefit, has superior bargaining power ("take it or leave it" situations).

D. Agreements for the commission of crimes or torts—Courts will not aid parties who found their causes of action on criminally or civilly wrongful acts.

E. Contracts obstructing the administration of governmental function or injuring public service.

   1. Influencing governmental action improperly.

      a. Corrupting legislators or other public officials.

      b. Distinguish valid lobbying activities.

   2. Obstructing judicial process by concealing commission of a crime or promising not to prosecute.

   3. Surrendering right of access to justice.

      a. Forum selection clauses are usually upheld. ·

      b. Agreements to submit present disputes and future disputes (because of statutes) to arbitration are upheld.

F. Discriminatory contracts.

III. Effect of illegality.

A. General rule—Illegal bargains are void and, therefore, unenforceable by either party.

B. Exceptions.

   1. Severable contracts—Courts will enforce legal provisions if the illegal portions of a contract can be severed.

   2. Members of a class, intended to be protected by a statute prohibiting specific activities, may enforce contract.

   3. If the parties are not equally at fault, the innocent party may recover consideration paid to guilty party.

FILL-IN QUESTIONS

1. Contracts, which violate _____ or _____ are illegal bargains and, therefore, void and unenforceable.

2. _____ statutes provide the maximum rate of interest that may lawfully be charged for a loan or forbearance of money.

3. By statute a lender is prohibited from charging interest of more than ten percent per year on a loan of money. If Larry lent Bob $100 and Bob agreed that he would repay the $100 in a year and give Larry an additional $30 at the time of repayment, Bob will have to pay Larry _____.

4. Contracts which provide for the creation of risk are _____ contracts and are illegal in most states. Contracts which provide for _____ risk, such as contracts of insurance, are legal.

5. A promise not to compete with another is termed a _____. The promise will be enforced if it is _____ and no more extensive than necessary to protect a property interest of the promisee.

MULTIPLE CHOICE QUESTIONS

1. An agreement to engage in an illegal act, such as robbing a bank, is an example of a:
   a. void contract.
   b. voidable contract.
   c. valid contract.
   d. quasi contract.

2. Contracts that are entered into by one who has not complied with a statute requiring a license for the practice of a business, trade or profession:
   a. may be enforced by the unlicensed party if the licensing statute is a revenue raising one rather than a regulatory one.
   b. may be enforced by the unlicensed party if the licensing statute is a regulatory one rather than a revenue raising one.
   c. may be enforced by the unlicensed party unless the statute states that such contracts are unenforceable.
   d. may be enforced by the unlicensed party as long as they are reasonable and not injurious to the other party to the contract.

3. An attorney, who has been admitted to practice law in North Dakota, but not in Missouri, performs legal services and conducts a trial for a client in Missouri.
   a. The client will be required to pay the attorney a fee for the legal services performed.
   b. The client will be required to pay the attorney a fee for the legal services performed and for conducting the trial.
   c. The attorney cannot collect a fee for performing the legal services but can collect a fee for conducting the trial.
   d. The attorney cannot collect a fee for any legal services performed in Missouri.

4. A transaction will be found to be usurious if the following has occurred:
   a. a lender makes a loan of money to a borrower.
   b. the borrower is required to repay the loan.
   c. a sum of money, in excess of the interest allowed by statute, is to be paid by the borrower to the lender.
   d. all of the above.

5. An insurance contract is not treated as an illegal gambling contract:
   a. because all states have statutes that so provide.
   b. because it provides for shifting an existing risk.

     c. unless the premium paid bears no reasonable relationship to the value of the property insured.

     d. unless it is for life insurance and the life insured is that of a child who is less than 18 years of age.

6. Smith purchased the Tiny Department Store from Timothy. All of the terms of the sale were contained in a writing, signed by Smith and Timothy. One of the terms provided that Timothy would not engage in the same business for ten years within a radius of five hundred miles of the Tiny Department Store. One year later Timothy opened the Hugh Department Store a half mile from the Tiny Department Store.

     a. Timothy has not breached the covenant because he did not use his own name or that of "Tiny" at his new store.

     b. The contract is unenforceable because the parties failed to comply with the Statute of Frauds.

     c. The covenant is contrary to public policy and is, therefore, illegal and void.

     d. The covenant is neither illegal nor void.

7. Johnson purchased the Warehard Hardware Store from Ware for $90,000. All of the terms of the sale were contained in a writing, signed by Johnson and Ware. One term provided that Ware would not engage in the same business for two years within one mile of the Warehard Store. Five months later Ware opened the Quick Hardware Store two blocks from the Warehard Store.

     a. Johnson can obtain an injunction because Ware has breached the contract.

     b. The contract is illegal because it provides for resale price maintenance by Johnson.

     c. This is an example of a restraint of trade which is unreasonable and, therefore, illegal and void.

     d. The contract violated the federal antitrust laws.

8. Seller Manufacturing Company produced widgets and contracted to sell 1000 widgets to Buyer Retail Store. Buyer agreed that it would sell the widgets at a price of at least $7 each.

     a. Although the agreement is contrary to public policy, Buyer's promise is enforceable if the quantity being sold is insufficient to give Buyer a monopoly on such goods in its trading area.

     b. Although the agreement is contrary to public policy, Buyer's promise is enforceable because the federal antitrust laws so provide.

     c. The agreement will be treated as a restraint of trade today because it provides for resale price maintenance.

     d. The provision of the agreement is legal and Buyer may, therefore, be sued for breach of contract if it sells the widgets for $6 each.

10

Genuineness of Assent

Objectively the parties to a contract may have agreed to the same terms but subjectively the assent of one or both of them may have not been real or genuine or voluntarily given because of mistake, fraud, misrepresentation, undue influence or duress. If a party was coerced or induced to assent to a contract to which he or she would not have agreed had he or she known the true circumstances, the contract is often voidable.

THINGS TO KEEP IN MIND

One who was prevented from freely exercising his or her own will when assenting to a contract has a number of options:

1. Enforce the contract by suing on it, or

2. Avoid the contract by bringing an action for rescission or, in some instances, sue for damages for wrongful conduct, or

3. Raise the defense that the contract was voidable in an action brought by the other party.

OUTLINE

I. Mistake.

   A. Unilateral mistake of material fact—In general, if only one party has made a mistake, he or she cannot avoid a contract unless the other party was responsible for the mistake or knew of it or should have known of it and failed to correct it.

B. Bilateral mistake of material fact—If both parties have made a mistake of material fact, the contract is voidable at the option of either party.

    1. Mistake as to a past or present material or essential fact.

        a. Mistake as to the existence of the subject matter essential for performance of the contract.

        b. Mistake as to identity or nature of the subject matter of the contract.

    2. Mistake as to value or a future contingency does not result in a voidable contract.

II. Fraud and misrepresentation.

A. Fraud in the execution—If a party has been led to believe that an act, which he or she is performing, is something other than executing a contract, his or her assent is not real and any contract that appears to have been formed is void.

B. Fraud in the inducement—A contract is voidable if a party was damaged by being induced to enter the contract because he or she reasonably relied upon a false representation of a material fact.

    1. Elements of fraud in the inducement.

        a. Intentional misrepresentation.
          1) Representation of past or present fact.
          2) Words or conduct may have been used.
          3) Not opinion, prediction, promises, "puffing" unless made by an expert.
          4) Misrepresentation of law.
            a) Not fraudulent if domestic (local) law misrepresented.
            b) May be fraudulent if made:
              (1) To one who is not a resident of state whose law was misrepresented, or
              (2) By lawyer or one who, because of his occupation, is presumed to know the law.

        b. Misrepresentation made with knowledge that it was false.
          1) Knowledge of falsity may be inferred from circumstances surrounding the transaction.
          2) If misrepresentation was made by one with reckless indifference to its truth or falsity, he or she may be treated as having had knowledge that it was false.

        c. Misrepresentation made with intent to deceive—The evidence that the representation was made to induce the deceived party to enter the contract is the fact that the contract was actually formed.

        d. Reliance on representation—Reliance must have been such that a reasonable person would have been justified in relying on the representation.

       e. Injury to the deceived innocent party—The contract would not have been formed or would have been more valuable if the representation had been true.

   2. Fraud because of silence or concealment.

       a. There is no duty to inform contracting party of facts.

       b. Exceptions.
          1) Seller must disclose latent defects, which are not ordinarily discoverable but which cause object to be dangerous.
          2) Seller, with superior knowledge, may not conceal facts, knowing that other party lacks knowledge.
          3) Party must correct if previously misstated fact.
          4) When parties have a confidential relationship, party with knowledge of relevant facts has obligation to disclose them.

  C. Innocent misrepresentation—If a party unintentionally makes a representation, without knowledge of its falsity, the other party, who relied upon the representation and was damaged, may rescind the contract.

III. Undue influence.

  A. When a party, who is in a dominant position, because of a confidential relationship, secures an unfair advantage in a contract with a weaker, dominated party, the contract may be voidable by the dominated party.

  B. There is a rebuttable presumption of undue influence:

   1. When the parties are in a familial or fiduciary relationship based on trust and confidence, and

   2. The contract is extremely unfair to the dominated party.

  C. Presumption may be rebutted by showing:

   1. Full disclosure was made.

   2. Consideration received was adequate.

   3. Independent advise received by weaker party.

IV. Duress.

  A. If a party is coerced into entering a contract because of the wrongful use of force or a threat of force, the contract is voidable.

  B. Assent may have been induced by fear of:

   1. Bodily injury to party or relative.

    2. Criminal (but not civil) prosecution of party or relative.

    3. Harm to property or business under unusual circumstances.

V.   Adhesion contracts and unconscionability.

    A. Adhesion contract arises when one party, with overwhelming bargaining power, takes such unfair advantage of other party that the latter has no choice but to adhere to dictated terms or do without a particular good or service.

    B. Resulting contract may be held to be voidable because of unconscionability (U.C.C. Sec. 2-302).

FILL-IN QUESTIONS

1. One whose assent was not real or genuine when he or she entered a contract may enforce the contract against the other party or he or she may _____ the contract because the contract is usually treated as being _____ rather than void.

2. A contract induced by fraud in the _____ is void; a contract induced by fraud in the _____ is voidable.

3. A contract may be rescinded if there has been a _____ mistake concerning a material fact rather than a _____ mistake.

4. Joan agreed to sell and Mary agreed to buy a painting valued at $10,000 for $100. Joan, who is 100 years of age, may be able to disaffirm the contract if she can show that there was mental coercion employed by Mary, who was a relative or a fiduciary. In other words, _____ was used to obtain Joan's assent.

MULTIPLE CHOICE QUESTIONS

1. When courts decide that one should not be held to a contract that was not entered into voluntarily, they may be referring to:
    a. duress.
    b. duress or undue influence.
    c. a felony.
    d. mistake of law.

2. A fiduciary is one occupying a confidential relationship with another. If a fiduciary uses the relationship to induce the other person to enter a contract, the fiduciary:
    a. will be considered as having used duress.
    b. will be considered as having used duress if the resulting contract is grossly unfair.
    c. will be considered as having used undue influence if the resulting contract is grossly unfair.
    d. will be considered as having used duress if he has made an intentional misrepresentation of a material fact.

3. F claimed that G owed him $100. G insisted that he did not owe F any money. F told G, "If you don't pay me $100, I'll 'beat you up'!" G immediately wrote a check for $100, payable to F, and gave it to F. Soon after leaving F, G stopped payment on the check, and the bank upon which it was drawn refused to honor it.
    a. F will not be successful in a suit to make G pay because F used fraud in order to obtain G's assent.
    b. F will not be successful in a suit to make G pay because F used duress in order to obtain G's assent.
    c. F will be successful in a suit to make G pay because G objectively manifested his assent to the agreement.
    d. F will be successful in a suit to make G pay because G's apparent assent was manifested.

4. A court will rescind a contract if:
    a. there is a mistake between the parties concerning the existence of the subject matter.
    b. there is a mistake between the parties concerning the value of the subject matter.
    c. there is a misrepresentation concerning the value of the subject matter.
    d. all of the above.

5. Smith, intending to order two apple pies, mistakenly ordered twenty apple pies at a price of $3 per pie from the Jones Bakery, which delivered the twenty pies without knowledge of Smith's mistake.
    a. The contract is void.
    b. Smith may disaffirm the contract at any time.
    c. Smith must pay the reasonable value for twenty pies.
    d. Smith must pay $60 for the pies.

6. S was the owner of a sailboat, which he offered to sell to B for $300. The day before B accepted the offer by telegram the boat was stolen.
    a. There is no contract between S and B because there was a mistake as to the existence of the subject matter.
    b. There is no contract between S and B because there was a mistake as to the identity of the subject matter.
    c. There is a contract between S and B but it may be disaffirmed by S.
    d. There is a contract between S and B but it may be disaffirmed by B.

7. If fraud in the inducement is to be used as the basis for rescission of a contract, the defendant must have made a misrepresentation relating to some material past or existing fact:
    a. with knowledge that the misrepresentation was not true.
    b. in order to induce the plaintiff to enter the contract.
    c. upon which the plaintiff reasonably relied.
    d. all of the above.

8. A necessary element to be shown in an action brought to recover damages for fraud in the inducement is that the defendant:
    a. misrepresented a material fact.
    b. innocently misrepresented a material fact.

     c. intentionally misrepresented a material fact.

     d. any of the above.

9. A seller is obligated to disclose to the buyer:
   a. all defects concerning the subject matter of the sale.
   b. latent defects concerning the subject matter of the sale.
   c. obvious defects concerning the subject matter of the sale.
   d. no defects concerning the subject matter of the sale.

10. Ellen painted over a number of damaged areas in furniture she sold to Van. Such conduct might be the basis for an action for fraud:
    a. in the inducement even though Ellen made no verbal misstatements with regard to the furniture.
    b. in the inducement only if Ellen made a verbal misstatement with regard to the furniture.
    c. in the execution even though Ellen made no verbal misstatements with regard to the furniture.
    d. in the execution only if Ellen made a verbal misstatement with regard to the furniture.

11. A contract induced by misrepresentation is:
    a. voidable.
    b. void.
    c. implied by conduct.
    d. all of the above.

Writing and Form

Although it is advantageous, contracts generally need not be reduced to writing in order to bind the parties. Some contracts, however, must be in writing and signed by the party against whom they are to be enforced because of the Statute of Frauds. Recall from Chapter 5 that one of the elements of a contract is that, if a form is required by law, an agreement must be in that form in order to be enforceable.

If a written instrument is regarded as an integration of the agreement of the parties to it, other evidence, which changes the effect of the writing, is not admissible because of the Parol Evidence Rule.

THINGS TO KEEP IN MIND

1. The Statute of Frauds does not require a formal document. All that is usually necessary is a signed memorandum indicating the essential terms.

2. If a contract does not comply with the Statute of Frauds, it is unenforceable, rather than void or voidable. This means that it cannot be proven in the manner required by law.

3. Usually the Statute of Frauds is raised as a defense. If the issue is not raised, an oral contract will be enforced.

OUTLINE

I. The Statute of Frauds.

  A. In order to be enforceable, some contractual promises must be evidenced by a writing, which is signed by the parties against whom they are being enforced.

B. Contracts that must be in writing.

    1. Contracts for sales of interests in real property.

        a. Interests in land include:
            1) Conveyances—Transfers of land for consideration. Usually a conveyance requires a contract for the sale of the land, the delivery of a deed and payment of the consideration.
            2) Life estates—Interests in land which lasts only for the lifetime of a named person.
            3) Mortgages—Conveyances given as security to lenders.
            4) Easements—Rights to use land.
            5) Leases—Rights to use and possess land for stated periods of time. Most states require that leases for more than one year be in writing.

        b. Contract may be taken out of the Statute of Frauds.
            1) Full performance of oral contract by one or both parties.
            2) Substantial part performance by a purchaser if his or her action is only explainable as being pursuant to an agreement.
                a) Part payment of consideration,
                b) Take possession, and
                c) Make substantial improvements in reliance on oral contract.

    2. Contracts not to be performed within one year.

        a. If performance is possible, even if improbable, within one year, an oral contract is enforceable.

        b. The year begins from the date of the contract.
            1) Not the date performance is to begin.
            2) If time for performance is of uncertain duration, but depends upon some contingency, which may occur within a year, oral contract is enforceable.

        c. Full performance by one party within a year takes contract out of the Statute of Frauds.

        d. Some states have statutes requiring that contracts, not performable within the lifetime of the promisor, must be in writing.

    3. Promises to answer for the debts or to discharge duties of another.

    Creditor   direct, original, primary promise to perform   Principal debtor
    obligee   <—————————————————   obligor
            consideration given or promised

    secondary, collateral
    promise to perform if principal   Secondary promisor
    obligor does not   guarantor

    a. A promise is within the Statute of Frauds and must be in a signed writing if:
      1) The promise is made to the obligee (rather than the principal obligor) by one who is not presently liable for the debt or duty.
      2) The liability of the guarantor is secondary or collateral to that of the principal obligor.

    b. If the main purpose or leading object of the secondary promisor is to protect his or her own interest or to materially benefit, an oral promise will be enforced.

4. Promises by executors or administrators to personally pay the debts of decedents' estates.

5. Unilateral promises made in consideration of marriage.

6. Contracts for the sale of goods and other personal property (covered by U.C.C.).

    a. Contract for sale of goods for a price of $500 or more (U.C.C. Sec. 2-201). Exceptions:
      1) Partial performance—Buyer pays for or receives and accepts goods.
      2) Goods (not ordinarily suitable for resale) to be specially manufactured for buyer by seller, who has begun production of the goods.
      3) Sale between merchants, when either party, within a reasonable period of time, sends a written confirmation to which the other party fails to object within ten days.
      4) Admission, in pleadings or in court, that contract existed.

    b. Other Code provisions.
      1) Contracts for sale of securities (U.C.C. Sec. 8-319).
        a) Statute of Frauds satisfied by payment or delivery and acceptance of securities.
        b) Statute of Frauds satisfied by written confirmation.
      2) Security agreements (U.C.C. Sec. 9-203).
      3) Contracts for sale of miscellaneous personal property when price is more than $5000 (U.C.C. Sec. 1-106).

C. Sufficiency of writing—Memorandum evidencing the contract need only contain basic, essential terms of the contract.

II. Parol evidence rule.

A. If a written instrument is regarded by the parties as their complete, integrated agreement, other oral or written evidence is inadmissible for purposes of changing, altering or contradicting the effect of the writing.

B. Parol evidence is admitted to show:

1. A modification of the writing.

2. The contract was void or voidable.

3. The meaning of ambiguous or vague language.

4. The writing was incomplete.

5. A prior course of dealings or a trade usage (U.C.C. Sec. 2-203).

6. Gross typographical or clerical errors.

7. Another separate contract with a different subject matter.

FILL-IN QUESTIONS

1. Promises, required by the Statute of Frauds to be in writing and signed by the party against whom they are being enforced, include those _____
    _____
    _____
    _____.

2. Johnson said to the manager of a local store, "If Cooper does not pay for his pur-
    chases this month, I will pay for them." Johnson's promise is unenforceable because
    the Statute of Frauds requires that a promise _____
    _____ must be in
    writing and signed by the promisor. If Johnson told the manager of the store that
    he would pay for the purchases made by Clark, Johnson's employee, Johnson's
    promise would be enforceable because _____
    _____ and, there-
    fore, is not within the Statute of Frauds.

3. A contract for the sale of goods when the price is $_____ or more is
    required to be in writing.

4. The Parol Evidence Rule provides that if a written instrument is regarded by the
    parties as a complete, integrated statement of their agreement, other oral or
    written statements, agreements or promises are _____ for purposes of
    adding to, deleting from, changing, altering or contradicting the effect of the
    writing, which is the final expression of the rights and duties of the parties.

5. Parol evidence is admissible to show that a contract is _____ because of
    illegality, fraud in the execution, mistake as to the existence of the subject matter,
    or judicially determined incapacity, or _____ because of lack of
    capacity (minority, insanity, intoxication), fraud in the inducement, misrepresenta-
    tion, mutual mistakes of fact, duress or undue influence.

6. With regard to a written contract, oral evidence is admissible to prove that the
    writing was not intended as the entire agreement of the parties or to prove _____
    _____
    _____
    _____.

MULTIPLE CHOICE QUESTIONS

1. The Statute of Frauds requires that certain contracts be in writing and signed by the party against whom they are being enforced. If such a contract does not comply with the Statute:
   a. it is voidable.
   b. it is void.
   c. it is unenforceable.
   d. it is illegal.

2. The Statute of Frauds:
   a. is an old English statute that has no relevance today.
   b. applies to all contracts which, by their terms, require the payment of $500 or more.
   c. defines what constitutes fraudulent conduct by a party in inducing another to enter a contractual relationship.
   d. requires that a contract for the sale of an unimproved piece of real property for $100 be in writing.

3. A contract must be in writing and signed by the party to be charged if it provides for:
   a. a sale of goods when the price is more than $300.
   b. a lease of equipment for more than one month.
   c. a promise made to a third party to answer for the default of another.
   d. a promise made to a debtor to answer for his or her debt to another person.

4. The section of the Statute of Frauds dealing with suretyship refers to:
   a. promises to pay debts of others.
   b. contracts for the sale of securities.
   c. contracts for the sale of real property.
   d. mutual promises to marry.

5. On November 1, 1979, Richards orally agreed to employ Everett for one year as a clerk at a salary of $170 per week. Everett began working a week later and performed satisfactorily, but on December 20, 1979, Richards terminated Everett's employment because of business reversals. Everett is suing Richards for damages for breach of contract.
   a. Everett will be successful if, on November 1, the parties had not fixed the date upon which Everett was to begin work.
   b. Everett will be successful if, on November 1, the parties had fixed November 8 as the date upon which Everett was to begin work.
   c. Whether or not the agreement stated the date upon which employment was to commence, it will not affect the outcome of the lawsuit.
   d. As the salary to be paid was more than $100 per week, Everett will not be successful because the agreement was not in writing.

6. Marco Manufacturing Co. orally agreed to sell and the Reed Retail Store agreed to buy $2000 worth of merchandise.
   a. If Marco fails to deliver the merchandise and Reed fails to pay the $2000, Reed can enforce the contract against Marco.

b. If Marco fails to deliver the merchandise and Reed fails to pay the $2000, Marco can enforce the contract against Reed.

c. If Marco delivers and Reed accepts the merchandise, the contract can be enforced by Marco against Reed.

d. The Statute of Frauds does not apply to a sale of goods between merchants and the contract is therefore enforceable.

7. The Parol Evidence Rule:
   a. requires that certain contracts be in writing or evidenced by a writing in order to be enforceable.
   b. affects the evidence that may be offered if a prisoner wishes to be released from jail.
   c. prevents the introduction of oral testimony to alter the terms of a written agreement.
   d. applies to a contract for the sale of miscellaneous personal property when the price is more than $500.

8. Gordon and Henry entered into a contract for the sale of goods. All of the terms were reduced to writing. Gordon is attempting to introduce another writing in evidence. In which of the following circumstances will Gordon *not* be able to introduce the evidence?
   a. The evidence relates to another agreement between the parties concerning a different subject matter.
   b. The written contract indicates that it was intended as the "entire contract" between the parties and the point is covered in detail.
   c. The evidence relates to statements made by Henry, to which Gordon assented, that the contract for the sale of the goods would become effective if the price of gasoline rose to $2 per gallon.
   d. The written contract contains an obvious typographical error concerning the point in issue.

9. Karla and Victor entered a contract for the delivery of goods, all of the terms of which were reduced to writing. Karla is attempting to introduce oral evidence. She will be prevented from doing so if the evidence related to:
   a. a mistake concerning the value of the goods.
   b. the subject matter of the contract which was heroin.
   c. another agreement concerning a loan of money.
   d. a modification of the contract made a week after the writing of the contract.

12

Third Party Rights

A contract between two parties may involve a third party, who has rights or assumes obligations. The parties to a contract may expressly provide that a benefit be conferred upon a person, who is not a party to the contract (third party beneficiary contract). A party to an existing contract may transfer rights he or she has to a stranger to the contract (assignment) or delegate performance of his or her duties to a third person (delegation).

THINGS TO KEEP IN MIND

1. In a third party beneficiary situation there is only one contract. When there is an assignment of rights or delegation of duties, usually there are two relevant contracts.

2. The one to whom performance is to be given under the terms of a contract has a "right," which may be assigned. The one who is required by a contract to render performance has a "duty," which may be delegated.

OUTLINE

I. Third party beneficiary contracts.

$$X = \text{Third Party Beneficiary}$$

performance $\nearrow$

Promisor = B $\longleftarrow$ consideration $\longrightarrow$ A = Promisee

A. The third party beneficiary is a stranger to the contractual relationship of the parties to the contract; he or she makes no promises and gives no consideration to the promisor, who is to render performance, but the intention of the parties is to confer a benefit upon him or her.

B. Creditor beneficiary—The promisee's intention is to discharge an obligation, owed to a third party, by having the promisor, with whom the promisee contracts, render performance to the third party.

C. Donee beneficiary—The promisee's intention is to confer a gift upon a third party by having the promisor, with whom the promisee contracts, render performance to the third party.

D. Rights of third party beneficiary.

1. An intended donee or creditor beneficiary has a legal right to enforce the contract against the promisor. (Note that a creditor beneficiary also has rights against his debtor, the promisee.)

2. Original contracting parties cannot modify, alter, or terminate contract if third party beneficiary:

   a. Learns of and assents to the contract, or

   b. Sues on the contract, or

   c. Materially changes his or her position in reliance on the contract.

3. The beneficiary acquires rights, subject to the right of the promisor to raise any defenses he or she might have against the promisee, against the beneficiary.

E. Incidental beneficiary—One, who is to receive an incidental benefit from the performance of a contract, may not enforce the contract if there was no intent to confer a benefit upon him or her.

II. Assignment of contract rights.

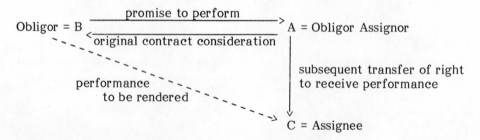

A. Assignment is an act whereby one party to an existing valid contract (the assignor) transfers the rights he or she has to another person (the asignee), who is a stranger to the original contract, but who may enforce the contract.

B. No special formality is necessary in order to make an effective assignment.

     1. Compliance with Statute of Frauds.

     2. Consideration need not be given.

        a. Promise to make a future assignment must be supported by consideration in order that it be effective.

        b. If no consideration is given by assignee, assignment is revocable by assignor.

C. Rights that may be assigned without assent of obligor.

     1. Right to receive the payment of money.

     2. Right to delivery of a deed or goods.

D. Some rights may not be assigned because of express prohibitions.

     1. Statutory prohibitions.

     2. Reasonable contractual prohibitions.

     3. Claims for injuries due to torts may not be assigned prior to judgment.

     4. Rights of an insured against an insurer may not be assigned prior to an actual insured loss.

     5. At law, future or potential rights may not be assigned.

E. The right to receive personal services may not be assigned without the consent of the obligor.

F. An obligee, who is making an assignment, may not change the nature of the non-personal performance (which he has a right to receive) so as to increase the burden or risk to the obligor, without the assent of the obligor.

G. Effect of assignment.

     1. Assignee can enforce the contract against the obligor.

     2. Assignee takes claim subject to all defenses available against obligee-assignor even if consideration was given for the assignment.

     3. Clause, providing for waiver of right to assert defenses, in original contract is strictly construed.

H. Although it is not necessary to give notice of assignment to obligor, it is wise to do so.

I. Multiple assignments.

    1. Successive assignments of same rights by obligee to more than one assignee, who takes in good faith and for value.

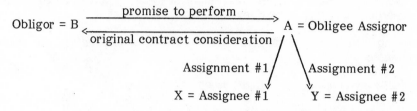

        a. Majority rule—Assignee, who first takes assignment, prevails even if he or she did not first give notice of assignment to obligor.

        b. Minority rule—Assignee, who first notifies obligor of assignment, will prevail.

    2. Partial assignments will be effective.

    3. An assignee may reassign the contract rights to another person (sub-assignment).

III. Delegation of duties.

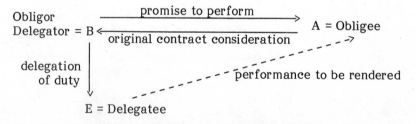

A. Performance of non-personal duties may be delegated by obligor.

B. Personal duties may not be delegated without assent of party to whom performance is to be rendered.

C. If a delegatee fails to perform, the obligee may sue:

    1. The obligor, with whom the obligee had contracted, and

    2. The delegatee. The obligee is treated as a third party creditor beneficiary of the contract formed by the obligor (delegator) and delegatee.

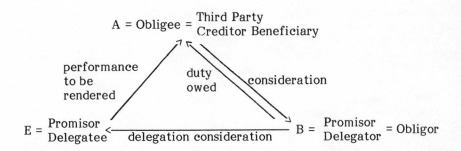

FILL-IN QUESTIONS

1. Adams and Brady have made an agreement which provides that Adams will pay Brady $20 per week for twelve weeks, if Brady promises to cut the grass on Cotton's and Delmer's property. If Delmer is a friend of Adams', Delmer will be treated as a third party _____ beneficiary if Adams intends to give him a gift of having his grass cut. If Adams owed Cotton $120, Cotton will be treated as a third party _____ beneficiary. Both Cotton and Delmer can enforce the contract but Nailer, a neighbor of Cotton's, although he will benefit from the performance of the contract, cannot enforce the contract because he is merely an _____ beneficiary.

2. If one transfers to another the rights he or she has because of a contract, he or she has made an _____. The transferor is called the _____ and the transferee is called the _____.

3. The performance of non-personal duties may be _____ by the party, who, under the terms of a contract, is required to render performance to the other contracting party.

MULTIPLE CHOICE QUESTIONS

1. Roberts took out a $10,000 life insurance policy on her own life with ABC Insurance Company and named Sanders as the beneficiary. Roberts paid all the premiums until her untimely death a year later. The insurance company has not paid Sanders, who is, therefore, suing it.
   a. Sanders is entitled to the payment of the $10,000 because he is a third party donee beneficiary.
   b. If Roberts made misrepresentations concerning material facts in the application for insurance, the ABC Insurance Company can successfully raise the defense that the contract was voidable because of fraud or misrepresentations against Sanders.
   c. Although Sanders gave no consideration and was not a party to the contract between Roberts and ABC Insurance Company, he is a proper party to enforce the insurance contract.
   d. All of the above.

2. A has agreed to pay B $400 if B promises to paint C's house.
    a. If C gave no consideration to A or B, C has no standing to sue B because there is no privity of contract between B and C.
    b. If C gave no consideration to A or B, C will be treated as a third party donee beneficiary and may enforce the contract against B.
    c. As C is a third party beneficiary, C may enforce the contract against B, who will be barred from raising any defenses against C that he could have raised against A.
    d. C is an assignee because A transferred his rights to have his (A's) house painted by B.

3. Hendon owed Borhan $200. On Monday, Borhan have $200 to Katz, who promised to give the money to Borhan on the following Friday in order to discharge Hendon's debt. Katz did not deliver the money to Borhan. Borhan, a third party creditor beneficiary, will be successful if she sues Katz:
    a. because the parties to a contract, which provided for conferring a benefit upon a third person, cannot terminate their agreement if the third person learns of the original contract and detrimentally changes his or her position in reliance upon it.
    b. even though Hendon and Katz altered their agreement on Wednesday before Borhan learned of it and gave her consent.
    c. even though Hendon and Katz altered their contract on Tuesday before Borhan materially changed her position in detrimental reliance on the contract.
    d. because the parties to a contract, which provides for conferring a benefit upon a third person, lack the power to alter or terminate their contract, after they confer a benefit upon the third person.

4. The Acme Construction Co. contracted with Granite City to build a new court house. It was foreseen that blasting would be necessary, and Acme promised that it would pay for "any and all property damage caused by the blasting."
    a. MacDonald, a homeowner, can recover from Acme for damage to his home caused by the blasting, because he is an incidental beneficiary.
    b. Naughton, a homeowner, cannot recover from Acme for damage to her home caused by the blasting, because she is an incidental beneficiary.
    c. Oppenheimer, a tourist, can recover for damage to her car caused by the blasting, because she is a third party beneficiary.
    d. Only the city can recover from Acme for damage to its property, because it was a party to the contract.

5. The right to recover under a fire insurance policy may be assigned:
    a. by the insured at any time.
    b. by the insured after the policy has been in force for a reasonable period of time without incurring a loss.
    c. after a fire when the duty of the insurer to pay is fixed.
    d. never.

6. Simple Oil Distributing Co. contracted with Vital Service Station to supply its gasoline requirements for one year, estimated to be one million gallons, at a price of twenty cents above the price per gallon paid by Simple. All of the terms of the contract were reduced to writing. Simple was having difficulty obtaining gas

supplies and, therefore, agreed with Best Oil Corp. that Best would "take over" Simple's contract with Vital by supplying Vital's requirements and receiving payment therefor from Vital.

a. Simple was not obligated to deliver gasoline to Vital if it was unable to obtain supplies because the quantity of gasoline to be delivered and the price were uncertain.

b. Simple cannot assign its right to be paid by Vital to Best without the assent of Vital.

c. Simple has effectively assigned its rights and delegated its duties under the terms of its contract with Vital to Best.

d. Simple is effectively released from any further obligation to perform under the terms of the contract with Vital.

7. Manson orally agreed to sell his truck to Jackson, who orally promised to pay Manson $510 within one week and $800 one year after delivery of the truck. Prior to delivering the truck, Manson orally assigned his right to be paid to Thompson.

a. Thompson cannot enforce Jackson's agreement because the Statute of Frauds requires that the contract and the assignment be in writing.

b. Thompson cannot enforce Jackson's agreement because he gave no consideration to Manson for the assignment.

c. Thompson cannot enforce Jackson's agreement because Jackson did not assent to the assignment by Manson.

d. Thompson can enforce Jackson's agreement.

8. On April 4, the Barnes Store sold $100 worth of merchandise on credit to Ames, who promised that she would pay the Barnes Store $100 on May 1. On April 6, the store assigned its right to be paid to the Careful Credit Corp. for $90.

a. Careful Credit Corp. may not assign its rights to Doubtful Claims Inc.

b. Careful Credit Corp. may not enforce Ames' promise to pay because Ames did not consent to the assignment.

c. If Ames returns the merchandise to the Barnes Store, which accepts it, on April 8, Ames can raise a good defense if Careful Credit Corp. sues her for $100 after May 1.

d. Since the Barnes Store is a merchant, it is prohibited from assigning its right to be paid by Ames until May 1 when the $100 is due and owing.

9. Rawson has a contract with Green, the owner of a professional basketball team, to play basketball for one year. In most states:

a. Green may assign his contractual rights to the owner of another basketball team without Rawson's consent.

b. Rawson may delegate his duty to play basketball and assign his right to be paid to Hubbard, without Green's consent, if Hubbard is a better basketball player than Rawson.

c. Rawson may assign his right to be paid for playing basketball after he has rendered his performance without Green's consent.

d. Rawson may not assign any rights or delegate any duties that he has because of his contract with Green to another person.

13

Performance and Discharge

Most contracts are fully performed by the parties, resulting in their discharge. Contracting parties may be discharged by full performance, by breach of contract, by agreement and by operation of law.

THINGS TO KEEP IN MIND

1. If a party fails to perform an absolute contractual promise, he is breaching the contract and is liable to the other party, who is discharged and, therefore, excused from performing.

2. If a contractual promise is conditional and the conditioning event occurs, the promisor's duty to perform does not arise or is terminated so that no liability attaches for failing to perform.

OUTLINE

I. Conditions—A condition is an operative event, the occurrence or nonoccurrence of which changes, limits, precludes, gives rise to or terminates a contractual obligation.

    A. Types of conditions.

        1. Condition precedent—Conditioning event must occur before performance by promisor is required. Until then the promisee has no right to receive performance.

        2. Condition subsequent—Occurrence of conditioning event extinguishes an existing contractual duty.

      3. Condition concurrent—Performance of each party is conditioned on the performance of other party.

  B. How conditions arise.

      1. Express—Condition clearly stated by parties.

      2. Implied in fact—Condition that is understood or inferred.

      3. Implied in law (constructive)—Imposed by court in order to achieve justice and fairness.

II. Discharge by performance.

  A. Full, complete performance in manner prescribed by contract discharges performing party.

  B. Tender of complete performance—An unconditional offer to perform by one ready, willing and able to do so, discharges party if his or her tender is not accepted.

  C. Time for performance.

      1. If time for performance is not stated, performance is to be rendered within a reasonable period of time.

      2. If parties stipulate that time is of the essence (vital), the time requirement must be complied with.

      3. If time for performance is stipulated, but not vital, performance prior to or within a few days of the stated time satisfies contract.

  D. Part performance.

      1. If partial performance is accepted, performing party can recover value of performance.

      2. If performance is substantial (i.e., minor, trivial deviation from contractual obligation) and not in bad faith, performing party is discharged but liable for failure to render complete performance.

      3. Partial performance, which is not substantial performance, is a breach of contract and results in the discharge of the party entitled to receive performance but not the discharge of the partially performing party.

  E. Effect of contractual conditions on discharge by performance.

      1. Strict compliance with express conditions is necessary.

      2. Substantial performance of constructive conditions is necessary.

3. Express personal satisfaction condition—Promise of one party to pay may be conditioned on that party's satisfaction with the other party's performance.

   a. If personal taste, preferences, esthetics, fancy or comfort is involved, payment is excused if dissatisfaction is honest and in good faith, even though a reasonable person would have been satisfied.

   b. If satisfaction relates to operative fitness, merchantability or mechanical utility, payment is excused when dissatisfaction is honest and a reasonable person would have been dissatisfied.

III. Discharge by agreement of the parties.

A. Provision in original contract.

B. New, subsequent, valid, enforceable contract.

   1. Elements of contract, including consideration, must be present.

   2. Mutual rescission—Parties agree to discharge and relieve each other of their obligations.

      a. If original bilateral contract was executory, consideration is present because each party gives up existing rights.

      b. If original contract was a unilateral or a bilateral one that was executed by one party, new consideration must be given to the party who performed in exchange for his or her promise to relieve the nonperforming party of his or her contractual duty to render the originally promised performance.

   3. Release—Statement by one party relieving other party of contractual duty. A release often includes a promise not to sue for breach of contract.

   4. Accord and satisfaction—Parties agree that a substitute performance will be rendered by one party in satisfaction of his or her original obligation and such performance is rendered and accepted.

   5. Substituted agreement—Parties agree to enter a new agreement with different terms as a substitute for an original contract, which is expressly or impliedly discharged.

   6. Novation—Parties agree with a third person that the contractual duties of one of the original parties will be assumed by the third person. The third person is substituted for one of the original parties with the consent of the party entitled to receive the performance.

IV. Discharge by breach of contract.

A. A party, who fails to perform totally or who materially breaches a contract, is not discharged and is liable for damages.   The other party is, however, discharged and need not hold himself or herself ready to perform.

B. If there is a minor, nonmaterial breach of contract, the breaching party is liable for damages if the breach is not cured.   The nonbreaching party is not discharged and is required to perform.

C. Anticipatory breach of contract.

   1. If a party repudiates a contract before he or she is required to perform, the other party may sue immediately and does not have to hold himself or herself ready to perform.

   2. The doctrine of anticipatory breach does not apply to a promise to pay a stated sum of money, a unilateral contract or a bilateral contract that is executory on one side only.

V.   Discharge by operation of law.

A. Material alteration of a written contract without consent.

B. Running of the Statute of Limitations.

C. Decree in bankruptcy.

D. Impossibility—Occurrence of a supervening, unforeseen event, making it impossible to perform.

   1. Object of contract becomes illegal.

   2. Death or serious illness of a party, who was to perform personally.

   3. Destruction of subject matter of contract.

   4. Economic frustration—An unforeseen event occurs which frustrates the purpose for which one of the parties entered the contract so that the value of the expected performance he or she is to receive is destroyed.

   5. Commercial Impracticability—An extreme change in conditions makes performance impracticable because it will be extremely difficult, burdensome or costly to render.

FILL-IN QUESTIONS

1.   If parties to a contract agree that one of them will not be required to perform upon the happening of some event, their contract contains a condition _____; if, however, they agree that the occurrence of some event will terminate an existing contractual obligation, the contract contains a condition _____.

2. A party, who renders or tenders _____ in the manner prescribed by a contract, is discharged.

3. The parties to a contract may subsequently agree to discharge and terminate their existing agreement by making a new contract. The new agreement may be an accord and satisfaction, _____ or _____ .

4. Parties to a contract are discharged by operation of law if there has been a material alteration of a written contract by one party without the assent of the other party or _____ _____ .

5. A contract is discharged because of _____ if the subject matter has been destroyed or one of the parties, who was to perform personal services, has died.

MULTIPLE CHOICE QUESTIONS

1. Aunt Alice promised to give her niece, Betty, $5000 if Betty spent her two month summer vacation in Europe. Betty is legally entitled to the $5000 if she:
   a. spends three weeks in Europe and works at home for the remainder of her vacation.
   b. spends two months in Mexico and Brazil.
   c. spends seven weeks in Europe.
   d. all of the above.

2. On November 1, S and B entered into a written contract for the sale by S of a fully described tract of land for $20,000, delivery of the deed and payment by B to be due on December 1.
   a. If B advises S on November 15 that he no longer wishes to purchase the land and is repudiating the contract, S can successfully sue B for breach of contract on November 17.
   b. If S advises B on November 15 that he no longer wishes to sell the land and is repudiating the contract, B can successfully sue S for breach of contract on November 17.
   c. If B advises S on November 15 that he no longer wishes to purchase the land and is repudiating the contract, S can successfully sue B for anticipatory breach of contract on November 17.
   d. If S advises B on November 15 that he no longer wishes to sell the land and is repudiating the contract, B can successfully sue S for anticipatory breach of contract on November 17.

3. If a breach of contract is:
   a. material, the nonbreaching party may sue for damages but must perform his or her part of the contract.
   b. material, the nonbreaching party may not sue for damages if he or she has accepted the improper performance.
   c. minor, the nonbreaching party is excused from performing.
   d. minor, the nonbreaching party may sue for damages for the breach.

4. On July 10, Fred, the owner of a farm, contracted to sell 3,000 bushels of grade A
    tomatoes on September 1 to the Prince Pizza Co. The tomatoes on Fred's farm
    were destroyed in a hail storm on August 8. If Fred fails to deliver 3,000 bushels of
    tomatoes on September 1:
    a. Fred may be sued for breach of contract successfully by Prince Pizza Co.
    b. Fred is discharged because of a condition subsequent.
    c. Fred is discharged by operation of law because of impossibility.
    d. Prince Pizza Co. may successfully sue Fred for anticipatory breach of contract.

5. On June 1, Frank, the owner of a farm, contracted to sell 2,000 bushels of grade A
    corn from his farm on August 10 to Careful Corn Canners Inc. The corn on Frank's
    farm was destroyed by locusts on August 1. If Frank fails to deliver 2,000 bushels
    of corn on August 10:
    a. Frank may be sued for breach of contract successfully by Careful Corn Canners
        Inc.
    b. Frank is discharged because of a condition subsequent.
    c. Frank is discharged by operation of law because of impossibility.
    d. Careful Corn Canners Inc. may successfully sue Frank for anticipatory breach
        of contract.

6. Larry rented a room from Mike along Main Street on a Saturday for the purpose of
    watching a parade. Mike knew that this was the reason for renting the room.
    Unfortunately there was a bad snow storm and the parade was cancelled. Mike has
    sued Larry for the rent. In most states a court will determine that:
    a. the contract is discharged because of impossibility.
    b. the contract is discharged because of economic frustration.
    c. the contract is discharged because of the occurrence of a conditioning event.
    d. the contract is not discharged.

7. On March 1, Pick and Quick entered a valid written contract that provided for the
    sale by Pick of 1000 yo-yos to Quick for $1000. All of the terms were clearly and
    unambiguously contained in the writing. A week later Pick delivered 400 yo-yos
    but he has failed to deliver the remaining 600 yo-yos.
    a. Pick is not discharged and is liable to Quick for a material breach of the
        contract.
    b. Quick must remain ready, willing and able to pay Pick the $1000.
    c. Even if Quick accepted the 400 yo-yos, he would not have to pay for them
        because there has been a material breach of contract.
    d. If Quick accepted the 400 yo-yos, Pick is discharged without liability and does
        not have to tender delivery of the remaining 600 yo-yos.

8. Don promised to pay Cathy $100 if Cathy painted Don's portrait.
    a. If Cathy dies before completing the portrait, Cathy and Don are discharged.
    b. If Ellen, Cathy and Don agree that Ellen will paint the portrait and Don will pay
        Ellen rather than Cathy, the parties have entered a novation.
    c. If Cathy paints the portrait but Don fails to pay the $100, Cathy is discharged
        but Don is not discharged.
    d. All of the above.

Breach of Contract and Remedies

A breach of contract occurs when a party fails to fully and correctly perform a contractual duty. The party to whom the duty is owed may sue the breaching party in order to enforce his or her rights or obtain an appropriate remedy.

THINGS TO KEEP IN MIND

If there has been a breach of contract, the remedy that usually will be afforded, when the nonbreaching party sues, will be compensatory money damages, which will be adequate in order to put him or her in the position that he or she would have been in had the contract not been breached.

OUTLINE

I.   Remedies at law—Money damages.

    A. Compensatory damages—Awarded to a nonbreaching party in order to compensate him or her for the actual harm or loss caused by the breach.

        Measure of damages—Factual question.

        1. How much money will place the plaintiff in as good a position as he or she would have been in if the defendant had correctly performed?

        2. Usually this amounts to the loss of normal, expected profit plus any sums previously paid or incidental expenses incurred by the nonbreaching party.

          a. Sales of goods—Difference between the contract price and market price.

    b. Sale of land—Usually the difference between the contract price and market price.

    c. Construction contracts—Damages vary depending upon which party breaches contract and at what stage construction is at time of breach.

    d. Employment contracts.
      1) Breach by employer—Salary for unexpired term less earnings of employee from job of similar nature or, if such job is available, compensation which the employee would have received if he or she had accepted the position.
      2) Breach by employee—Cost of procuring replacement employee less contracted salary or wages.

B. Consequential or special damages—Speculative, non-foreseeable, remote, indirect or unexpected damages, which do not ordinarily flow from a breach of contract, are not recoverable unless contemplated by breaching party because he or she was given notice thereof.

C. Punitive or exemplary damages—Unusual award by court to punish for willful, wanton, malicious harm caused to a nonbreaching party.

D. Nominal damages—Inconsequential sum, which establishes that plaintiff had a cause of action but suffered no measurable pecuniary loss.

E. Mitigation of damages—A party, who suffers damages, must reduce actual damage, if he or she is able to do so.

F. Liquidated damages—The parties may provide in their contract that a stated sum of money or property will be paid or, if previously deposited, forfeited, if one of the parties breaches the contract. Such provisions will be enforced unless they are unreasonable and, therefore, are penalties.

II. Equitable remedies.

A. Not available.

    1. Remedy at law (usually money damages) is adequate, determinable and available.

    2. Aggrieved party has shown bad faith, fraud, etc.

    3. Aggrieved party has delayed in bringing action unnecessarily.

    4. Court will have to supervise execution of remedy.

B. Rescission and restitution.

    1. Rescission means cancellation or abrogation of a contract. It may be

mutually agreed to by parties to a contract or awarded as a remedy by a court.

2. Usually restitution is also given by a court so that previously rendered consideration, or its value, is returned.

C. Specific performance—An order by a court to render a contractually promised performance.

1. Specific performance will be granted when:

a. Contract involves unique personal property or real property, which is always considered to be unique.

b. Performance that is to be rendered is clear and unambiguous.

2. Specific performance will not be granted when performance to be rendered involves personal services.

D. Injunction—An order enjoining or restraining a person from doing some act.

E. Reformation—A court may correct an agreement to conform to the intentions of the parties.

F. Quasi contract—A court may require that one who has received a benefit pay for the benefit conferred in order to prevent unjust enrichment.

III. Election of remedies.

A. Waiver of breach—A party may relinquish, repudiate or surrender a right that he or she has to seek a remedy for breach of contract.

B. Contractual limitations on liability will be enforced unless they are unconscionable or the result of unequal bargaining power.

1. Parties may agree to limit liability for certain types of breaches of contract or conduct but may not exclude liability for gross negligence or intentional torts.

2. Parties may agree to fix a maximum sum that can be recovered if there is a breach of contract.

3. Parties may agree to limit remedies.

FILL-IN QUESTIONS

1. A plaintiff, who is suing a party with whom he has contracted, may recover _____ damages to compensate him or her for the foreseeable injury sustained because of a breach of contract.

2. In an action based on a breach of a contract for the sale of property, the measure of damages will usually be the difference between _____ and _____ .

3. If a provision in a contract states that a certain sum of money will be forfeited by a party who breaches the contract, the provision is referred to as a _____ clause and will be enforced as long as the amount _____ _____ .

4. _____ will be granted by a court if a minor or a party, whose assent was not real, wishes to disaffirm a voidable contract to which he or she was a party.

5. Equitable relief, such as _____ _____ and _____ , will be granted if a legal remedy, such as compensatory damages, is _____ or unavailable.

MULTIPLE CHOICE QUESTIONS

1. In an action based upon a refusal of a buyer to accept and pay for $100 worth of pencils instituted by the seller, a court will probably:
    a. award nominal damages only.
    b. award compensatory damages only.
    c. grant a decree of specific performance.
    d. grant a decree of specific performance and damages.

2. In an action based on a breach of an employment contract by an employee, a court will probably:
    a. award nominal damages.
    b. award punitive damages.
    c. award compensatory damages.
    d. grant a decree of specific performance.

3. Nominal damages refer to:
    a. a small sum awarded to a plaintiff whose rights have been infringed upon as a result of a defendant's breach of contract if the plaintiff incurred no actual loss.
    b. a specific sum of money that one party agrees to pay to another in the event that he breaches a major provision in a contract.
    c. an award by a court when it is determined that a liquidated damages clause in a contract was excessive because it did not bear a reasonable relationship to the actual damage incurred.
    d. the difference between the contract price and the market price of goods that were the subject matter of a contract that has been breached by either the buyer or seller of the goods.

4. When a contract provision requires that a party, who breaches a contract, pay a specified sum to the other party, the amount is referred to as:
    a. specific performance.
    b. nominal damages.

    c. liquidated damages.
    d. punitive damages.

5. Specific performance is:
    a. the remedy used when the subject matter of a contract is unique.
    b. the first remedy a court will grant if a contract is breached.
    c. used when a party has failed to mitigate damages.
    d. infrequently used in cases of breach of contracts for the sale of real property.

6. In an action based on a breach of a contract:
    a. whenever possible a court will require specific performance.
    b. if a party can be adequately compensated by money damages, he will not be granted an injunction.
    c. the party to whom damage is done because of the breach will be awarded money damages only if the contract is rescinded.
    d. the party to whom damage is done because of the breach will usually be awarded money damages as well as rescission or an injunction.

7. One who suffers damage, because the party with whom he has contracted has breached the contract, has a duty to reduce his actual damages if possible. This is referred to as:
    a. making an election of remedies.
    b. limiting liability.
    c. liquidating damages.
    d. mitigating damages.

8. David contracted to sell a set of dueling pistols to John for $50,000. Both David and John believed that the pistols had been owned by Aaron Burr. It is learned that they made a mutual mistake of fact and John wishes to avoid the contract. The most appropriate remedy is:
    a. nominal damages.
    b. compensatory damages.
    c. rescission.
    d. reformation.

9. Reynolds promised to sell 500 shares of stock to Ingram for $10,000 but has failed to deliver the stock certificates to Ingram. A court will issue a decree for specific performance if it is established that:
    a. Ingram used false representations of fact in order to induce Reynolds' assent to the contract.
    b. the shares of stock are those of a corporation, whose shares are publicly traded on a national stock exchange.
    c. a provision of the contract stipulated that if Reynolds breached the contract she would pay Ingram $100, which was the foreseeable amount of damages that would be incurred.
    d. the shares of stock are those of a small corporation which are not readily available for purchase.

UNIT III

Personal Property and Bailment

The objective of Unit III is to introduce you to the concept of property, which, in law, is considered to be a collection of rights and interests associated with ownership of things. The subject of real property, land and things affixed to it or beneath its surface, is covered in Unit IX. All other things, which are capable of being owned, are treated as personal property, the subject of this unit. Contracts, the topic of the previous unit, frequently affect the rights of owners of personal property. It is personal property that is the subject matter of commercial transactions, which are covered in the next unit.

In the chapters in this unit, you will learn about the nature of personal property, how it may be acquired and transferred and the relationship created when one, who has possession of personal property, transfers possession of it to another.

Personal Property

Personal property includes rights and interests in things, other than real property, which are capable of being possessed. Personal property may be tangible or intangible. The chapter deals mainly with the ways in which such property may be acquired and transferred.

THINGS TO KEEP IN MIND

Property is not an object itself. Rather, it is the collection of rights and interests, associated with ownership, that are protected by law.

OUTLINE

I. The nature of personal property—The rights and interests in things, other than real property, which are moveable and capable of being possessed and controlled (chattels).

A. Tangible personal property—Rights in moveable property that is subject to physical possession.

B. Intangible personal property—Rights in a thing that lacks physical substance, e.g., contract rights, ideas, stocks, bonds.

II. Acquisition and transfer of ownership of personal property.

A. Possession or occupation.

1. Possession, with intent to control and exclude others, gives one rights with respect to personal property.

2. One may take possession of unowned property, such as wild animals, fish in their native state and personal property that has been voluntarily abandoned.

B. Purchase—Subject of Uniform Commercial Code and Chapters 17 to 22.

C. Gift—Voluntary transfer of ownership rights without receipt of consideration.

1. Requirements for effective gift.

   a. Delivery by donor.
      1) Actual physical transfer of possession to donee.
      2) Constructive delivery by transferring symbol, such as key to safe deposit box or stock certificate, to donee without retention of control or dominion.
      3) Constructive delivery to a third person with unconditional and absolute instructions to deliver to donee. (Gifts to minors by delivery to a custodian are covered by a Uniform Act.)

   b. Donative intent—Donor intends to presently transfer rights of ownership and relinquishes control.

   c. Acceptance by donee.

2. Types of gifts.

   a. *Inter vivos*—Absolute, present, irrevocable transfer during donor's lifetime.

   b. *Causa Mortis*—Transfer given in contemplation of imminent death as a result of illness or peril. Revocable:
      1) Expressly by donor while living.
      2) If and when donor recovers or survives peril.
      3) Upon death of donee before donor.

D. Accession—Annexation or addition of new value through labor or materials to existing personal property.

1. Without consent of owner.

   a. If innocent accession is not severable and the identity of the original object is changed or the value added exceeds the prior value of the property, improver has ownership rights, but original owner recovers value of lost property.

   b. If accession is willful, original owner is usually entitled to improved property.

2. Annexation pursuant to contract, with owner's consent.

   a. Owner retains rights to property with the improvements.

b. If owner fails to pay for contracted improvements, the improver may exercise possessory artisan's or mechanic's lien by selling property, retaining part of the price to reimburse himself and giving balance to owner.

E. Confusion.

1. Goods, owned by a number of people, may be commingled so that they cannot be identified.

2. Fungible goods—Every unit is exactly the same as every other unit, e.g., grain, oil, livestock, steel, logs, money.

3. If confusion occurs because of an agreement, an innocent mistake or an act of a third person:

   a. If proportionate ownership shares are known, all parties have rights to their proportionate shares.

   b. If amounts owned are unknown, each party shares equally in ownership.

4. If confusion is caused intentionally or because of negligence of a party:

   a. If there has been no loss, each party shares as in 3 above.

   b. If there has been a loss, only the innocent parties share in the manner set forth in 3 above.

F. Lost, abandoned and mislaid property.

1. Mislaid or misplaced—Owner intentionally left property at a location that was inadvertently forgotten. Owner of premises, where property has been found, is entrusted with holding property as a bailee for owner.

2. Lost—Property is accidentally, involuntarily left by owner.

   a. Finder's right of possession is good against all but true owner.

   b. In many states, if found on private property by one who is trespassing, owner of the premises holds lost property as bailee for true owners.

   c. If found by an employee, employer holds lost property as bailee.

3. Abandoned—Owner discarded property without intending to reclaim it. Property belongs to first person who takes possession with intention of owning it.

4. Treasure trove—Nontrespassing finder has right to possession of money, which has been hidden so long in the past that it is unlikely owner will return.

   5. Estray statutes—Finder of lost property becomes owner after publication of notice, if property is not reclaimed by true owner within statutory period.

G. Inheritance—Discussed in Chapter 55.

H. Creation or production—Property created through mental or physical labor belongs to producer or creator.

   1. Patents—Federal statute gives inventors monopolies on use of their inventions for 17 years in exchange for full disclosure.

   2. Trademarks—(Federal Statute)—Perpetual protection from infringement is given to one who first adopts and uses a distinctive symbol, design or mark.

   3. Copyright—Federal statute prohibits reproduction of literary or other creative works, without permission, for the life of the creator plus fifty years. This is subject to some exceptions, such as "fair use," library reproduction and works created prior to 1978.

FILL-IN QUESTIONS

1. Property is a concept that deals with _____ in things. Those things, which are not real property, which are moveable and _____ are considered to be personal property.

2. Usually personal property is transferred by purchase, but it may also be acquired by _____.

3. In order to transfer ownership of personal property by gift, it is necessary that three things occur. They are _____, _____ and _____.

4. Personal property is mislaid if the owner _____, but it is considered to be lost if the owner _____.

MULTIPLE CHOICE QUESTIONS

1. When a judge refers to personal property, he or she means:
   a. rights associated with ownership of things other than real property.
   b. rights associated with ownership of physical objects.
   c. tangible physical things that are not part of real property.
   d. property that is privately owned.

2. A United States Treasury Bond is considered to be:
   a. intangible personal property.
   b. intangible real property.
   c. tangible personal property.
   d. public property.

3. Peg will acquire ownership of a rabbit by occupation if:
    a. the rabbit was previously wild and she took possession of it when it came on her property.
    b. the rabbit was previously wild and she took possession of it when she went to visit a wildlife preserve owned by the state.
    c. the rabbit had run away two years before from its owner, who had not been able to find it.
    d. all of the above.

4. Sara, who had never flown in a plane because of her fear of flying, wanted to see Disneyland and booked an airplane ticket. Before leaving, she signed over title to her automobile and gave the keys therefor to Fred, her dear friend, saying, "I'll probably never make it back alive and I don't want my relatives to have my car, so it's yours." Fred drove off. Later, he opened the glove compartment and found a box, inside of which was a ring and a note to Gloria, Fred's ex-girlfriend, in which Sara stated that the ring was for Gloria.
    a. Gloria becomes the owner of the ring by accession.
    b. When Sara safely returns, she may not reclaim the car from Fred, because she made an irrevocable *inter vivos* gift.
    c. When Sara safely returns, she may reclaim the car from Fred because she made a revocable gift *causa mortis*.
    d. Sara has made a valid, *inter vivos* gift of the ring to Gloria by constructive delivery.

5. Pat has received a gift of the contents of a safe deposit box by constructive delivery if her father put the key to the box in an envelope with Pat's name on it and:
    a. placed it in a drawer in his desk.
    b. left it in Pat's desk, with instructions to keep it for him.
    c. gave it to his attorney with instructions to give it to Pat in three years if he (father) did not reclaim it.
    d. mailed it to Pat, who received it.

6. Martha left her watch with a jeweler to be cleaned and repaired. The charges were $20.
    a. The jeweler may sell the watch and retain the proceeds because Martha has failed to reclaim the watch within one year.
    b. The jeweler may retain possession of the watch and use it because Martha has failed to pay the $20.
    c. The jeweler acquires ownership rights in the watch by occupation.
    d. The jeweler may sell the watch, retain $20 and hold the balance for Martha.

7. R, S and T stored varying quantities of grain in M's silo. Half of the grain and M have disappeared. R can prove that he stored 100 bushels of grain in the silo, and S and T are able to prove that they stored 200 bushels each. M had stored 100 bushels of his own grain in the silo.
    a. R is entitled to 60 bushels and S and T are each entitled to 120 bushels.
    b. R is entitled to 50 bushels and S and T are each entitled to 100 bushels.
    c. R is entitled to 50 bushels and S and T are each entitled to 100 bushels. R, S and T then share equally in M's share.
    d. R, S and T share equally in the grain.

8. Johnson has invented a device which enables the user to produce gasoline from walnut shells. If he obtains a patent, he can prevent others from using his idea:
    a. for as long as he uses the idea.
    b. for his lifetime, even if he does not use the idea.
    c. for a statutory period of 17 years, even if he does not use the idea.
    d. for a statutory period of 28 years, if the patent was obtained before 1978.

9. Harry dumped an old painting, which he no longer wanted, in a street waste container and Tom found and kept it:
    a. Tom will be treated as a bailee of the painting, which was mislaid.
    b. Tom's right to possession is good against all but Harry who is the true owner.
    c. The painting is now Tom's property because he found it after it was abandoned.
    d. If Tom paints over the picture, Harry is still entitled to reclaim the painting.

Bailments

A bailment is a legal relationship that is created when one person, the bailor, delivers temporary possession of personal property to another, the bailee, who has a duty to return the property to the bailor or deliver it or dispose of it as directed by the bailor.

THINGS TO KEEP IN MIND

1. Usually, but not always, bailments are created by contract.

2. In most instances, problems involving bailment relate to the contract or tort liability of a bailee, who has not carried out his or her duty of returning or correctly disposing of the bailed property.

OUTLINE

I. Elements of a bailment.

   A. Subject matter of bailment is personal property, in which the bailor has a possessory interest.

   B. Actual or constructive delivery of possession to the bailee.

      1. In a voluntary bailment, the bailee must be given exclusive possession and control over the property.

      2. The bailee must knowingly accept possession.

      3. Constructive delivery.

         a. Bailee may be given some symbol, which evidences right to possession.

    b. Bailee may have possession of property belonging to another under circumstances which obligate him or her to deliver property to rightful owner (involuntary bailment).
       1) Finder of lost property.
       2) Bailee to whom stolen property was delivered or who has knowledge of an adverse claim to the property.
       3) One who has absolute control over area in which property is deposited.
       4) One to whom a container is delivered has sufficient control over contents to be considered a bailee of objects, which normally would be expected to be in the container.

C. Bailment agreement may be express or implied. Generally it need not be in writing.

D. Duty of bailee to return specific property to bailor or dispose of it in manner which bailor directs.

    1. Bailee receives possession only. He or she does not receive ownership interests, such as title to the property.

    2. Duty of bailee is to deliver identical property, unless the bailed property consists of fungible goods, in which case only the same quantity is to be returned to the bailor.

II. Types of bailments—Liability of a bailee is determined to some extent by the type of bailment.

A. Special bailments—Carriers, warehousemen and innkeepers.

B. Ordinary bailments—Bailee must exercise reasonable care. What is reasonable depends upon the type of bailment.

    1. Bailment for the sole benefit of the bailor (gratuitous)—No consideration is given by the bailee.

    2. Bailment for the sole benefit of the bailee (gratuitous)—No consideration is given by the bailor.

    3. Bailment for mutual benefit—Most bailments envision that consideration (usually a fee or other compensation is given) be given to each party.

III. Rights and duties of bailee.

A. Rights of bailee.

    1. Temporary control and possession of bailed property. Bailee can, therefore, recover from a third party, who interferes with bailee's possession.

    2. Utilize the property in accomplishing purpose of the bailment.

3. Receive compensation, for a nonrental bailment, if bailment is not gratuitous.

B. Duties of bailee.

1. Exercise reasonable care of the property in his or her possession. What is proper care depends upon:

   a. Time and place of bailment.

   b. Facilities of bailee.

   c. Nature of property and bailee's knowledge of its nature.

   d. Type of bailment:
      1) For benefit of bailor—Slight care.
      2) For benefit of bailee—Great care.
      3) Mutual benefit—Ordinary care.

2. Contractual duty to relinquish property at end of bailment in same condition in which it was when received.

   a. Allowance is made for normal wear, depreciation and deterioration.

   b. If bailee was to perform services in order to repair or improve the property, he is required to do so.

   c. There is a presumption that a bailee was negligent if the property is not in correct condition or not relinquished at end of bailment.

IV. Rights and duties of bailor.

A. Rights of bailor—Bailor has right to expect that bailee will:

1. Use reasonable care to protect bailed property.

2. Correctly relinquish property at end of bailment.

3. Perform contract of bailment.

   a. If the bailee has the right to use the property, he or she does so in the agreed manner.

   b. If bailee is to compensate bailor, bailee makes agreed upon payment.

   c. If bailee is to render services on the property, he does so correctly.

B. Duties of bailor.

1. Tort liability—Bailor has duty to furnish property that is free from certain defects.

   a. Mutual benefit bailment—Bailor must notify bailee of known and latent defects (hidden and not ordinarily discoverable).

   b. Bailment for sole benefit of bailee—Bailor must inform bailee of defects of which he or she has actual knowledge.

2. Contract liability—Bailor warrants that property is fit for intended purpose of the bailment.

V. Contractual limitations on liability of bailee—If bailor knows of the limitations on liability or if his or her attention is called to them, they will be enforced. Absolute disclaimers and exculpatory clauses, however, are rarely enforced.

VI. Termination of bailments.

A. If bailment is for a specified term, it ends at expiration of term.

B. If bailment is not for a specified period, it may be terminated by demand of either party or completion of the purpose of the bailment.

C. A bailment may also be terminated by:

   1. Mutual agreement,

   2. Act of a party which is inconsistent with the terms of the bailment, or

   3. Operation of law.

VII. Special bailments.

A. Carriers—Transport goods.

   1. Contract carrier—Provides transportation services under individual contracts to selected users.

   2. Private carrier—Maintains transportation facilities that are privately owned and operated for the sole benefit of the owner and not for hire.

   3. Common carrier—Holds self out to furnish transportation to the public for compensation, without discrimination, as long as it has available facilities. Usually it has a definite route and/or schedule.

      a. Mutual benefit bailment.

      b. Extraordinary liability approaches that of an insurer. Carrier is absolutely liable for loss, destruction or damage to property carried, without regard to fault, unless due to:

1) Act of God.
2) Act of war.
3) Order of public authority.
4) Act of the shipper.
5) Inherent nature of the goods.

   c. Carriers issue documents of title, bills of lading.

   d. Carrier may limit its liability by contract to:
     1) Stated losses but may not relieve itself of liability based on intentional wrongful acts or negligence.
     2) Some maximum dollar amount, but must afford shipper an opportunity to obtain a higher limit by paying a higher charge.

B. Warehouses—Engage in business of storing personal property of others for compensation, without discrimination. Their rights and duties are those of bailees for mutual benefit, modified by statutes.

   1. A public warehouse is liable for its failure to exercise reasonable care.

   2. If property is lost, damaged or destroyed, while in the possession of the warehouse, it has the burden of proving its nonliability.

   3. Warehouses issue documents of title, warehouse receipts.

C. Article 7—Uniform Commercial Code.

   1. Documents of title—Warehouse receipts and bills of lading—Functions:

     a. Receipt for property bailed.

     b. Represents the goods so that the person holding it has right to the property represented by it.

     c. Contract for shipment or storage.

   2. Possessory liens of common carriers and public warehouses.

   3. Other federal and state regulatory statutes.

D. Innkeepers, hotels, motels, etc.

   1. At common law, one, who offered living accommodations to transients, was practically an insurer with respect to the personal property of guests.

   2. Statutes limit liability or provide methods by which liability may be limited by a hotel, etc.

     a. Typically a hotel will not be liable for valuables unless they are deposited in a safe provided by the hotel, notice of which is given to guests.

   b. Hotel will be liable for ordinary negligence, resulting in the loss of property of guests, which are necessary or part of usual wearing apparel and not put in a safe.

FILL-IN QUESTIONS

1. A bailment arises when one person, called the _____, delivers temporary possession of _____ property to another, called the _____, who is obligated to _____ the property to the person who delivered it or dispose of it in the manner which he or she directed.

2. Property may be actually or _____ delivered to a bailee. If the bailee is given some symbol, evidencing a right to possession, or has possession involuntarily, under circumstances which obligate him or her to deliver it to the rightful owner, there has been _____ delivery of the property.

3. A bailee owes a duty of reasonable care with respect to bailed property. If a bailment is for the sole benefit of the bailee, the bailee must exercise _____ care; if it is for the sole benefit of the bailor, the bailee will be liable if he or she fails to exercise _____ care. Most bailments are _____ _____, in which case bailees owe a duty of _____ care.

MULTIPLE CHOICE QUESTIONS

1. In a bailment relationship:
    a. the bailee has temporary title to the bailed personal property.
    b. consideration is necessary to form the relationship.
    c. the bailee has temporary possession of the bailed property.
    d. the property is returned to the bailor or one who the bailee believes has valid title to the property.

2. Which of the following statements is *not* true?
    a. One, who is not an owner of personal property, may be a bailor of the property.
    b. One, in possession of personal property, may not avoid liability to the owner of the property, if he or she sells it to a third person.
    c. One need not be given actual physical possession of personal property in order to be considered a bailee.
    d. One, in possession of personal property, is not a bailee unless the owner of the property entered into an express bailment agreement.

3. Jackson brought his car to a local garage for a tune-up and a number of repairs.
    a. The garage will be liable to Jackson for the value of the car, if it was stolen because the mechanic left the keys in the ignition.
    b. The garage will be liable to Jackson for the value of golf clubs that had been in the trunk but are now missing.
    c. The garage will be liable to Jackson, if it refuses to deliver the car to him because he has not paid for the repairs.

d. The garage will be liable to Jackson for damage done to the car while on its premises a month after it notified Jackson that the work on the car was completed.

4. A parking lot is liable to the owner of an automobile:
    a. who had parked and locked his own car, retaining the keys, if the car is stolen.
    b. who had parked and locked his own car, delivering the keys to an attendant, if the car is stolen.
    c. whose car was parked by an attendant, even if there is a large sign stating that it will not be liable for cars which are damaged by persons other than its employees, if the car is damaged by another user of the parking lot.
    d. whose car was parked by an attendant, if his briefcase, containing business papers and securities worth $3,000, was stolen from the car while it was parked in the lot.

5. Lukins placed a suitcase, containing clothing, in a self-service locker at an airport. He put a quarter in the slot, locked the door and took the key. Marlin checked his suitcase, containing clothing, in a checkroom at the same airport. In this case an attendant took the case from him and put it in a rack in full view of all the attendants in the checkroom. The attendant charged $1 for the storage and gave Marlin a claim check with nothing but a number printed on it. Both the lockers and the checkroom were owned and maintained by the airport.
    a. The airport will be liable to Lukins, if his suitcase is missing when he returns to reclaim it.
    b. The airport will be liable to Marlin, if the suitcase is missing when he returns to reclaim it.
    c. The airport will be liable to Lukins, if the suitcase cannot be returned because an explosion wrecked the checkroom, if the explosion was caused by a bomb left by terrorists and in no way due to the fault of the airport.
    d. The airport will be liable to Marlin, if the suitcase cannot be returned because an explosion wrecked the lockers, if the explosion was caused by terrorists and in no way due to the fault of the airport.

6. A common carrier is:
    a. liable for damage, caused to food carried by it, which is harmed by unseasonably warm temperatures.
    b. not liable for livestock destroyed by an insane railroad engineer.
    c. not a contract carrier.
    d. not liable for injuries to its passengers.

7. A common carrier is *not* liable for damage to property being shipped, if the damage is caused by:
    a. theft.
    b. a tornado.
    c. rioters.
    d. negligence of a trespasser.

8. A public warehouse may limit its liability for loss, destruction or damage to goods it stores in the contract with an owner, who delivers goods to it for storage:

    a. but it is required to offer the owner higher limits of liability at increased rates.

    b. by using exculpatory clauses.

    c. but must obtain a release from the owner in the warehouse receipt which functions as the contract of bailment.

    d. by calling the owner's attention to the limitation on its liability following the delivery of the goods.

9. The common law liability of hotels has been changed by statute so that, if a hotel provides a safe and posts notices of its availability and a guest has been robbed, the hotel will be:

    a. liable for a $200 gold watch, even if it is not deposited in the safe by the guest.

    b. not be liable for a $300 gold watch, even if it is not deposited in the safe by the guest.

    c. liable for $400 worth of uncut diamonds if they were not deposited in the safe by the guest.

    d. never be liable for the property of guests.

10. Traveler was staying at the Buena Vista Motel in a state which permits innkeepers to limit their liability by providing safes for valuables belonging to its guests and notifying them of its availability. Traveler did not use the safe. Among his belongings were a rare 1882 inverted stamp worth $10,000, diamond cuff links worth $5,000, which he wears a few times a week, and dirty laundry of uncertain value. All of these items have disappeared from Traveler's motel room. The motel is:

    a. liable for the loss of the rare 1882 stamp.

    b. not liable for the dirty laundry.

    c. liable for the cuff links.

    d. liable for the loss of the 1882 stamp, the dirty laundry and the cuff links.

UNIT IV

Commercial Transactions and the Uniform Commercial Code

The objective of this unit is to familiarize you with some of the more frequently occurring types of business transactions. Much of the law relating to such transactions has been codified in the Uniform Commercial Code, an internally consistent, comprehensive statement of applicable basic principles of law.

The Code applies to most aspects of a commercial transaction, involving personal property, but does not relate to those involving real property or the performance of services. Included are rules relating to agreements for the sale of goods by original manufacturers, by wholesalers and other distributors and, ultimately, by retailers, who sell them to the final consumers; the transportation and storage of goods; methods available for financing the purchase of goods and for securing payment of the purchase price. Note that, if the parties wish that a rule, different than that provided for by the Code, apply to their dealings, they may so agree.

References are given in the material in the subsequent chapters to sections found in the Uniform Commercial Code, the provisions of which are reproduced in the text. (See Appendix A.)

Introduction to Sales Contracts and Their Formation

The law of sales deals with the rights and duties of the buyers and sellers of goods in the entire chain of purchases-and-sales, from their original production to their ultimate purchase for consumption or other use. Transactions involving sales of goods for consideration are covered by Article 2 of the Uniform Commercial Code. The Code provides for flexibility and establishes standards of good faith and reasonableness for parties engaging in sales transactions. Provisions of the Code, that change some of the rules of law with which you became familiar when you studied the law of contracts, are highlighted.

THINGS TO KEEP IN MIND

1. An agreement for the sale of goods is a contract. All of the elements of a contract, therefore, must be present for it to be valid and enforceable. Some of the rules of contract law, however, are relaxed under the U.C.C.

2. Often special rules are applicable if one or, in some cases, both parties are merchants.

OUTLINE

I. Nature of sales transactions.

   A. The most common commercial transaction is the sale and purchase of goods (tangible personal property).

   B. Modern sales law is derived from the Law Merchant. Today many of the principles of the law of sales are codified in Article 2 of the U.C.C.

C. A sale is a present transfer of ownership rights (title) to existing, identified goods for consideration, known as the price, by a seller to a buyer.

   1. Goods—Items that are tangible and moveable.

      a. Goods associated with realty (real property) (Sec. 2-107):
         1) Mineral or similar natural resources, found beneath the surface, to be severed by the seller.
         2) Growing crops and similar things attached to land to be severed by the buyer or seller.
         3) Things attached to realty to be severed by the buyer or seller, without material harm to the land.

      b. It is sometimes difficult to distinguish goods from services, to which the Code is not applicable.

      c. Special classifications (Sec. 2-105):
         1) Unborn young of animals.
         2) Rare coins and money treated as a commodity.
         3) Items specially manufactured.

   2. Merchants, to whom special rules apply (Sec. 2-104):

      a. Deal in goods of the kind involved in the transaction, or

      b. Hold themselves out, because of their occupation, as having knowledge and skills peculiar to the business or goods involved in the transaction, or

      c. Employ merchants to act on their behalf.

II. Formation of sales contract.

   A. Contract law principles apply to sales agreement, unless modified by the Code. (See Table 17-1 in text for summary.) The Code applies standards of good faith and reasonableness in many instances.

   B. Offer.

      1. Moment at which contract became effective may be undetermined (Sec. 2-204).

      2. If intention to form a contract is found, contract will not fail for indefiniteness because some terms are left open.

         a. Quantity—Requirements and output contracts (Sec. 2-306).

         b. Price (Sec. 2-305).
            1) If parties intended to form contract, but did not set price or provide method by which it was to be determined, the price will be the reasonable price at the time of delivery.

2) If buyer or seller is to set price, he or she must do so in good faith.
3) If price is not fixed through fault of one party, other party may treat contract as cancelled or fix a reasonable price.

c. Place of delivery (Sec. 2-308)—If not specified:
   1) Seller's place of business or, if he or she has none, his or her residence.
   2) If goods are at a location other than seller's place of business, and both parties know it, at that location.

d. Time of delivery (Sec. 2-309)—If not specified, reasonable time.

e. A party, terminating an ongoing contract for delivery of goods, when no period is specified for its duration, must give reasonable notice Sec. 2-309).

f. If the terms for payment are not specified, payment is due at the time and place at which the buyer is to receive the goods (Sec. 2-310).

g. Merchant's firm offer will be irrevocable without consideration, if it is in writing and signed by the merchant (Sec. 2-205).

C. Acceptance.

1. Method of acceptance—If none is specified, any commercially reasonable means of communication may be used (Sec. 2-206).

2. Offer to buy for prompt shipment is accepted when seller promises to ship or promptly ships conforming goods. If seller ships nonconforming goods as an accommodation, it is not an acceptance. (Sec. 2-206.)

3. Offeree communicates that he or she intends to accept an offer, but adds different or new terms (Sec. 2-207).

   a. If the parties are not merchants, it is an effective acceptance of terms agreed upon and proposal for new or different terms.

   b. If the parties are merchants, the new or different terms become part of the contract unless:
      1) Offer expressly limits acceptance to only its terms, or
      2) The terms materially alter the offer (such that they result in hardship or surprise), or
      3) The offeror notifies the offeree of his or her objections to the terms within a reasonable period of time.

4. If an offeree to a unilateral contract does not notify the offeror within a reasonable period of time that he is beginning his or her performance, the offer lapses (Sec. 2-206).

D. Consideration.

1. Consideration is not necessary for contract modifications if made in good faith (Sec. 2-209).

2. A writing is, however, necessary if:

    a. Agreement of the parties so provides, or

    b. The contract, as revised, is required to be in writing in order to be enforceable under the Statute of Frauds.

3. See also Chapter 7—Consideration for contracts.

E. Statute of Frauds (Sec. 2-201).

1. If price for the sale of goods is $500 or more, a writing or memorandum (indicating the parties, nature of goods, price and quantity, unless covered by open term provisions), signed by the party against whom it is being enforced, is required.

2. Sales between merchants—If one party sends a written confirmation of oral agreement within a reasonable time, and the other party does not object within ten days, both parties are bound.

3. Writing not required in following cases:

    a. Contract for goods to be specially manufactured for a particular buyer when:
        1) Goods are not suitable for resale in the ordinary course of business, and
        2) Seller has begun production.

    b. Party admits in court or pleadings that contract had been formed.

    c. Receipt and acceptance of goods.

    d. Payment for goods.

F. Parol evidence rule—Even if writing is a complete statement of the agreement of the parties, parol evidence is admissible to explain or supplement the writing by showing trade usage, a course of dealings or a course of performance, which is not inconsistent with the terms of the writing (Sec. 2-205 and 2-208).

1. Trade usage—Any regular or customary practice or method of dealing in the particular place, trade or vocation, which one is justified in expecting will be observed with regard to the transaction.

2. Course of dealings—Prior conduct of the parties, while engaged in similar transactions.

3. Course of performance—Subsequent conduct of the parties, which is indicative of their intentions.

G. Unconscionability—Contracts or severable contract provisions, that are grossly unfair or one-sided, will not be enforced (Sec. 2-302).

FILL-IN QUESTIONS

1. A sale is a contract which provides for a _____ of title or ownership rights to existing, identified _____ for consideration known as the _____ .

2. Article 2 of the Uniform Commercial Code contains special rules if the parties to a contract are _____, because they _____
_____ or
hold themselves out, because of their occupations, as having the special knowledge and skills peculiar to the business or goods involved in the transaction, or employ others with such knowledge and skills

3. In order for an offer to be effective at common law, all of the material terms must be clear, definite and certain. This rule is relaxed by the Uniform Commercial Code. For example, the _____ and/or the _____ of goods, which are the subject matter of a contract of sale, may be left open.

4. A buyer and seller, in good faith, may modify a contract for the sale of goods in order to change the date upon which the goods are to be delivered without any _____ . The modification would have to be in writing, signed by the seller, in order to be enforceable by the buyer, if _____
_____ or the agreement of the parties so provides.

MULTIPLE CHOICE QUESTIONS

1. A contract providing for the transfer of title to four automobile tires is not covered by Article 2 of the Uniform Commercial Code if:
   a. the bargained for consideration is services to be performed by the recipient.
   b. there is no bargained for consideration given by the recipient.
   c. the tires are to be specially manufactured for an antique fire engine.
   d. the price for the tires is less than $500.

2. Article 2 of the Code applies to the sale of tangible moveable personal property, including:
   a. minerals, if removed from realty by the buyer.
   b. things attached to realty, which are to be severed by the seller, without regard to the harm to the realty.
   c. things not yet in existence.
   d. unborn young of animals.

3. Polk owns 100 acres of woodland. He agrees to sell a specified amount of the timber growing on it to the Lewiston Lumber Co. and the right to extract coal from the land to the Comet Coal Co. for one year.
    a. The transaction with Lewiston Lumber Co. involves a sale of goods if the timber is to be cut by Lewiston.
    b. The transaction with Comet Coal Co. does not involve a sale of goods.
    c. The transaction with Lewiston Lumber Co. involves a sale of goods if the timber is to be cut by Polk.
    d. All of the above.

4. Ware orally contracts to specially manufacture two pairs of glasses with prescription lenses for Ohl for $600.
    a. The transaction is not covered by Article 2 of the Code because it provides for the sale of goods to be specially manufactured.
    b. The transaction is not covered by Article 2 of the Code because it is a contract for the performance of services.
    c. Although the agreed upon price is more than $500, the contract will be enforceable against Ohl because Ware sent a written confirmation of the agreement immediately and Ohl failed to object within ten days.
    d. Although the agreed upon price is more than $500, the contract will be enforce able against Ohl, if Ware has begun grinding the lenses, because the glasses are not suitable for resale in the ordinary course of business.

5. If it is established that a buyer and seller had contractual intent, their contract will be enforced even though:
    a. the buyer had not communicated his assent to the seller's offer.
    b. it provides for the sale of an illegal substance.
    c. it calls for the sale of all the carpeting manufactured at the seller's plant for one year, although the quantity of goods to be sold is indefinite.
    d. it calls for the sale of all the carpeting that the buyer may wish to buy for one year, because the quantity of goods to be sold is indefinite.

6. Lee is the owner of a clothing store. On January 2, she called the Demarre Dress Manufacturing Co. and placed an order for 100 dresses, at a price of $20 per dress, to be delivered on January 20. Lee refused to accept the dresses, which conformed to the contract, on January 20.
    a. Lee is liable to Demarre, if Demarre sent a writing on January 3, confirming the agreement, which was received by Lee, who did not respond.
    b. Lee is liable to Demarre, if Demarre sent a writing on January 3, stating that the price would be $25 per dress, which was received by Lee, who did not respond.
    c. Lee is liable to Demarre because the Statute of Frauds provision of the Code is not applicable when the buyer and seller of goods are both merchants.
    d. Lee is not liable to Demarre because the dresses were not delivered to her place of business.

7. A merchant's offer to sell goods states that it will remain open and not be revoked by the seller. The offer is revocable:
    a. unless consideration is given by the buyer if the offer is oral.
    b. unless the period of time, during which it is to be held open, is stated in the offer.

c. unless the offer is evidenced by a writing, signed by the buyer.

d. if the period of time, during which it is held open, is reasonable.

8. Wright Box Corp. offered to sell 1,000 #4 cardboard boxes at a price of $100 to the Pomfert Packing Co. and stated that it would not withdraw the offer for one month:

a. The offer is a firm offer and irrevocable, without consideration, for three months, if it is in writing.

b. The offer is a firm offer and irrevocable, without consideration, for the period stated, if it is in writing.

c. The offer is a firm offer and irrevocable, without consideration, for a reasonable period of time, if it is oral.

d. Pomfert Packing Co. is bound by the agreement, if it does not object within ten days.

9. Kabot agrees to sell and Long agrees to buy 100 pounds of flour at a price to be determined by Kabot, the seller.

a. The flour is to be delivered at Long's place of business, because the parties did not expressly state where it was to be delivered.

b. There is no contract, because the parties did not agree to the place of delivery.

c. There is no contract, because Long did not agree to a price.

d. Long will be required to pay the price set in good faith by Kabot.

Title, Risk and Insurable Interest

Although for some purposes, such as taxation, inheritance and creditors' rights, it is necessary to determine which party has title (rights of ownership) to the goods that are the subject matter of a contract for sale, under the Uniform Commercial Code, the concept of title does not have major importance in determining the rights and responsibilities of the parties to a sales transaction. To a great extent, it has been replaced by concepts of identification, risk of loss and insurable interest, which are explained in this chapter. These concepts affect the liabilities of the parties, if the goods are damaged, destroyed or lost, their rights to obtain insurance, as well as the rights of their creditors.

THINGS TO KEEP IN MIND

1. The rules discussed in the chapter apply only if the parties have not specified in their contract when identification of the goods or transfer of the risk will occur.

2. Goods that are in existence are usually identified when the contract is made, at which time the buyer has an insurable interest although he may neither have possession nor title nor bear the risk of loss.

3. If a buyer has a contract right to receive goods that are not in existence (future goods), the earliest point at which he or she has an insurable interest, bears the risk of loss or obtains title, is when the goods come into existence and are identified.

OUTLINE

I. Identification—Designation of goods that are the subject matter of a sales contract (Sec. 2-501).

A. Identification determines when the buyer has a right to obtain insurance on the goods, recover from a third person, who damages the goods and, in some cases, obtain the goods from the seller.

B. The parties may specify in their agreement when identification will occur.

C. If parties do not so specify, identification occurs:

   1. At the time the contract is made, if goods are existing and identified.

   2. In general, at the time future goods come into existence and are marked, shipped or identified by the seller.

II. Passage of title (Sec. 2-401).

A. Title does not pass until goods are in existence and identified.

B. Parties may agree on manner of and conditions under which title passes.

C. Applicable rules, if parties have not otherwise agreed.

   1. Existing goods, identified at the time of contracting.

      a. If contract does not provide for issuance of a document of title or delivery to a bailee, other than for movement—Title passes at time of contracting.

      b. If contract provides for delivery of document of title by the seller—Title passes at time and place document of title is delivered.

      c. If contract provides for goods to be held by a bailee without issuance of document of title—Title passes at time and place of contracting.

   2. Future goods—Title passes when seller completes duty of physically delivering goods.

      a. Contract provides for shipment to buyer (F.O.B. point of shipment)—Title passes at time and place goods are delivered to carrier.

      b. Contract provides for delivery at destination (F.O.B. point of destination)—Title passes at time and place goods are tendered at specified destination.

D. Sale of goods on trial basis—Buyer has privilege of returning conforming goods to seller (Sec. 2-326).

   1. Sale on approval—Goods are delivered primarily for use.

      a. Title passes to buyer upon approval (acceptance by buyer).

      b. Until that time, buyer's creditors have no rights with respect to the goods.

2. Sale or return—Goods are delivered primarily for resale.

    a. Title passes to buyer in accordance with II.B and II.C. *supra*, unless seller reserves title.

    b. Goods are subject to buyer's creditors' claims while they are in buyer's possession.

III. Transfer of risk of loss to buyer (Secs. 2-509 and 2-510).

  A. Risk of loss does not shift to buyer until goods are in existence and identified.

  B. Parties may agree as to how and when risk of loss will shift to buyer.

  C. Applicable rules, if parties have not otherwise agreed.

    1. Existing goods identified at time of contracting.

      a. If contract does not provide for issuance of document of title or delivery to a bailee, other than for movement, risk is transferred to buyer:
      1) When buyer receives goods from merchant seller.
      2) When nonmerchant seller tenders the goods.

      b. If contract provides for delivery of document of title, risk is transferred to buyer at time and place of buyer's receipt of document of title.

      c. If contract provides for goods to be held by bailee, without issuance of document of title, risk is transferred to buyer at time and place bailee acknowledges buyer's right to possession.

    2. Future goods—Seller completes duty of physically delivering goods.

      a. Shipment contract—Risk shifts to buyer at time and place goods are delivered to carrier.

      b. Destination contract—Risk shifts to buyer at time and place goods are tendered at specified destination.

  D. Sale of goods on trial basis.

    1. Sale on approval—Goods are delivered for use.

      a. Risk of loss remains with seller until goods accepted.

      b. Buyer must exercise right of returning goods within specified time or, if none is specified, a reasonable time, in which case seller bears expense of returning goods.

    2. Sale or return—Goods are delivered for resale.

      a. Risk of loss is on buyer.

         b. Buyer bears expense and risk of return.

     E. Effect of breach of sales contract on risk of loss.

        1. Breach by seller.

           a. Defect in goods discovered immediately—Risk does not pass until defect cured or buyer knowingly accepts defective goods.

           b. Defect in goods discovered after goods accepted—Buyer can revoke acceptance. To the extent buyer is not covered by insurance, seller bears the loss.

        2. Breach by buyer.

           a. Loss shifts to buyer for a reasonable period of time after seller learns of breach by buyer, if goods are identified.

           b. To the extent seller is not covered by insurance, buyer bears the loss.

IV. Bulk transfers—A transfer (usually a sale) in bulk of a major portion of assets, such as inventory, materials, furniture, fixtures, etc., that is not in the ordinary course of the transferor's business.

     A. Effect is to jeopardize creditors' ability to collect debts owed by seller.

     B. Article 6 of the Code provides for giving notice to seller's creditors.

        1. As between seller and buyer, sale is valid, without compliance with Article 6.

        2. Buyer notifies seller's creditors at least ten days before sale so that they can protect their own interests.

           a. Seller furnishes list of creditors.

           b. Seller and buyer provide schedules of property.

        3. If Article 6 is not complied with, property in hands of buyer is subject to claims of seller's creditors within a specified period of time.

V. Sales by nonowners (Sec. 2-403).

     A. One, who sells goods, can only transfer to another that interest which he or she has.

     B. Imperfect title.

        1. Void title—Purchaser, in good faith for value, from a seller, whose title was void, does not acquire title.

2. Voidable title—A seller may avoid a contract for the sale of goods if he or she is a minor or if the buyer used fraud to induce the contract, etc., while the buyer has possession of the goods. If the buyer has resold them to a good faith purchaser for value, the subsequent purchaser acquires valid title.

C. Entrusting—If an owner of goods entrusts possession of them to a merchant, who deals in that kind of goods, the merchant has power to transfer the entruster/owner's title to a purchaser in the ordinary course of business.

D. Seller's retention of sold goods—Goods, which are retained by a seller, after their sale, are treated as entrusted to the seller, who, therefore, has the power to effectively sell them to another purchaser for value in good faith.

VI. Insurable interest (Sec. 2-501).

A. A buyer has an insurable interest:

1. In existing goods that have been identified as soon as a sales contract is made.

2. In future goods when the goods come into existence and are identified.

B. A seller has an insurable interest as long as he or she retains title and, after title has passed, if he or she retains a security interest in the goods.

FILL-IN QUESTIONS

1. A contract for the sale of goods may provide for a sale of goods presently in existence or _____ .

2. Identification of existing goods occurs at the time _____ ; identification of goods not yet in existence does not take place until the goods come into existence and are properly _____ or identified by the seller.

3. If a buyer, who purchased goods for his or her own use, has a right to return conforming goods to the seller, the sale is a sale _____ ; if he or she purchased the goods for resale, the transaction is a sale _____ .

4. If parties have not otherwise agreed in their contract for the sale of existing goods to be delivered by a merchant seller to the buyer, title passes and the buyer has an insurable interest at the time _____ but the risk of loss is not transferred to the buyer until _____ .

5. If parties have agreed in their contract for the sale of future goods that the goods are to be shipped F.O.B. to a carrier in the city in which the seller maintains its business, it is a _____ contract. Title and risk of loss to the buyer will pass when the goods are _____ , although the buyer has _____ when the goods come into existence and are identified.

MULTIPLE CHOICE QUESTIONS

1. Under a contract for sale of goods, a buyer may return goods after they have been delivered but before they are accepted.
    a. If the goods are the kind that are used by the buyer, the buyer's creditors can make a claim with regard to the goods.
    b. If the goods are the kind that are used by the buyer, and they are stolen, the risk of loss falls on the buyer.
    c. If the goods have been purchased for ultimate resale by the buyer, the buyer's creditors can make a claim with regard to the goods.
    d. If the goods have been purchased for ultimate resale by the buyer, the seller bears the expense of returning the goods, if the buyer exercises his right of returning the goods.

2. In general, the buyer is deemed to have waived his right of inspection when an agreement for sale is:
    a. a shipment contract.
    b. a destination contract.
    c. an identification.
    d. a documentary sale.

3. Frank lent his bicycle to his friend, Pat. Pat then sold the bicycle to Bob for a fair price. Bob did not know how Pat had acquired the bicycle. When Frank learned what Pat had done, he demanded that Bob return the bicycle to him.
    a. Frank can enforce his demand.
    b. Frank cannot enforce his demand, because he was not a minor.
    c. Frank can enforce his demand only if Pat was the owner of a bicycle store and Bob was a customer.
    d. Frank can enforce his demand only if Pat was insolvent at the time of the sale.

4. On Monday, Frankel purchased a bicycle for $150 from The Cycle Shop but left it with the seller so that some adjustments could be made. On Tuesday, Brady purchased the bicycle for $155, without knowing that it was Frankel's property. The sale to Brady was:
    a. effective because the Cycle Shop's title was voidable, because Frankel was a minor.
    b. effective because Frankel had entrusted the bicycle to the Cycle Shop, which dealt in bicycles.
    c. not effective because the Cycle Shop did not have title to the bicycle.
    d. not effective because the Cycle Shop's title was void.

5. The Bulk Sales Act:
    a. protects the creditors of the seller. As a general rule, if the Act is complied with, such creditors must look to the proceeds of the sale only.
    b. protects the creditors of the buyer. As a general rule, if the Act is not complied with, such creditors must look to the proceeds of the sale only.
    c. requires that a list of creditors and a schedule of property be filed with a designated official of the State or County.
    d. must be complied with in order that the contract of sale be enforceable by a seller against a buyer.

Performance and Obligation

As is true of any contract, the parties to a contract for the sale of goods assume certain express duties to perform in accordance with their agreement—the seller to transfer and deliver and the buyer to accept and pay for goods that conform to the contract. In addition, the Uniform Commercial Code imposes obligations on each of the parties to exercise good faith in performing and to do nothing to impair the expectations of the other party that the contract will be duly performed.

THINGS TO KEEP IN MIND

1. Many of the seemingly intricate rules explained in this chapter are effective if the parties have used certain commercial terms, with which you should become familiar.   Often, if you give some thought to it, you will realize that the consequences of using a particular term is implicit from the wording of the term itself.

2. In the law of sales, the word "delivery" does not necessarily mean a physical delivery of the goods.   A seller is required to make the goods available to the buyer, which may be accomplished by a tender of delivery of a document of title, rather than the goods themselves.

OUTLINE

I.   Duty of good faith and commercial reasonableness—Standards of good faith and commercial reasonableness are read into every contract for the sale of goods.

    A. If a party is to fill in particulars of performance, he or she must do so "in good faith and within limits set by commercial reasonableness" (Sec. 2-311).

B. In the case of a merchant, this means honesty and "observance of reasonable commercial standards of fair dealing" (Sec. 2-103(1)(b)).

C. Parties are expected to be cooperative and not take advantage of each other.

II. Performance of a sales contract—The seller has an obligation to transfer and deliver goods that conform to the contract and the buyer has an obligation to accept and pay for them (Sec. 2-301).

A. If the parties have not otherwise agreed, the obligations of the seller and buyer to perform are concurrent conditions.

B. A party must either perform as required by the contract or, under certain circumstances, tender correct performance or be excused from tendering his or her performance.

III. The seller's obligations.

A. Tender of delivery (Sec. 2-503).

1. A seller, holding conforming goods, must give reasonable notice to the buyer to enable him or her to take delivery.

2. Place of delivery.

a. In situations in which the place of delivery is not specified and transportation by carrier is not required, the place of delivery is:
   1) Seller's place of business; if he or she has none, seller's residence.
   2) When the parties know that goods are at a location, other than the seller's place of business, at that location.
   3) When the goods are held by a bailee, seller tenders delivery of document, which will enable the buyer to obtain goods (Sec. 2-308).

b. Carrier cases (Sec. 2-319—2-322).

   1) Shipment contract—Seller must:
      a) Put goods in carrier's possession, and
      b) Make reasonable contract for transportation of the goods, and
      c) Notify buyer promptly of shipment.

   2) Destination contract—Seller must tender conforming goods at specified destination. Typically this is accomplished by tendering documents of title, often through customary banking channels.

   3) Delivery F.O.B. (free on board) at a named place.
      a) Seller's duty, risk and expense ends when goods are at the designated place.
      b) Seller must bear risk and expense of loading, if a particular vehicle of transportation is specified.

   4) Delivery F.A.S. (free alongside) named vessel—Shipment contract—Seller's duty, risk and expense ends when goods are delivered to dock

and seller obtains receipt (usually the bill of lading), which is tendered to the buyer.

    5) Delivery Ex-ship (from the carrying vessel)—Destination contract—Seller bears duty, risk and expense until the goods are unloaded.

    6) C.I.F. (purchase price includes cost of the goods, insurance during transit and freight charges)—Shipment contract.
       a) Seller is obligated to load goods, pay freight, obtain proper insurance, receipt and other necessary documents, prepare invoice and tender all documents to buyer.
       b) Risk of loss is borne by buyer.
       c) C & F—Price includes cost of goods and freight charges.

B. Perfect tender rule—In order to be entitled to payment, the seller is required to tender conforming goods in a manner that accords completely to the terms of the contract.

  1. If the goods and/or tender do not conform to the contract, the buyer may:

    a. Reject all the goods, or

    b. Accept all the goods, or

    c. Accept some and reject the rest of the goods (Sec. 2-601).

  2. Exceptions.

    a. Parties may agree otherwise.

    b. Cure—Seller may repair, replace or, in some cases, make a price adjustment for nonconforming goods.
      1) Buyer is required to disclose nature of defect.
      2) If time for delivery has not expired, seller is merely required to give notice of intention to give proper delivery and make such delivery within contracted time.
      3) If seller had reason to believe that the buyer would accept nonconforming tender and the time for delivery has expired, seller has a reasonable time within which to make proper delivery after giving notice to buyer (Sec. 2-508).

    c. If there is no material delay or loss because of inappropriate shipping arrangements, the buyer may not reject the goods (Sec. 2-504).

    d. Seller may substitute a different means of delivery, if the agreed manner of delivery becomes impracticable or impossible to use, without fault of the seller (Sec. 2-614).

    e. Installment contract—Delivery of goods in installments may be contemplated in the contract or because of circumstances necessitating delivery in lots (Secs. 2-307 and 2-612).

1) Buyer may reject a nonconforming installment, which cannot be cured and which impairs the value of the installment.
2) Entire contract is breached if one or more nonconforming installment substantially impairs the value of the entire contract.

f. Commercial impracticability—If performance of a contract is commercially impracticable because of an unforeseen supervening occurrence, not contemplated by the parties at the time of contracting, nondelivery or a delay in delivery does not constitute a breach (Sec. 2-615).

g. Destruction of identified goods before risk of loss passes to buyer (Sec. 2-613).
1) Seller is excused from performing, if the goods are totally destroyed.
2) If the goods are partially destroyed, the buyer may:
  a) Treat the contract as avoided, or
  b) Accept the goods with a deduction from the contract price.

IV. The buyer's obligations.

A. The buyer is obligated to accept the goods and to pay for them in accordance with the terms of the contract for sale (Secs. 2-301 and 2-607).

B. Payment—If no provision is made in the contract:

1. Payment is to be made at the time and place that the goods are received by the buyer (Sec. 2-511).

2. Payment can be in cash or another commercially acceptable medium (Sec. 2-511).

3. If sale is made on credit, the credit period begins on the date of shipment (Sec. 2-310).

4. Buyer has a right to inspect goods before making payment unless buyer has agreed to:

a. C.O.D. (collect on delivery) shipment, or

b. Payment upon presentation of document of title. (This is so when a bill of lading is tendered with a C.I.F. or C & F contract.) (Sec. 2-513.)

C. Acceptance (Sec. 2-606).

1. Manifested expressly or by conduct if buyer:

a. After opportunity to inspect, indicates that the goods are conforming or that they are acceptable despite nonconformity.

b. After opportunity to inspect, fails to reject the goods.

c. Performs an act that is inconsistent with the seller's ownership.

2. Acceptance may be revoked by notifying seller of a breach within a reasonable period after buyer discovers or should have discovered the breach (Sec. 2-607).

V. Anticipatory repudiation—If, prior to the time for performance, either party communicates his or her intention not to perform to the other party, the aggrieved party may:

A. Wait for the other party to perform correctly or retract the repudiation.

B. Resort to an appropriate remedy.

C. Suspend his or her own performance (Sec. 2-610).

FILL-IN QUESTIONS

1. In order to perform a seller is obligated to transfer and deliver goods _____ _____ to the buyer, who has an obligation to accept and _____ the goods. If the parties have not otherwise specified, the seller's and buyer's obligations are to be rendered at the same time because they are _____ conditions.

2. If a seller is to deliver goods to a carrier under a shipment contract, the seller is required to (1) _____, (2) make a commercially reasonable contract for transportation, and (3) promptly notify the buyer.

3. Delivery F.A.S. and Ex-ship are terms used when goods are to be transported by ship. If delivery is F.A.S. a named vessel, the seller's duty ends when the goods are _____ and the seller obtains a receipt, which is duly tendered to the buyer. If the goods are to be delivered Ex-ship, the seller's duty, risk and expense continue until the goods are _____.

4. The distinction between a C.I.F. and a C & F contract is that, with a C.I.F. contract, the purchase price includes the cost of the goods, _____ and _____, whereas with a C & F contract, only the _____ are included. With both C.I.F. and C & F contracts, the risk of loss during shipment is borne by the _____.

5. If a seller tenders goods that do not conform to the contract, the buyer has a number of options. He or she may (1) _____, (2) _____, or (3) _____ _____.

6. When the parties have not indicated any terms of payment but goods have been properly tendered for delivery by a seller, a buyer has an obligation to pay at the time and place the goods are _____ by using cash or _____ for payment.

MULTIPLE CHOICE QUESTIONS

1. Upon the delivery of nonconforming goods, a buyer may:
    a. reject all the goods.
    b. accept all the goods.
    c. accept those units which conform but reject the rest.
    d. all of the above.

2. Beyer, in Kansas City, Missouri, ordered 1000 fully described pots and pans from Deelar, a wholesaler, in Pittsburgh, Pennsylvania. The pots and pans were in existence and to be shipped by truck. If the pots and pans were to be shipped:
    a. F.O.B. Kansas City, and the goods were lost in transit, the risk of loss is borne by Beyer.
    b. F.O.B. Kansas City, and the goods were lost in transit, the risk of loss is borne by Keelar.
    c. C.I.F. and the goods were lost in transit, the risk of loss is borne by Deelar.
    d. C & F and the goods were lost in transit, the risk of loss is borne by Deelar.

3. The New England Candy Co. of Boston, Massachusetts, contracted for the purchase of a stated quantity of sugar from Sweet Sugar Inc. of Louisiana. Assume that the contract provided that the sugar was to be shipped:
    a. F.O.B. Boston. The expense of loading is borne by New England Candy Co.
    b. F.A.S. Coastal Queen (a freighter), New Orleans. The expense of loading is borne by Sweet Sugar Inc.
    c. Ex-ship Boston. The expense of loading is borne by Sweet Sugar Inc.
    d. C & F. The expense of loading is borne by New England Candy Co.

4. The New England Candy Co. of Boston, Massachusetts, contracted for the purchase of a stated quantity of sugar from Sweet Sugar Inc. of Louisiana. Assume that the contract provided that the sugar was to be shipped by sea, to arrive November 1.
    a. Assume that Sweet Sugar learns that shipment by truck will be less expensive and ships by truck rather than by sea, in accordance with the contract. New England Candy Co. may reject the goods, which arrived on October 30 in Boston because of the seller's failure to make a perfect tender.
    b. Assume that there is a hurricane off the coast of New Orleans and that Sweet Sugar, therefore, ships the sugar by truck, rather than by sea. New England Candy Co. may not reject the goods, which arrived on October 30 in Boston, because of Sweet Sugar's failure to perform in accordance with the contract.
    c. Assume that the goods arrived by ship in Boston on October 30 but were stolen from the vessel on October 31. New England Candy Co. bears the risk of the loss, even though Sweet Sugar failed to notify it that the goods were being shipped.
    d. Assume that the goods arrived by ship in Boston on October 30 but were stolen from the vessel on October 31. Sweet Sugar bears the risk of loss, even though it sent and New England Candy received the bill of lading through normal banking channels.

5. Shuman Auto Parts Inc. entered into a contract for the sale of 3000 spark plugs to Wright Auto Supplies Distribution Co. The 3000 spark plugs were marked, packaged and held by Shuman at its plant. Wright was notified that the spark plugs were

available. A week later, a fire occurred at Shuman's plant and the spark plugs were destroyed.

    a. If no delivery terms were specified in the contract for the sale of the spark plugs, Shuman made a tender of delivery and has fully performed its contractual obligations.

    b. Shuman is excused from performing because identified goods were destroyed before the risk of loss was transferred to Wright.

    c. Both Shuman and Wright are excused from performing because of commercial impracticability.

    d. Wright may treat the contract as avoided because the goods have been destroyed.

6. The Bertown Bridge Club placed an order for 100 decks of playing cards with McDonald. No date was specified for delivery. A week later, McDonald tendered 100 decks of cards to the Bridge Club. The Bridge Club discovered that 50 of the decks were missing the ace of diamonds and immediately notified McDonald that the goods were nonconforming and unacceptable.

    a. McDonald's action may be treated as an anticipatory repudiation. The Bertown Bridge Club can, therefore, suspend its performance.

    b. The Bertown Bridge Club's action may be treated as an anticipatory repudiation. McDonald may, therefore, sue the Bridge Club for damages.

    c. McDonald will cure the defect by supplying the missing aces of diamonds within a reasonable period of time.

    d. McDonald will cure the defect by reducing the price of the 50 decks by three percent.

7. Selk and Buckingham had a contract for the sale of three electric typewriters, which were delivered by the seller, Selk, in the manner prescribed by the contract. Buckingham has a right to inspect the typewriters before paying for them:

    a. unless Selk notified Buckingham that the typewriters did not conform to the contract because they were green instead of blue and were being shipped as an accommodation.

    b. unless the contract specified that the typewriters were to be shipped C.O.D.

    c. only if the contract so provided.

    d. only if Buckingham accepts delivery at Selk's place of business.

8. Schain had delivered ten window screens to Barton in the manner prescribed by the contract of sale, and Barton paid for the screens.

    a. If Barton resells the screens to a third person, Barton will be treated as having accepted them.

    b. If Barton discovered that the screens were defective three months later, while she was putting them up, and notified Schain of the defect, Barton will not be treated as having accepted them.

    c. If Barton discovered that the screens were defective three months later, while putting them up, but did not notify Schain of the defect for six months, Barton will not be treated as having accepted them.

    d. If Barton inspected the screens when they were delivered, without noticing the defects, which became apparent when she put the screens up, Barton may not revoke her acceptance.

Introduction to Sales
Warranties

A manufactured item, that had been the subject matter of a contract of sale, may prove to be defective or not fit for the normal or a particular use for which it was purchased, causing personal or property damage to the buyer; or the seller may not have had the right to sell the item, so that, after it was in the hands of the buyer, a third person asserted claims to it. Often a buyer, seeking redress, may rely on a contractual theory of warranty.

A seller has certain obligations to the buyer, because he or she makes warranties, or assurances, concerning the goods he or she sells. The seller is responsible for transferring good title and for furnishing goods that function in the expected manner and are suitable for the buyer's need.

THINGS TO KEEP IN MIND

All sellers of goods are treated as making certain implied warranties, unless they have made effective disclaimers. Warranties may also be expressly made by sellers, who make factual assertions, affirmations, representations, etc.

OUTLINE

I.   Warranties of title (Sec. 2-312).

    A. In most contracts for the sale of goods, the seller makes warranties concerning his or her right to sell the goods free of claims to them by other persons.

        1. Good title—Seller warrants that he or she has valid title to the goods and that the transfer of title to the buyer is rightful.

2. No liens—Seller warrants that there are no liens, security interests or other encumbrances, of which the buyer has no knowledge.

3. No infringements—If seller is a merchant, he or she warrants that the goods are free from any adverse copyright, patent, trademark or similar claims. This warranty against infringement does not apply if the goods were made to the buyer's specifications.

B. Warranties of title may be expressly excluded, disclaimed or modified in the contract.

C. Warranties of title are excluded if sale occurs under circumstances which clearly indicate that no such assurances are being made by the seller.

II. Warranties of quality.

A. Express warranties—A factual assertion, representation, affirmation or promise, relating to the goods, or description, model or sample of the goods, which becomes "part of the basis of the bargain" (Sec. 2-313).

1. Assurances and representation made by a seller before, at the time of and after contracting.

2. No particular words need be used to create a warranty.

3. Statements of opinion and value do not create warranties as to quality, unless made by experts.

4. In some cases, a seller may not make any warranties or may effectively disclaim those which he or she has made, by unambiguous language to that effect in the contract.

B. Implied warranties—Arise, unless expressly excluded.

1. Merchantability (Sec. 2-314).

a. Made by merchant, who deals in the kind of goods sold.

b. Goods are merchantable if:
    1) Of the average or usual quality existing in the market.
    2) Reasonably fit for the normal, ordinary purposes for which they are used.
    3) Properly "contained, packaged and labeled."

c. Merchant seller is absolutely liable for breach.

d. Warranty of merchantability is made in a sale of food or drink for consumption on the premises or elsewhere.

e. Warranty of merchantability may be disclaimed or modified by:

        1) Using expressions such as, "as is" or "with all faults."
        2) Using conspicuous language, which must include the word, "merchantability."
        3) An inspection conducted by the buyer, or a refusal by the buyer to examine the goods or a sample. (There is no warranty as to defects, which a reasonable examination would reveal.)
        4) Trade usage, course of dealing or course of performance (Sec. 2-316).

  2. Fitness for particular purpose (Sec. 2-315).

    a. Seller warrants that the goods are fit for the particular purpose intended by the buyer.

    b. The warranty is made by a seller, who need not be a merchant, having reason to know the particular purpose for which the buyer purchases the goods.

    c. The buyer relies on the skill and judgment of the seller in selecting the goods.

    d. Warranty of fitness for particular purpose may be disclaimed or modified by:
        1) Using expressions such as, "as is" or "with all faults."
        2) The disclaimer must be in writing and conspicuous, but need not have a reference to fitness for particular purpose.
        3) An inspection conducted by the buyer, or a refusal by the buyer to examine the goods or a sample. (There is no warranty as to defects, which a reasonable examination would reveal.)
        4) Trade usage, course of dealing or course of performance (Sec. 2-316).

III. Disclaimers, exclusion and modifications of warranties.

  A. Express and implied warranties may be excluded, or disclaimed or modified, as discussed herein at I.B, II.A.4, II.B.1.e and II.B.2.d.

  B. Note that the Magnuson-Moss Warranty Act, discussed in Chapter 21, may limit the Uniform Commercial Code provisions.

IV. Overlapping warranties—More than one warranty may be made by a seller in a sales transaction (Sec. 2-317).

  A. If the warranties are consistent with each other, a buyer can base an action against the seller on all of them.

  B. If multiple warranties are inconsistent, the intention of the parties will determine which will prevail. The following rules are used as guides to determine their intentions.

    1. Specifications prevail over inconsistent models, samples or general descriptions.

2. A "sample from an existing bulk" prevails over inconsistent general descriptions.

3. Implied warranty of fitness for particular purpose takes precedence over express warranties.

4. Express warranties take precedence over implied warranties, of merchantability and title.

FILL-IN QUESTIONS

1. A seller, whether or not he or she is a merchant of goods, impliedly warrants that he or she is transferring good title to the buyer, that he or she has the right to do so and that the goods are _____ _____ ; a seller, who is a merchant, also warrants against infringements, which means that the goods are _____ _____ .

2. A seller, who makes a statement or representation concerning the quality of the goods that he sells, has made an _____ warranty if the assertion, statement or representation deals with a _____ characteristic of the goods, as distinguished from a statement of opinion or value.

3. Even though a seller of goods makes no express warranties concerning the quality of the goods that he or she is selling, it is implied that the goods are _____ and _____ .

4. A merchant, who deals in the kinds of goods that are the subject matter of a sale to a consumer, makes an implied warranty of merchantability. He or she warrants that the goods are (1) _____ , (2) _____ and (3) contained, packaged and labeled as provided in the contract, unless he or she has effectively disclaimed or modified the implied warranty. He or she may do so by using conspicuous language, which includes the word, _____ .

5. If the intentions of the parties are not clear as to whether or not an express warranty made by the seller was to take precedence over an inconsistent implied warranty, the implied warranty of _____ will prevail over an inconsistent _____ warranty. If, however, an express warranty is inconsistent with an implied warranty of merchantability or title, the _____ warranty will prevail over the inconsistent _____ _____ .

MULTIPLE CHOICE QUESTIONS

1. In a contract for the sale of goods, express warranties are created by the seller, if he or she:

a. represents that the goods will increase in value by at least 20 percent in two months.

b. states that in his or her opinion, the goods will prove satisfactory for the buyer's purpose.

c. assures the buyer that the goods will be the same as a sample, which he exhibits.

d. says that his or her goods are better than those of his competitors.

2. Obedin owned and operated a small precision machine manufacturing business. Kendall contracted with Obedin for the manufacture of a metal cutting machine, for which Kendall supplied specifications. Obedin produced and delivered the machine, which conformed to the specifications, and Kendall paid the contract price. The machine performed satisfactorily. Six months after delivery of the machine to Kendall, Cutter Machine Tools brought action against Obedin and Kendall for infringement of its patent rights. Kendall, in turn, brought an action against Obedin, based upon breach of warranty. Kendall will *not* be successful, if his action is based upon breach of:

a. an express warranty, because an implied warranty against infringement takes precedence over a conflicting express warranty.

b. an implied warranty against infringement, because the machine was made in accordance with specifications furnished by the buyer.

c. an implied warranty of good title, because an implied warranty of good title is displaced by an implied warranty against infringement when the seller is a merchant.

d. an implied warranty that the machine was free of liens or other encumbrances because such a warranty is not made when goods are specially manufactured.

3. Langer, who was not a merchant, sold a computer to Vannan for use in an educational project. Langer made no express warranties. Vannan claims and is able to show that the computer does not perform the operations needed for her project. She, therefore, sues Langer for breach of warranty. Vannan will probably be successful because Langer breached the implied warranty:

a. of merchantability.

b. of fitness for a particular purpose.

c. that the item sold was fit for the ordinary purpose for which computers are normally used.

d. that there were no security interests or other encumbrances which would interfere with Vannan's use of the computer.

Questions 4, 5 and 6 are based on the following fact situation: Charlotte went to Katherine's store in order to purchase a new ladder so that she could paint the trim on her 15-foot ceilings. Charlotte asked to see a ladder manufactured by X, which Katherine showed her. Katherine also showed Charlotte a ladder manufactured by Y and one by Z, stating that she believed that the Y ladder was the "best buy" of the three and that X ladder would not prove satisfactory for Charlotte's purposes. You are to assume that the entire transaction was conducted orally.

4. Charlotte purchased the X ladder. She was injured when the ladder collapsed while she was painting the trim on her ceiling. With regard to a breach of warranty of fitness for a particular purpose, which of the following statements is true?

a. There has been a breach of warranty of fitness, because Katherine knew the purpose for which Charlotte was making the purchase.
b. There has been no breach of the warranty of fitness, because Charlotte did not rely on Katherine's skill and judgment in making her selection.
c. There has been no breach of the warranty of fitness, because Katherine used conspicuous language to effectively exclude the warranty of fitness.
d. There has been a breach of warranty of fitness, because the ladder was not fit for the normal purpose for which ladders are used.

5. Charlotte purchased the Y ladder. She was injured when the ladder collapsed while she was painting the trim on her ceiling. With regard to a breach of warranty of merchantability, which of the following statements is true?
a. The warranty of merchantability was breached because the ladder was not reasonably fit for the purpose for which one usually uses a ladder.
b. A warranty of merchantability takes precedence over express warranties.
c. Katherine effectively disclaimed the warranty of merchantability.
d. Katherine's express statements created an express warranty of merchantability.

6. Charlotte purchased the Z ladder. She was injured when the ladder collapsed while she was painting the trim on her ceiling.
a. Katherine has not breached any warranties because she made no assertions or representations of facts concerning the Z ladder.
b. An implied warranty of merchantability can be expressly excluded by contract if the seller is a nonmerchant, but not by Katherine because she was a merchant.
c. An implied warranty of merchantability would have been effectively excluded if the defect had been revealed by Charlotte's inspection.
d. A disclaimer of the warranty of merchantability by Katherine would not be effective unless it was conspicuous and in a writing, which included the word, "merchantability."

7. Cautious T.V. and Radio Store wished to exclude implied warranties as to quality from its future sale of television and radio sets. It can effectively do so by:
a. selling only brand name merchandise.
b. using a written contract form which states conspicuously that, "All warranty protection by Cautious T.V. and Radio Store is expressly excluded by the seller."
c. using a written contract form which states conspicuously that, "There are no warranties which extend beyond the description contained in this contract of sale."
d. Using a written contract form which states conspicuously that, "The merchandise is sold as is and with all faults."

8. Freyberg became violently ill after eating a hamburger purchased at Speedy Burger Palace, and it has been determined that his illness was caused by poisonous substances in the hamberger, causing it to be unfit for human consumption. Freyberg sues the Speedy Burger Palace, basing his cause of action on a breach of implied warranty of merchantability and warranty of fitness for a particular purpose.
a. Freyberg may base his cause of action upon either of both of the warranties.

b. Freyberg may base his cause of action upon one of the warranties but not both of them.
c. The implied warranty of merchantability does not apply, because Freyberg did not consume the hamburger at the Speedy Burger Palace, but ate it while seated in his own car.
d. The implied warranty of fitness for a particular purpose does not apply, because Speedy Burger Palace was not informed by Freyberg of the particular purpose for which he was purchasing the hamburger.

9. Huber purchased a case of beer from Beere's Beverages. He drank one can of the beer without any harmful effects and used the remainder of it to wash his car. As a result, the paint on the car was permanently damaged.
a. Beere's Beverages is liable to Huber for breach of the warranty of merchantability.
b. Beere's Beverages is liable to Huber for breach of the warranty of fitness for a particular purpose.
c. Beere's Beverages is not liable for breach of any implied warranties as to quality, because Beere's Beverages did not know the purpose for which Huber was purchasing the beer and Huber used the beer for an unusual purpose.
d. Beere's Beverages is not liable for breach of any implied warranties as to quality, because such warranties do not apply to food or drink.

Products Liability

If a manufactured product is defective, it may be the cause of personal or property injuries to the purchaser or third persons, such as other users or bystanders. The product may have been the subject matter in a chain of numerous sales transactions and, as a result, many sellers may have potential liability to those injured by the defective item. Who bears the burden of liability is determined by the theory of law, upon which the injured person bases his or her cause of action. Liability for defective products may be imposed because of tort, contract and/or statutory law.

The diagram below illustrates the numerous potential parties. Some may be parties because they have been injured and are plaintiffs; others may be parties because they were in the "chain" of purchases and sales. Note that often it is the remote user or bystander, rather than the ultimate buyer, who will seek to impose liability on one of the sellers in the vertical chain of sales.

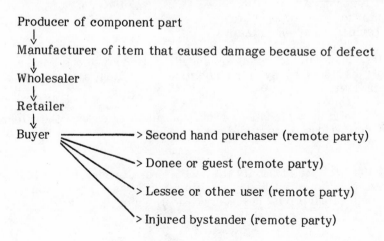

Producer of component part
↓
Manufacturer of item that caused damage because of defect
↓
Wholesaler
↓
Retailer
↓
Buyer ————————> Second hand purchaser (remote party)

> Donee or guest (remote party)

> Lessee or other user (remote party)

> Injured bystander (remote party)

THINGS TO KEEP IN MIND

1. In the diagram, those in the vertical chain are potential defendants; remote parties in the horizontal chain represent potential plaintiffs. The ultimate buyer may be a defendant as well as a plaintiff.

2. Many of the concepts of contract and tort law were formulated before modern methods of production and distribution for mass consumption existed.

OUTLINE

I. Contract liability—Based on the theory that a seller is regarded as making certain warranties relating to the products that he or she sells. (See Chapter 20.)

A. Common law doctrine of privity of contract.

   1. One, who has not consented to a contractual relationship, neither acquires rights nor assumes obligations.

   2. There are obligations and, therefore, liabilities for failure to carry out obligations only if there is privity of contract.

   3. If there is a breach of an express or implied warranty by a seller:

      a. The buyer can sue his seller for the breach, but

      b. An injured user or other remote, noncontracting party, who was not in privity with the seller, cannot sue a seller for the breach. (Remember, this is the common law rule, which is subject to change.)

   4. Prior to the adoption of the Uniform Commercial Code, the limitations on liability, based on the concept of privity, had been eroded in many states, in which courts recognized that, with modern marketing techniques, consumers purchased products because of the name of the manufacturer and its advertising campaigns, and held that:

      a. Warranties, made by a seller, extended to those persons who could reasonably be foreseen by a manufacturer as potential users of the manufactured item.

      b. Warranties, relating to food and drink, and, in some cases, other items, which, if deleterious, were dangerous to human life, extended to remote users.

B. Modification of the doctrine of privity in the Uniform Commercial Code (Sec. 2-318)—With regard to potential liability arising from breach of warranty, the requirement of contractual privity has been considerably obviated by the Code.

1. The effect is to make certain persons, such as lessees, family members, donees and bystanders, third party beneficiaries of express and implied warranties that are made by sellers of the goods. Note that three alternative provisions have been proposed by the drafters of the U.C.C.

   a. Persons:
      1) Alternatives A and B extend only to natural persons.
      2) Alternative A extends only to those in the family or household or guests in the home of the purchaser.

   b. Who are reasonably expected to use, consume or be affected by the goods, and

   c. Who are injured—Alternatives A and B extend only to those who incur personal injuries and, therefore, exclude property damage.

2. A seller may not exclude or limit liability for personal injuries.

II. Tort Liability—(Note: In an action based on tort, an injured party need not show that privity of contract existed.)

A. Fraudulent misrepresentation.

   1. A buyer, who is injured because he or she relied upon a representation of material fact that was false and made to induce a contract, may recover for the tort of fraud.

   2. If a misrepresentation is innocently made by a seller, without the intention of deceiving a buyer, in some jurisdictions, the buyer may also recover in tort for the injuries he incurred because of the misrepresentation.

B. Negligence—Failure to exercise reasonable care.

   1. Manufacturer (as well as other sellers) must exercise reasonable care to make products that are safe for the purpose for which they are intended to be used.

   2. A manufacturer is liable to one who is injured because of a defective product if:

      a. It was foreseeable that the defect would cause the product to be dangerous to life, and

      b. The manufacturer failed to correct the defect or make a reasonable inspection, which would disclose the defect.

C. Strict tort liability—Manufacturer or other seller is liable, without fault, if:

   1. The product was defective,

2. The defect resulted in the product being unreasonably dangerous, when used for its ordinary purpose,

3. The defect was the proximate cause of the injury,

4. The product reached the user without any substantive change in its condition after its sale by the defendant, and

5. The defendant is normally engaged in selling such products.

6. The injured party need not establish privity of contract or that the manufacturer, or other seller, was negligent or that its conduct was intentional.

7. Defenses—In some of those states in which the strict liability theory is applied, the following defenses may be effective:

   a. Property damage, rather than personal injuries, was incurred.

   b. The product was misused.

   c. The defect occurred after the product left the defendant's control and possession.

   d. The plaintiff's existence was not foreseeable—he or she is too remote a party.

   e. With regard to automobiles, "ordinary use" of an automobile does not include involvement in a collision. (Some courts, however, have adopted the "crash worthiness doctrine.")

   f. Plaintiff, while knowing of and appreciating the risk, created the defect, unreasonably and voluntarily engaged in the risk although he or she realized the potential danger. (Assumption of the risk.)

III. Statutory liability—Federal and state statutes, in addition to the Uniform Commercial Code, impose duties on manufacturers of goods purchased for consumption with regard to labeling, advertising, selling, etc.

A. If a manufacturer has violated such a statute, it may be treated as negligence *per se.*

B. Some relevant federal legislation.

1. The Consumer Product Safety Act provides for regulation of all potentially hazardous consumer products.

2. The Federal Trade Commission Improvement Act (The Magnuson-Moss Warranty Act) provides for conspicuous disclosure of information, concerning written warranties, extended to buyers of goods, purchased for consumption, when the price is more than $10.

FILL-IN QUESTIONS

1. A buyer of goods that prove to be defective may bring an action against the seller, with whom he contracted, based on contract, if he or she can show that there was a breach of an express or implied _____. If the buyer bases his cause of action on tort, he or she will have to establish that the seller was either _____ or strictly liable.

2. If a seller of goods made representations concerning the goods which were false, but induced the buyer to purchase the goods, the buyer may recover in contract from the seller, based on a theory of breach of _____ and, in tort, based on fraud in the inducement, if the buyer _____ and was _____.

3. Prior to the adoption of Sec. 2-318 of the Uniform Commercial Code, in many states, one, who was not a purchaser, but was injured by a manufactured product, could not recover from the seller of the product in an action based on breach of warranty because of lack of _____. For this reason, he or she would base his or her cause of action on the tort of _____, but would have to show that the seller _____.

4. Today, under the U.C.C., one who was not a purchaser, but was injured by a defective manufactured product, may recover from the seller, based on a breach of an express or implied warranty, because he or she is treated as a _____ _____ of the sales contract. In all states, however, he or she will have to show that he or she was a person who was reasonably expected to _____ by the goods.

5. Based on the tort doctrine of strict liability, any person who is injured by a manufactured product, including the buyer, a bystander or remote user, may successfully recover from the manufacturer or other seller of the item by establishing that he or she was injured by the product, which was defective, and that _____ _____ _____.

MULTIPLE CHOICE QUESTIONS

Unless otherwise indicated in a question below, assume that the fact situations, given in the following questions, arise in a state which has adopted the Uniform Commercial Code and which is following the recent trends in the United States so that the courts are imposing strict liability on all the sellers of defective products.

Questions 1, 2 and 3 are based on the following fact situation: Thirsty purchased a 25¢ bottle of soda, manufactured by the Soke Company, at a neighborhood grocery store. Thirsty took the bottle home, where he drank some and shared the rest with Parched. Thirsty and Parched became violently ill because they swallowed slivers of glass that were in the bottle of soda. The grocery store and Soke Company exercised extraordinary care to prevent such an occurrence.

1. At common law, the grocery store would be liable to:
    a. Thirsty for breach of warranty of merchantability, because there was privity of contract between it and Thirsty.
    b. Parched for breach of warranty of merchantability, because there was privity of contract between it and Parched.
    c. Thirsty for the tort of negligence.
    d. Parched for the tort of negligence.

2. With regard to the liability of Soke Company, which of the following statements is *incorrect*?
    a. It is liable to Thirsty and Parched for breach of warranties.
    b. It is liable to Thirsty and Parched in tort, even though it exercised a high degree of care.
    c. It is not liable to Thirsty and Parched for the tort of negligence, because it used due care in the manufacture of its product in order to insure that it was safe, if used for the purpose for which it was intended.
    d. It is not liable to Thirsty and Parched in tort because a reasonable person would have inspected the bottle and its contents before consuming the soda.

3. Which of the following statements is correct?
    a. Soke Company could have effectively disclaimed all liability to buyers and other consumers of its product by putting a carefully worded disclaimer on the label.
    b. Federal and state consumer product safety protection statutes would not apply to Soke Company, because soda is not normally a hazardous product.
    c. The Magnuson-Moss Warranty Act does not have any applicability to Soke Company's liability to Parched or Thirsty.
    d. The Magnuson-Moss Warranty Act insures that the implied warranty of merchantability is extended to Parched as well as Thirsty.

Questions 4 and 5 are based on the following fact situation: Tillie purchased a new typewriter, manufactured by the BMI Corp., from a seller of business equipment, for $350. When she brought the typewriter home, she tested it by typing her name. As she touched the "L" key, all of the keys flew out of the machine, severely injuring Tillie. On her written contract of sale there was a conspicuous statement to the effect that the sale was covered only by the manufacturer's warranties and that the seller did not warrant that the typewriter was fit for the particular purpose intended by the buyer nor make any warranties as to its merchantability. There was a conspicuous written twelve month warranty attached to the typewriter, promising that BMI Corp. would replace the typewriter if it proved to be defective.

4. With regard to the seller from whom Tillie purchased the typewriter:
    a. it is liable to Tillie for breach of the warranty of merchantability.
    b. it is liable to Tillie for breach of warranty of fitness for a particular purpose.
    c. it is not liable to Tillie for negligence, if it can show that it exercised reasonable care.
    d. it is not liable to Tillie in tort for personal injuries but is liable for property damage.

5. The warranty statement attached to the typewriter:
    a. was binding on BMI Corp. and the seller with whom Tillie dealt.

b. was binding on BMI Corp. only.

c. does not have to comply with the Magnuson-Moss Warranty Act, because the typewriter was purchased for Tillie's personal use.

d. limits BMI Corp.'s liability to Tillie for personal injuries.

6. Acro purchased a set of Goodmonth tires from Tyre, a dealer in tires, who made no express warranties. The tires were put on Acro's delivery truck. After the truck had been driven 100 miles on the new tires, one of them blew out, causing the truck to go out of control. As a result, the truck was completely wrecked and Ernest, the driver employed by Acro, was injured, as was Innocent, the driver of the automobile into which Acro's truck collided. Neither Ernest nor Innocent was negligent.

a. Tyre is the only party liable to Acro for breach of warranty.

b. Goodmonth is liable for personal injuries, incurred by Ernest, in tort and in contract for breach of warranty.

c. Goodmonth is not liable for personal injuries, incurred by Innocent, in tort or in contract for breach of warranty.

d. Tyre is relieved of any liability because he did not manufacture the defective tire.

7. Conny Sumer purchased a television set from Rea Taylor, who had purchased the set (and nine others, which she had sold to other buyers in her applicance store) from the Manu Facturing Co. When Conny's son turned the television set on, the screen shattered, severely cutting his face. Conny Sumer and her son are, therefore, suing Rea Taylor and Manu Facturing Co., basing the actions on torts and contract.

a. Conny Sumer's son can recover for his personal injuries from either Rea Taylor or Manu Facturing Co. in contract and tort.

b. Conny Sumer can recover for property damage from either Rea Taylor or Manu Facturing Co. in contract.

c. In some states, Conny Sumer cannot recover for property damage from Rea Taylor or Manu Facturing Co. in tort unless she can show that they were negligent.

d. All of the above.

Remedies of Buyer and Seller for Breach of Sales Contract

If one of the parties to a sales contract breaches or repudiates the contract or becomes insolvent, a number of different remedies are available to an aggrieved party under the Uniform Commercial Code. The reason for the variety of remedies is to insure that appropriate relief will be afforded to an aggrieved party in order to put him or her in as good a position as he or she would have been had the other party correctly performed (Sec. 1-106). Parties to a sales contract may, if they wish, create or provide their own remedies as well.

THINGS TO KEEP IN MIND

Some of the Code remedies revolve around acceptance by a buyer of identified, conforming goods. Acceptance usually is signified by (1) receipt and retention of goods by a buyer, after inspection reveals that the goods conform to the contract, or (2) an indication by a buyer that he or she will take nonconforming goods, or (3) the failure of a buyer to reject.

OUTLINE

I.   Rights and remedies of the seller.

    A. Seller's lien (Sec. 2-703)—Seller has a right to retain possession of goods until payment of the price, unless right is waived or lost by:

       1. Express agreement of the parties.

       2. Acts inconsistent with its existence. If transaction is a sale on credit, seller has no right to lien until credit period expires or buyer becomes insolvent.

3. Payment or tender of payment by buyer. If buyer gives a promissory note, lien is not discharged until note is paid.

4. Unconditional and voluntary delivery of the goods to the buyer or a bailee or agent of the buyer.

B. Withhold delivery of goods—Seller may retain goods if:

1. Buyer breaches contract or repudiates part of contract by wrongfully rejecting, revoking acceptance or failing to make proper payment (Sec. 2-703).

2. Buyer becomes insolvent (Sec. 2-702(1)).

C. Stop delivery of goods (Sec. 2-705).

1. Seller may stop the goods in hands of carrier or other bailee:

   a. If buyer breached contract, seller may stop carload or other large shipment.

   b. If buyer is insolvent, size of shipment is immaterial.

2. Seller must give timely notice to bailee and pay any charges resulting from the stoppage. Bailee need not obey, if negotiable document of title, which had been issued, is not surrendered.

3. Right to stop in transit ends when:

   a. Buyer receives goods.
      1) Physical possession, or
      2) Bailee, other than carrier, acknowledges to buyer that goods are held for the buyer.

   b. Carrier acknowledges to buyer that goods are held for buyer by reshipment or as a warehouseman.

   c. Negotiable document of title has been negotiated to buyer.

D. Reclaim goods in possession of an insolvent buyer (Sec. 2-702).

1. Within ten days after buyer's receipt of the goods.

2. Anytime, if buyer misrepresented his solvency, in writing, within three months prior to delivery of the goods.

3. Right to reclaim is lost, if buyer resold goods to good faith purchaser.

E. Identify goods to contract notwithstanding breach (Sec. 2-704).

1. When goods are identified to the contract, seller may hold buyer liable to pay purchase price or resell the goods.

2. Seller may identify:

   a. Goods that are finished and conform to the contract.

   b. Unfinished goods. Seller must exercise reasonable commercial judgment in order to mitigate loss and either:
      1) Cease manufacturing and resell for scrap or salvage value, or
      2) Complete manufacturing and identify goods.

F. Resell the goods (Sec. 2-706).

   1. Buyer breached or repudiated contract.

   2. Seller has possession of goods, because of proper withholding, stoppage in transit or reclaiming.

   3. Resale must be made in good faith in a commercially reasonable manner; it may be public or private.

   4. Seller must give buyer reasonable notice, unless goods are perishable.

   5. Seller may recover:

      a. Difference between resale price and contract price, and

      b. Incidental damages.

   6. Seller is not liable to buyer for any profits made at resale.

   7. Purchaser at sale takes free of any claims of buyer to the goods.

G. Recover purchase price plus incidental damages (Secs. 2-709 and 2-710).

   1. Buyer accepted goods and has not revoked acceptance.

   2. Conforming goods were lost or damaged after risk of loss passed to buyer.

   3. Buyer breached contract after goods were identified, but seller is unable to resell them at a reasonable price.

H. Sue for damages (Sec. 2-708)—Usually the measure of damages is the difference between the contract price and the market price at the time and place of tender of goods.

I. Cancel contract.

1. Buyer wrongfully rejects goods, revokes acceptance of conforming goods, fails to pay for the goods or repudiates (Sec. 2-703).

2. All unperformed duties of buyer and seller are terminated, but seller may sue for breach of contract (Sec. 2-106(4)).

J. No right to repossession of goods—Unless provided for in contract.

II. Rights and remedies of buyer.

A. Reject nonconforming or improperly delivered goods (Sec. 2-601)—Buyer may:

1. Reject all the goods,

2. Accept all the goods, or

3. Accept one or more commercial unit or units and reject remainder.

B. Revoke acceptance (Sec. 2-608).

1. Buyer accepted goods without knowing that they were nonconforming.

a. Defect difficult to discover.

b. Buyer assumed nonconformity would be cured, but it was not.

2. Buyer notified seller within a reasonable time after defect was discovered or should have been discovered, and before any substantial change in condition of goods, not caused by defect, occurred.

3. Defect substantially impaired the value of the goods to the buyer.

C. Cover (Sec. 2-712).

1. Buyer contracts for purchase of goods in substitution for those due from seller if:

a. Buyer rightfully rejected or revoked acceptance of goods.

b. Seller repudiated contract or failed to deliver goods.

2. Measure of damages is the difference between cost of cover (= market price) and contract price.

3. Buyer is not required to cover and may seek alternative remedy.

D. Recover damages.

1. For nondelivery or repudiation of contract (Sec. 2-713)—Measure of damages is difference between market price when buyer learned of breach and

contract price, plus any incidental and consequential damages, less expenses saved because of seller's breach.

2. For breach, although nonconforming goods were accepted by the buyer and notice given to seller.

    a. Damages resulting from seller's breach of contract.

    b. Damages resulting from seller's breach of warranty.
       1) Measure—Difference, at time and place of acceptance, between value of goods as accepted and value that they would have had if they had been as warranted.
       2) If goods were resold by the buyer and he or she is sued by his or her customer, buyer may:
          a) Notify original seller of pending litigation. Notice may provide that seller may come in and defend and, if seller does not do so, he is bound by determination.
          b) Defend against customer's suit and later bring action against seller.

E. Recover identified goods upon seller's insolvency (Sec. 2-502).

1. Seller becomes insolvent within ten days after receiving first payment.

2. Buyer tenders unpaid balance of purchase price.

F. Obtain specific performance (Sec. 2-716(1))—When goods are unique or buyer's remedy at law is inadequate.

G. Replevin the goods (Sec. 2-716(3))—Recover identified goods in possession of a seller, who is wrongfully withholding them, when buyer is unable to effect cover.

H. Retain and enforce security interest in the goods (Sec. 2-711(3))—After breach by seller, buyer may enforce a security interest for payment of price and reasonable expenses incurred.

I. Cancel the contract (Sec. 2-711(1)).

1. Seller wrongfully fails to make proper delivery or repudiates contract or buyer rightfully rejects or revokes acceptance of the goods.

2. Right to cancel may be lost, if buyer delays in exercising right.

3. All unperformed duties of buyer and seller are terminated, but buyer may sue for breach of contract occurring before cancellation.

J. Sue seller for fraud—Under applicable state law.

III. Statute of limitations.

A. Actions for breach of sales contract, brought under Uniform Commercial Code, must be commenced within four years after the cause of action arose (Sec. 2-725).

     1. Cause of action for breach of warranty accrues when seller makes tender of delivery, even though buyer did not know of defect.

     2. Future performance warranties are not breached until time for performance begins.

B. Causes of action, based on non-Code claims, are subject to applicable state statutes of limitations.

IV. Contractual provisions affecting remedies.

A. Liquidation of damages (Sec. 2-718)—Must be reasonable and approximately equal to anticipated or actual loss caused by the breach.

B. Limitation of remedies (Sec. 2-719).

     1. Buyer and seller may expressly provide for additional remedies, substitute remedies, a different measure of damages or that a particular remedy be an exclusive or sole remedy.

     2. If circumstances cause the purpose of an exclusive remedy to fail, the aggrieved party may pursue remedies provided by the Uniform Commercial Code.

     3. A limitation or exclusion of consequential damages will be enforced, unless it is unconscionable.

C. Waiver of defenses—The buyer may agree, in the contract for sale, that he or she will not assert defenses, which he or she has against the seller, against an assignee or holders to whom commercial paper is transferred.

FILL-IN QUESTIONS

1. If a buyer breaches a contract by wrongfully rejecting, revoking a prior acceptance, failing to make proper payment or repudiating part of a sales contract, or becomes insolvent, a seller may _____ or

_____ .

2. If a buyer wrongfully breaches or repudiates a sales contract, a seller may:
   (1) exercise his or her seller's lien;
   (2) _____ ;
   (3) _____ ;
   (4) _____ ;
   (5) _____ ; or
   (6) _____ .

3.   If a buyer becomes insolvent, the seller may, under certain circumstances, _____
_____.

4.   If a seller breaches a sales contract, prior to acceptance by the buyer, the buyer
     may:
     (1) reject nonconforming or improperly delivered goods;
     (2) _____;
     (3) _____;
     (4) _____;
     (5) _____;
     (6) _____;
     (7) _____; or
     (8) _____.

MULTIPLE CHOICE QUESTIONS

1.   Salisbury sold a refrigerator to Benton, who paid for it with a check. Benton
     stopped payment on the check before Salisbury cashed it.
     a. Salisbury has a right to take and retain the refrigerator.
     b. Salisbury does not have the right to exercise a seller's lien.
     c. Salisbury has the right to take and retain the refrigerator, if it is in the
         possession of a good faith purchaser in the ordinary course of Benton's business.
     d. Salisbury has the right to revoke the buyer's acceptance.

2.   If a buyer breached a contract of sale, the seller may stop the delivery of goods in
     the possession of a carrier when:
     a. the size of the shipment is a carload or less.
     b. the carrier acknowledged to the buyer that it was holding the goods for the
         buyer as a warehouseman.
     c. the seller gives timely notice to the carrier and surrenders a negotiable docu-
         ment of title to the carrier.
     d. a negotiable document of title has been negotiated to the buyer.

3.   Edson purchased a radio from the Radio Store for cash. Later Ogden, a competitor
     of the Radio Store, demanded that Edson turn over the radio to him, because he
     (Ogden) could prove that it had been stolen from his store. Edson relinquished the
     radio to Ogden and demanded his money back from the Radio Store.
     a. Edson will not be able to get his money back, because the doctrine of
         caveat emptor is applicable.
     b. Edson will not be able to get his money back, because the contract of sale
         provided that the seller make no express warranties.
     c. Edson will be able to get his money back, because the Radio Store breached its
         warranty of merchantability.
     d. Edson will be able to get his money back, because the Radio Store breached its
         warranty of good title.

*Questions 4 and 5 are based on the following fact situation: Fleur Sweater Co.
purchased yarn from Scott Yarns Inc., a manufacturer of yarn. The yarn was delivered,
accepted and paid for by the buyer. The yarn was used to manufacture 5,000 sweaters,*

which were subsequently sold throughout the United States. Months after the sweaters had been sold to consumers, Fleur Sweater Co. began to receive complaints that, due to defects in the yarn, the sweaters were disintegrating. Fleur Sweater Co. notified Scott Yarns Inc. that, unless it came into the litigation, it would be bound by any and all judicial determinations. Scott Yarns Inc. has not responded.

4. Fleur Sweater Co. can successfully:
    a. sue Scott Yarns Inc. for money damages, including the amounts consumers have recovered from it.
    b. revoke its acceptance of the yarn.
    c. exercise its remedy of cover.
    d. all of the above.

5. Assume that the contract for the sale of the yarn had been made in January 1976; the yarn was delivered and accepted by Fleur Sweater Co. in March 1976; the sweaters were manufactured in April 1976; the sweaters were sold to consumers in 1977 and 1978; and complaints were first received from consumers in February 1978.
    a. Scott Yarns Inc. can cancel its contract with Fleur Sweater Co.
    b. Fleur Sweater Co. will not be able to obtain money damages for breach of warranty.
    c. Fleur Sweater Co. will be able to exercise its remedy of replevin.
    d. The measure of damages recoverable by Fleur Sweater Co. is the difference between the market price, when it learned of the breach by Scott Yarns Inc., and the contract price.

23

Basic Concepts of
Commercial Paper

You are familiar with many types of writings that are used to facilitate commerce and trade. For example, money in the form of currency is used daily by most of us. Recall, from the material in Unit I, that many contractual agreements are reduced to writing and often the rights of the parties are assignable. In addition, in order to facilitate the delivery of goods, documents of title are issued, and investment securities, such as stocks and bonds, are issued by business organizations and frequently bought and sold. These writings are all forms of intangible personal property, for one who is in possession of them has rights associated with ownership. Such instruments are used in business because there is relative ease in transferring them.

Special kinds of paper, the subject of this and the following six chapters, are referred to as "commercial paper" when they contain written promises or orders to pay money. They are forms of personal property, representing contract rights, which are easily transferable and used to facilitate trade. You are familiar with checks, for you have probably received and/or used them to pay for goods and services. Checks are one type of commercial paper. In addition, there are also promissory notes, drafts and certificates of deposit. These kinds of instruments have been used in the business community for hundreds of years.

THINGS TO KEEP IN MIND

It is important to become familiar with the terminology presented in this short chapter. Be sure you understand the meanings of the terms discussed.

OUTLINE

I.   Purposes of commercial paper.

     A. Substitute for money—For convenience and safety.

B. Credit device—One wishing to extend the time for payment for goods, services or the use of money (a loan) may give a creditor a written instrument. The creditor, in turn, if he or she wishes to have cash immediately, may sell the instrument received from the debtor, but will have to "pay for" the immediate cash by paying interest in advance (discounting).

C. Historical origins of commercial paper.

  1. Used by traders and merchants.

  2. The Law Merchant.

  3. Court recognition of the legal rights of traders.

  4. Uniform Negotiable Instruments Act.

  5. Uniform Commercial Code—Article 3.

II. Types of commercial paper.

A. Promissory note—Written promise signed by the promisor, the maker, to pay a sum of money to another person, at a definite time, or on demand.

  1. Used to borrow money, buy goods, obtain services, or as evidence of indebtedness.

  2. Types of promissory notes.

    a. Mortgage note—Promise to repay a loan of money, secured by real property.

    b. Collateral note—Promise to repay a loan of money, secured by personal property.

    c. Certificate of deposit—Acknowledgement by a bank of a receipt of money with a promise to repay.

    d. Judgment notes—In some states the maker of a note authorizes the immediate confession and entry of a judgment against him or her by a court of record, if he or she fails to pay in accordance with the terms of the note.

B. Draft—Written order, direction or command by one person, the drawer, to another person, the drawee, to pay a sum of money to a third person, the payee.

  1. Parties to draft.

    a. Drawer—Issues paper, giving direction that a sum of money be paid.

    b. Drawee—Person, to whom draft is directed, who is to pay and who is already or may become obligated to the drawer.

    c. Payee—Person to whom money is to be paid.

    d. One person may be more than one party to a draft. I.e., drawer may be drawee or payee.

  2. Used to:

    a. Collect an account.

    b. Finance purchase of goods or the furnishing of services.

    c. Transfer funds.

  3. Drafts may be accepted—Drawee engages or promises that he will pay.

  4. Drafts may be payable on demand or at sight or at a future stated time or at a stated period of time after date or after sight (after it has been presented to the drawee).

  5. Types of drafts.

    a. Trade acceptance is a credit device, a draft, drawn by a seller of goods, payable in the future to a named payee (who is also the drawer), drawn on another person, who is usually the buyer of goods.

    b. Check—Demand draft, drawn on a bank by a drawer, who has money on account at the drawee bank, payable to another person.

III. Other ways of classifying commercial paper—Commercial paper may be classified as to:

A. When it is payable—Demand or time paper.

  1. Demand or sight paper—Payable whenever it is presented for payment by the person in possession of it.

  2. Time paper—Payable at a time in the future.

B. To whom it is payable—Commercial paper may be payable to:

  1. A named person, the payee, or his or her order, or

  2. Bearer, who is anyone in possession of the paper, which is payable to bearer, or cash, or other designation indicating that it is not payable to a named person.

IV. Parties.

A. Original parties.

    1. To a promissory note:

        a. Maker—Issuer who signs and is promising to pay.

        b. Payee—Party to whom promise is made; may be issued to bearer.

    2. To a draft:

        a. Drawer—Issuer who signs and is ordering the drawee to pay.

        b. Drawee—Party to whom direction or order to pay is directed.

        c. Payee—Party to whom payment is to be made; may be issued to bearer.

B. Other parties who may come in contact with commercial paper.

    1. Indorser—Transferor who signs his or her name on the back of the commercial paper.

    2. Indorsee—Transferee to whom or to whose order paper is payable.

    3. Holder—Person in possession of an instrument issued or indorsed to him (or her) or his (or her) order or to bearer.

    4. Holder in due course—A good faith holder to whom instrument is transferred for value, who has a special status because certain defenses cannot be raised by the person, required to ultimately pay the instrument, against a holder in due course.

    5. Holder through (or under) a holder in due course—A holder who is not himself or herself a holder in due course, but acquires his rights from or through another person who is a holder in due course.

FILL-IN QUESTIONS

1.

> January 4, 1980
>
> At sight, I promise to pay John Jones the sum of $20.
>
> *Mary Smith*

The instrument is a promissory _____. The _____ is Mary Smith and the payee is _____. It is a _____ instrument because it is not payable at a future time.

2.

```
                    January 6, 1980

    Pay to the order of bearer the sum
    of $100 on January 6, 1981.

    To:  Ben Beier

            David Duke
```

The instrument is a _____ . _____ is the drawer and _____ is the drawee. Since it is not payable to a named person, it is _____ paper. It is _____ paper because it is payable on a fixed date in the future.

MULTIPLE CHOICE QUESTIONS

1. A draft is:
    a. a collateral note.
    b. a time instrument.
    c. payable to bearer.
    d. a three party instrument.

2. On a check, the drawee is:
    a. the one who wrote the check.
    b. the person cashing the check.
    c. a bank.
    d. a bank or other person.

3. An essential difference between a draft and a promissory note is:
    a. a promissory note is payable on a specific date.
    b. a draft is payable to a specific person.
    c. the drawer and drawee of a draft have a debtor-creditor relationship.
    d. two or more persons are required to sign a promissory note.

4. Little owes Adams money. Instead of Adams being paid the money, the money is to be paid to Brown. The draft will be signed by:
    a. Adams.
    b. Little.
    c. Brown.
    d. Little and Adams.

5. Smith made a contract to purchase a washing machine on credit from the Acme Appliance Co. He signed a paper in which he stated that he promised to pay $350, the purchase price, in six months from the date of the writing. It also stated that the paper was secured by the washing machine. Acme Appliance Co. transferred the paper to Easy Finance Corp., which paid Acme eighty percent of the face value. Smith was notified that Easy Finance Corp. was now in possession of the paper.

    a. The instrument was discounted by Easy Finance Corp.
    b. The instrument was a mortgage draft.
    c. The drawer of the instrument was Acme Applicance Co.
    d. The drawee of the instrument was Easy Finance Corp.

24

Negotiability

Commercial paper may be negotiable, in which case unique, special rules, found in Article 3 of the Uniform Commercial Code, govern the rights and obligations of the parties to it, as well as others to whom it may be transferred, or it may be nonnegotiable, in which case the law of contracts applies. Recall, from the chapter on the rights of third parties, that an obligor can raise a defense, which he or she can assert against the obligee (who assigns his or her rights to a third person), against an assignee. As a result, negotiable promissory notes, certificates of deposit, drafts and checks are more freely transferable and more readily acceptable as substitutes for money and credit and are, therefore, more desirable than nonnegotiable instruments.

THINGS TO KEEP IN MIND

In order to be treated as a negotiable instrument, commercial paper must comply with certain formal requisites, all of which must be found within the four corners of the face of the writing. It must be in writing, signed by the maker or drawer, contain a single, unconditional promise or order to pay a sum certain in money, on demand or at a definite time in the future, and it must be payable to the order of a named payee or to bearer (Sec. 3-104).

OUTLINE

I. The forms of negotiable instruments (Sec. 2-104).

A. Promises to pay—Promissory notes and certificates of deposit.

B. Orders to pay—Drafts and checks.

II. Requirements for negotiability (Sec. 3-104).

   A. A writing which is relatively permanent, preservable, portable, moveable and tangible.

   B. Signed by the maker of a note or certificate of deposit, or the drawer of a draft or check.

      1. A symbol or mark intended by the user to authenticate the writing.

      2. Need not appear at bottom right hand corner of the writing (a subscription).

   C. Contains a single, express, absolute, unequivocable, unconditional promise or order to pay (Sec. 3-105).

      1. Promise—An express affirmative undertaking.

         a. Not merely an acknowledgment of indebtedness, without the inclusion of words such as, "due on demand."

         b. A promise is indicated from the terms used in a certificate of deposit.

      2. Order—An express, precise, mandatory direction or command to the drawee, who is identified.

      3. Unconditional—The holder does not have to look outside of the paper to determine his or her right to payment.

         a. Nonnegotiable, if promise or order is subject to or governed or burdened by another agreement, but *negotiable* if:
            1) Subject to implied or constructive conditions, such as good faith.
            2) States the consideration or transaction which gave rise to the instrument, by using notations such as, "as per contract" or "arising out of the sale of goods."
            3) Refers to another separate collateral agreement by using words such as, "secured by a mortgage" or "secured by a security interest in certain property." (These words "better" the paper.)

         b. Nonnegotiable, if paper states that it is payable out of a particular fund or source, because payment would depend upon the existence and sufficiency of the source of funds.
            1) Use of words such as, "payable only from account number 3," "pay out of proceeds of sale," etc.
            2) *Negotiable* if:
               a) Indicates particular fund out of which reimbursement is to be made or an account to be debited.
               b) Payable out of a particular fund, when paper is issued by a governmental body or agency, to be paid out of certain revenue funds, or by a partnership, estate or trust, payable only out of its assets.

D. Sum certain in money—At the time that the holder receives the instrument, the holder must be able to know the present value of the instrument, in terms of the existing medium of exchange, without referring to a source outside the paper.

1. Sum certain (Sec. 3-106).

   a. At the time that the holder receives the instrument, he or she must be able to ascertain, from the face, the exact minimum amount that he or she will receive when it is paid, and

   b. At the time or maturity, the holder must be able to determine the definite sum that he or she will be paid. The exact sum to be paid must be stated or capable of being made certain by computation from the face of the instrument.

   c. *Negotiable* if provides that instrument is to be paid:
      1) With stated interest or in stated installments.
         a) Negotiable if states:
            (1) Payable with interest at the contract (lawful) rate or at the judgment (legal) rate.
            (2) Payable with interest, which is interpreted as the statutory judgment rate of interest (Sec. 3-118(d)).
         b) Nonnegotiable if states that interest is to be payable at "prevailing" or "current bank rate."
      2) With different stated interest rates before and after default or on a specified date, or
      3) With reasonable court costs and attorney fees upon default, in those states which permit such clauses, or
      4) With a stated discount or additional sum if payment is made before or after the date fixed for payment.

2. Payable in money only.

   a. Money is the "medium of exchange authorized or adopted by a domestic or foreign government as a part of its currency" (Sec. 1-201(24)).

   b. If instrument is payable in foreign currency, it may still be negotiable, but it is deemed payable in equivalent United States dollars.

   c. If instrument provides for payment in a commodity (other than money), instead of or in addition to money, it is not negotiable.

E. Payable on demand or at a definite time.

1. Payable on demand—Payment is required whenever instrument is tendered, at sight or on presentment (Sec. 3-108).

   a. "At sight" or "on presentment."

   b. If no date is stipulated in an instrument for payment, it is payable on demand.

2. Payable at a definite time (Sec. 3-109)—The holder must be able to determine the latest possible date on which the instrument will be paid.

    a. An instrument is negotiable if it is payable:
       1) On or before a stated date.
       2) At a fixed period after a stated date or after issue or sight.
       3) At a definite stated time but subject to acceleration. (The time for
          payment will be accelerated upon the happening of some event, such
          as the failure of the obligor, who is usually the maker of a note, to
          make a payment of interest or an installment that is due.)
       4) At a definite, stated time but subject to an extension:
          a) To another stated date, so that the outer limit in time for
             payment is known. (Think of it as being payable at the date to
             which it may be extended, but subject to acceleration to the
             earlier stated date.)
          b) At the option of the holder, with no outer limit stated. (Think of
             it as being demand paper.)

    b. An instrument is not negotiable:
       1) If it is payable upon the happening of an event, the date of which is
          not certain (such as the arrival of a ship, death of a named person).
       2) At a definite stated time, subject to an extension at the option of the
          obligor.

F. Payable to order or to bearer—The words of negotiability.

  1. Order instrument (Sec. 3-110).

    a. Pay to the order of a named payee (who may be the maker, drawee or
       drawer as well).

    b. Pay to a named payee or order.

    c. Pay to the order of multiple payees, together or in the alternative.

    d. Pay to the order of the representative of an estate, trust, etc., or a
       partnership or unincorporated association.

  2. Bearer instrument (Sec. 3-111).

    a. Pay to bearer.

    b. Pay to order of bearer.

    c. Pay to the order of a named person or bearer (or his or her assigns).

    d. Pay to cash or payroll or similar designation.

III. Terms and omissions that do not affect negotiability (Sec. 3-112)—An instrument is
negotiable although it:

A. Omits a statement of consideration or the place where drawn or payable.

B. Contains a statement that collateral is given.

C. Contains a provision that the payee, by indorsing or cashing the instrument, acknowledges that it is accepted as full satisfaction of an obligation.

D. Does not state the date of issue, unless such date is necessary in order to determine the date at which payment is due.

FILL-IN QUESTIONS

1.

> To: Tenth State Bank   May 1, 1980
>
> Pay to John Jonry the sum of fifty-four dollars ($54.00).

The instrument satisfies the following requirements for negotiability _____
_____
but it is not negotiable because _____
_____.

2. You are given the following instrument:

> May 1, 1980
>
> On June 3, 1981, I promise to pay to the order of
> N. Barnes one hundred dollars ($100.00), this note being
> payable out of the proceeds of the sale of my 1928
> antique Ford automobile.

The instrument satisfies the following requirements for negotiability _____
_____
but it is not negotiable because it does not contain _____
_____
_____.

3. You are given the following instrument:

> May 1, 1979
>
> Fifty years from date I, *Cynthia Smart*   ,
> promise to pay to the order of Lucy Loring the sum of
> ($1000.00) one thousand dollars, but should my aunt,
> Pricilla Smart, die before the maturity date hereof, this
> note shall become payable two weeks after her death.

The instrument satisfies the following requirements for negotiability _____

_____

_____

but it is not negotiable because _____

_____.

MULTIPLE CHOICE QUESTIONS

1. The signature of the maker of a negotiable promissory note must appear:
    a. on the instrument.
    b. in ink.
    c. as a subscription.
    d. in the lower right hand corner.

2. The following writing is given to you:

> 8/19/80
>
> Pay to Jack Johnson fifty dollars ($50.00).
>
> To: The First State Bank
>
>   *John Jackson*

   a. It is an example of a negotiable demand draft.
   b. It is an example of an order bill of exchange.
   c. It is an example of a nonnegotiable promissory note.
   d. It is an example of a nonnegotiable sight draft.

3. When no time of payment is specified in a promissory note, the note is payable:
    a. on demand.
    b. within a reasonable period of time.
    c. within one year.
    d. thirty days after issue.

4. The following paper is given to you:

> Pay to the order of Peter Squires or bearer $33.00.
>
> To: R. Carey
>   5487 Main St.

   a. It is an example of a negotiable check.
   b. It is an example of a nonnegotiable check.
   c. It is an example of a time draft.
   d. It is an example of a negotiable sight draft.

5. A promise to pay out of a particular fund does not destroy negotiability of an instrument, provided the promise is made by:
   a. a banker.
   b. a business corporation.
   c. a municipal corporation.
   d. none of the above.

6. The negotiability of an instrument is destroyed if it contains the terms:
   a. this note is secured by a chattel mortgage, date June 4, 1979.
   b. this note is subject to the terms of a mortgage dated September 22, 1977.
   c. this check is given in payment of rent for June.
   d. this instrument is given as per agreement entered on the date of issue.

7. A so-called "I.O.U." is:
   a. a draft.
   b. a promissory note.
   c. order paper.
   d. an acknowledgment of an obligation.

8. The following words in a promissory note would destroy negotiability:
   a. subject to our agreement of March 2, 1980.
   b. payment for five crates of oranges.
   c. payable in three monthly installments.
   d. together with interest at the legal rate.

9. A check, payable "to the order of U.S. Treasurer," is:
   a. not negotiable because it is not payable to a named person's order or to bearer.
   b. a negotiable order check.
   c. a negotiable bearer check.
   d. treated as time paper.

10. The negotiability of an otherwise negotiable promissory note is affected by:
   a. post-dating the note.
   b. a clause authorizing payment in silver.
   c. a clause authorizing payment in Mexican pesos.
   d. a clause providing for acceleration of payment.

Transferability and Negotiation

The manner in which commercial paper is transferred depends firstly upon whether it is negotiable, in which case it is transferred by negotiation, or nonnegotiable, in which case transfer is by assignment. Negotiation of order paper is by delivery and indorsement, but bearer paper may be negotiated by delivery alone.

An indorsement will have certain characteristics, which are not mutually exclusive. An indorsement indicates (1) how subsequent negotiation is to be effected (blank or special), (2) limitations on the liability of the indorser (qualified or unqualified), and (3) the type of interest being transferred (restrictive or nonrestrictive).

THINGS TO KEEP IN MIND

1. One, who signs his name on a negotiable instrument, acquires liability to subsequent holders.

2. One, whose signature is not on a negotiable instrument, is not liable on the instrument, except if he or she had been a holder of a bearer instrument, he or she will be liable to his or her immediate transferee.

3. No indorsement can change the negotiable character of paper. If it is negotiable on its face, it remains negotiable.

OUTLINE

I. Methods by which commercial paper is transferred.

    A. Nonnegotiable—Transfer is by assignment and, therefore, delivery of the instrument by the maker or drawer, who issues the instrument (Sec. 3-102(1)(a)).

Thereafter, an assignee may make a subassignment, in order to transfer his or her rights.

B. Negotiable—Transfer is by "negotiation"—A transfer that results in the transferee being a holder, one in possession of a negotiable instrument, drawn, issued or indorsed to him or her or his or her order or bearer (Sec. 1-201(20)). The manner in which negotiation is effected depends on whether the instrument is order or bearer paper.

   1. Transfer of paper from original maker or drawer to the person to whom he or she intended to be the recipient—Contract law applies.

   2. Bearer paper is negotiated by physical delivery alone.

   3. Order paper is negotiated by a physical delivery and a necessary indorsement by the transferor (the payee or an indorsee).

II. Indorsement.

A. Signature of a transferor, usually on the back of the instrument.

B. If instrument is payable to the order of a named payee, the payee must indorse it in order to transfer his or her rights.

C. If instrument is payable to bearer, the transferee may request that his or her transferor indorse it.

D. If there is no space for an indorsement of the back of an instrument, indorsement is effective if written on an *allonge*, a separate paper that is firmly affixed to the original instrument.

E. One can change the manner required in order to transfer commercial paper by the type of indorsement used, but cannot change the negotiable character of the paper by indorsement.

F. One, who indorses, becomes secondarily liable to subsequent holders.

III. Types of indorsement.

A. Manner of indorsement determines how paper is transferred or negotiated in the future, what rights are transferred and the liability of parties.

   1. Indorser is liable to pay subsequent holder if primarily liable party does not pay.

   2. One, who indorses without indicating that he or she is indorsing in a representative capacity, is liable in his or her individual capacity.

B. Future manner of negotiating instrument is determined by blank or special indorsement (Sec. 3-204).

1. Blank indorsement.

    a. Holder or one in possession signs name.

    b. Results in paper being considered bearer paper. Negotiation is by delivery alone.

2. Special indorsement.

    a. Holder or one in possession indicates a specific person, to whom he or she intends to make the instrument payable, by writing, "Pay to the order of," or, "Pay to," the specified person and signs name.

    b. Results in paper being considered order paper. Negotiation thereafter is by delivery and indorsement of indorsee.

3. Order paper can be changed to bearer paper and *vice versa* by using a blank indorsement and special indorsement.

C. Liability of indorser is described by qualified or unqualified indorsement (Sec. 3-414).

    1. Qualified—Indorser signs name and writes, "without recourse," so that he or she has limited liability to subsequent holders.

    2. Unqualified—Indorser signs, in blank or specially, without qualification and is secondarily liable to subsequent holders.

D. Type of interest being transferred is described by restrictive or nonrestrictive indorsement (Sec. 3-205 and 3-206).

    1. Restrictive—Restricts or conditions rights of indorsee, but does not change obligations of party who created the paper.

        a. An instrument is not negotiable if the issuer imposes such restrictions. A restriction or condition in an indorsement, however, does not destroy the negotiability of the paper.

        b. Transferee from an indorsee, whose rights were restricted by a restrictive indorsement, must comply with direction in indorsement.

        c. Kinds of restrictive indorsements.
            1) Conditional—Rights of indorsee are subject to the happening of some event. (Pay X only if he delivers the merchandise.)
            2) Prohibition against further transfer—Interpreted as a special indorsement. (Pay to X only.)
            3) Indorsement for deposit or collection—Results in the indorsee (usually a bank) being an agent for purposes of obtaining payment for indorser.
            4) Trust indorsement—Payment to indorsee must be consistent with the restriction.

2. Nonrestrictive—No conditions or restrictions are imposed upon the indorsee.

IV. Miscellaneous.

A. Indorsement on negotiable instrument, with reference to assignment, is a negotiation (Sec. 3-202).

B. If name of indorsee is misspelled, indorsee may negotiate by indorsing in misspelled name, correct name, or both (Sec. 3-203).

C. Depository bank is agent of customer for purposes of supplying a missing indorsement of customer (Sec. 4-205).

D. Multiple payees (Sec. 3-116)—If payable:

   1. In the alternative—Either may indorse.

   2. Jointly—All must indorse.

E. Unindorsed order paper (Sec. 3-201)—Transferee is treated as an assignee but may obtain transferor's indorsement, if transfer was made for value.

F. Instrument drawn or indorsed payable to an estate, partnership, unincorporated association, etc., may be indorsed by an authorized representative of the organization (Sec. 3-110).

V. Forged or unauthorized indorsements and imposters.

A. Forgeries and signatures of unauthorized persons (Sec. 3-404)—Loss falls on one who took from forger.

   1. Forger or unauthorized indorser is personally liable.

   2. Not considered to be the signature of the person, by whom it appears to have been written.

   3. If signature was necessary for negotiation, transferee is not a holder.

   4. Payor is liable to rightful owner.

B. Imposters (Sec. 3-405)—Loss falls on maker or drawer if:

   1. Imposter, representing that he or she was another person, convinces maker or drawer to issue instrument in name of person that he or she is representing.

   2. Employee or agent issues instrument to a named payee, who may be ficticious, intending that the payee have no interest in the instrument.

3. Employee or agent supplies the name of a payee, or ficticious person, to employer or principal, who issues instrument.

VI. Warranties—See Chapter 27.

FILL-IN QUESTIONS

You are given the following instrument:

```
                                              30 March 1980


Pay to the order of Lucy Low-----------------------$25.00
Twenty-five and 00/100---------------------------dollars

Tenth State Bank
                            Howard How
```

1. Write the appropriate indorsement in order to transfer the instrument to Tom Trustee for the benefit of Benny Fishiary: _____
_____ .

2. Write the appropriate indorsement in order to transfer the instrument from Tom Trustee to Henry Hunt so that it becomes bearer paper: _____
_____ .

3. Write the appropriate indorsement so that Henry Hunt can deposit or cash the check at his bank: _____ .

MULTIPLE CHOICE QUESTIONS

1. An order instrument:
   a. is merely an assignment.
   b. may be changed to bearer paper by indorsement.
   c. may be negotiated without an indorsement.
   d. is payable to bearer.

2. An instrument that is bearer on its face:
   a. is always bearer paper.
   b. is a draft.
   c. cannot be a check.
   d. may be changed to order paper.

3. An indorsement that specifies the person to whom the instrument is payable:
   a. changes order paper to bearer paper.
   b. is a restrictive indorsement.
   c. is a special indorsement.
   d. cannot be transferred subsequently to another person.

4. Delivery and indorsement are the two elements of a valid negotiation for:
    a. negotiable instruments.
    b. commercial paper.
    c. order paper.
    d. bearer paper.

5. A qualified indorsement is best epitomized by the words:
    a. For deposit only.
    b. Without recourse.
    c. Pay to the order of X only.
    d. Any of the above.

6. The payee of a check signed his name on the back and wrote, "Pay to Richard Roe."
    This is:
    a. a qualified, nonrestrictive, blank indorsement.
    b. an unqualified, nonrestrictive, special indorsement.
    c. an unqualified, restrictive, special indorsement.
    d. an unqualified, nonrestrictive, blank indorsement.

7. The last indorsement on the back of a check reads, "Arthur's Annex, for collection
    only." It is:
    a. a qualified, nonrestrictive, blank indorsement.
    b. a qualified, restrictive, blank indorsement.
    c. an unqualified, restrictive, special indorsement.
    d. an unqualified, restrictive, blank indorsement.

8. "John Doe, without recourse" is written on the back of a promissory note. It is:
    a. a qualified, nonrestrictive, blank indorsement.
    b. a qualified, restrictive, blank indorsement.
    c. an unqualified, restrictive, blank indorsement.
    d. an indorsement that will prevent the further negotiation of the note.

9. The "imposter rule" may be described as:
    a. an exception to the usual rule that a payor is liable to one whose signature is
        forged.
    b. a restatement of the general rule that a payor is not liable to one whose
        signature has been forged.
    c. a restatement of the general rule that a payor is liable to a true payee if the
        payor pays a forger rather than the payee.
    d. none of the above.

10. Zack wrote a check, payable to the order of Vera, who claimed that she was
    collecting money for the United Fund. Vera was not really collecting for the
    United Fund, but she cashed the check at Zack's bank.
    a. Zack must incur the loss.
    b. Vera had good title to the check.
    c. The bank must incur the loss because it paid out on a forged signature.
    d. The bank must incur the loss even though there was no forgery.

Holders in Due Course

As will become clearer in Chapter 27, a holder in due course possesses greater rights than a person who is simply a holder. It is important that you be able to recognize whether or not a particular holder of an instrument is a holder in due course. A holder in due course is a holder, who takes a negotiable instrument for value, in good faith, without notice that the instrument is defective or overdue or has been dishonored or that there are defenses or claims that may be asserted against it.

THINGS TO KEEP IN MIND

One who is not a holder, in possession of a negotiable instrument, drawn or issued to his or her order or to bearer or indorsed to him or her specially or in blank, cannot be a holder in due course.

OUTLINE

I.   Contract law versus law of commercial paper.

    A. Contract law of assignment.

        1. Contract law applies when contract rights are assigned to a third person, the assignee.

            a. Nonnegotiable commercial paper transferred to a third person.

            b. Negotiable instrument transferred, without a proper negotiation, to a third person.

2. Assignor transfers only those rights which he or she has. Original obligor can, therefore, raise defenses, existing between contracting parties, against the assignee, who was not a party to the original contract.

B. Special rules of Article 3 of the Uniform Commercial Code apply to transferee of a negotiable instrument that has been properly negotiated to him or her. The transferee may be deemed to be a holder or a holder in due course.

II. Holder—A person in possession of an instrument drawn, issued or indorsed to him or her or to his or her order or to bearer or indorsed in blank (Sec. 1–201(20)) so that he or she is entitled to receive payment (Sec. 3–301).

A. An original party to the issuance of an instrument, such as the payee, may be a holder.

B. A holder has the right to:

1. Transfer or negotiate the instrument.

2. Demand payment.

3. Assert any rights, which his or her transferor might have asserted. This is so because a holder has the status of an assignee.

III. Holder in due course—A holder of a negotiable instrument who takes the instrument for value, in good faith, without notice that it is overdue or that it has been dishonored or that any person has a defense against it or a claim to it (Sec. 3–302).

A. Value (Sec. 3–303).

1. Value must have been actually given rather than promised, unlike consideration for a contract.

2. A donee of a gift does not give value.

3. Holder takes instrument for value to the extent that the agreed consideration has been performed. Consideration may be services performed, property sold or money (not necessarily the face amount of the instrument).

4. Adequacy of consideration is immaterial. (The question of adequacy may, however, go to the issue of good faith.)

5. Value is given if an instrument is given as security.

6. Value is given if an instrument is given in payment of an antecedent (pre-existing) debt or claim.

7. Value is given if an instrument is exchanged for a negotiable instrument or if an irrevocable commitment is made to a third person.

8. Sufficient value is *not* given if a holder acquired instrument:

a. At a judicial sale or under legal process.

b. In taking over an estate.

c. As part of a bulk transfer that was not in the ordinary course of business (Sec. 3-302).

B. Good faith (Sec. 1-201(19)).

1. Holder acts honestly and subjectively believes that the instrument is regular, even if a more prudent person would have been suspicious or put on notice that something was wrong.

2. If the consideration given by a holder is inadequate, relative to the purported value of an instrument, the holder does not take it in good faith.

C. Without notice of certain defects (Sec. 3-304).

1. Notice.

a. At the time instrument is acquired.

b. Actual knowledge, receiving notification or having knowledge of available facts or circumstances, such that he or she should have known certain things. (Knowledge is, therefore, imputed.)

2. Without notice that the instrument was overdue.

a. Time instrument.
1) Considered overdue on the day after specified maturity date.
2) Presence of an acceleration clause in installment paper is not notice that instrument may be overdue.

b. Demand instrument.
1) Knowledge that a demand had been already made.
2) Acquire instrument after it has been outstanding an unreasonable period of time.
   a) Check—30 days (Sec. 3-304(3)(c)).
   b) Draft—Less than 60 days (business usage).
   c) Note—60 days (business usage).

3. Without notice that instrument was dishonored—Presented for payment or acceptance, which was refused.

4. Without notice that there are defenses against the instrument or claims to it.

a. Defects that are apparent from the examination of the instrument because it is incomplete or irregular—Erasures, alterations, incomplete or incorrect indorsements, material omissions or blanks, when author of paper did not authorize completion (Sec. 3-304).

    b. Defects that are extraneous to the instrument but apparent from facts surrounding the transaction.
       1) Knowledge that transferor's title is defective because of theft, illegality, fraud, etc.
       2) Knowledge that obligation of a party is void or voidable or that all parties were discharged.
       3) Knowledge will not be imputed if:
          a) Instrument is antedated or postdated.
          b) Public notice by filing, etc., has been given.

    5. Payee, who was not an actual party to issuance of instrument, may be a holder in due course.

IV. Holder through a holder in due course.

  A. A holder, who derives his interest or title from a holder in due course, may acquire the rights of a holder in due course because he or she is an assignee, who acquires the rights that his or her assignor possessed, unless he or she was a party to an irregularity, such as fraud or illegality (Sec. 3-201).

  B. Limitations.

    1. A holder, who reacquires an instrument, is entitled to the status he or she had previously.

    2. A holder cannot better his or her status by reacquiring an instrument from a holder in due course.

FILL-IN QUESTIONS

1. One is considered to be a holder if he or she is in possession of an instrument that is drawn, issued or indorsed to him or her or to his or her order or to _____ or indorsed _____ .

2. A holder in due course of a negotiable instrument is one who took the instrument, _____ and without notice that it was _____ or that it had been _____ or without notice of _____ or claims to it on the part of any person.

3. Giving value, as a requisite for being a holder in due course, differs from considera-tion necessary to support a contract because value must be _____ _____ , whereas consideration may be something promised. One is not considered as having given value if nothing is given or if something, such as _____ , is promised but not given, or if an instrument is acquired at a judicial sale or _____ _____ in taking over an estate or as part of a bulk transfer _____ _____ .

4. If you are in possession of a note, payable to the order of John Doe, and indorsed by John Doe, you are a _____. If you paid $10 to your transferor in exchange for the note, in good faith and without notice that _____ _____, you are also a holder in due course.

MULTIPLE CHOICE QUESTIONS

1. Henry Hunt needed $100 in a hurry. He asked Frank Franklin, an acquaintance, if Frank would give him $100 for a piece of paper that looked like this on its face:

> May 5, 1981
>
> To: Earl Earl
>
> Pay to the order of Paula Paul the sum of $120.00.
>
> *Roberto Roberts*
> Roberto Roberts

   The only writing on the back of the paper was Paula Paul's signature.
   a. Earl Earl was a holder but not a holder in due course.
   b. Paula Paul could not have been a holder because she was the payee.
   c. Henry Hunt will have to indorse the instrument in order for Frank Franklin to have the status of a holder in due course.
   d. Frank Franklin will be a holder in due course if he has no notice of any defects in the paper or defenses available against it.

2. Mary Munroe, the assistant to the treasurer of the XYZ Corporation, prepared the monthly payroll and the checks for the corporation. Ms. Munroe added the name of Jane Joker, a ficticious person, to the payroll and prepared a check to Jane Joker's order. The treasurer, who did not know the true facts, signed the check in good faith. Mary Monroe then indorsed the check with the name of Jane Joker, negotiated the check to Kevin Kansas, obtained the money and disappeared. Kevin Kansas cashed the check at the corporation's bank.
   a. XYZ Corporation can recover the amount of the check from the bank.
   b. Kevin Kansas was a holder in due course.
   c. Jane Joker was a holder in due course.
   d. Mary Munroe was a holder in due course.

3. Peter Pill, in exchange for $800, offers you a piece of paper. One side looks like this:

> I promised to pay to the order of Barney Beaker the sum of One Thousand and   dollars on November 30, 1984.
>
> *Arthur Aspirin*
> Arthur Aspirin

The back looks like this:

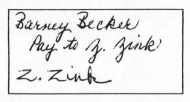

You will not be a holder in due course because:
a. there is a blank on the face of the instrument.
b. the date upon which the instrument was issued has been omitted.
c. the consideration you give will not be adequate value.
d. the name of Peter Pill, who will be your transferor, does not appear on the back.

4. Quoit paid Ridge for services performed by Ridge with a check payable to Ridge's order. Ridge indorsed it in blank and gave the check to Strata as a gift.
    a. Strata is neither a holder nor a holder in due course.
    b. Strata is a holder but not a holder in due course.
    c. Strata is a holder and a holder in due course.
    d. If Strata transfers the check for value to Tracer, Tracer will be a holder through a holder in due course.

5. Viper induced Walsh to write a check payable to Viper's order by making a misrepresentation of a material fact, upon which Walsh reasonably relied. The next day Viper gave the check to Houlder, who took it in good faith, for value, without notice of any defects in the paper or defenses against it or claims to it. Two days later, Houlder indorsed the check, payable to Ingram's order. Ingram, who knew of the original transaction between Viper and Walsh, gave value to Houlder and is the present holder of the check.
    a. Houlder was a holder in due course.
    b. Houlder was not a holder in due course but had the rights of a holder through a holder in due course.
    c. Ingram is a holder in due course.
    d. Ingram is not a holder in due course but had the rights of a holder through a holder in due course.

6. On June 1 Macon sold Norris defective goods, for which Norris paid with a check. On June 3 Norris discovered that the goods were defective and stopped payment of the check. On June 8 Macon learned of the stop order. On July 4 Macon specially indorsed the check to Loring for value. Loring knew neither of the defective goods nor the stoppage of payment.
    a. Macon was a holder in due course.
    b. Loring was a holder in due course.
    c. Loring was not a holder in due course because the instrument was overdue when he acquired it.
    d. Loring was not a holder in due course because he acquired the instrument on a national holiday.

Liability, Defenses and Discharge

Parties, who issue or transfer commercial paper, acquire liability to subsequent holders of such instruments. Recall that commercial paper is a special form of contract. For this reason, any party, whose signature appears on the instrument, is liable in contract. A party, who makes an unconditional promise to pay, such as a maker of a note or an acceptor of a draft, is absolutely and primarily liable in contract to pay. The contract liability of other parties to an instrument, such as a drawee of a draft, unqualified indorsers and accommodation parties, is secondary and conditioned upon (1) the proper and timely presentment of the instrument to one, who is required to pay or required, in the case of a draft, to accept, (2) dishonor, a refusal to pay or accept, and (3) notification of the dishonor.

In addition, parties, who transfer or present commercial paper, are treated as having made certain implied warranties, the effects of which are to cut off defenses, which ordinarily might be raised and, therefore, to impose additional unconditional liability on such parties.

A party to commercial paper, who is obligated to pay, may have one or more defenses, which can be raised against a holder seeking payment of an instrument. Certain defenses, termed personal defenses, are not available against a holder in due course; other defenses, referred to as real defenses, are available against all holders, including holders in due course.

The liability of one or more parties to pay the face amount of an instrument may be terminated or discharged. Normally commercial paper is discharged by payment or other satisfaction but some or all parties may be discharged by cancellation or renunciation; a correct tender of payment; impairment of a right of recourse (to obtain reimbursement) against a party or collateral security; reacquisition; a fraudulent, material alteration; certification of a check; a draft varying acceptance; an unexcused delay in presentment and/or notice of dishonor; or any act which would discharge a simple contract for the payment of money. No discharge, however, will be effective against a holder in due course, who lacked notice of the discharge when the instrument was negotiated to him or her.

THINGS TO KEEP IN MIND

In addition to the liability discussed in the chapter, remember that some underlying transaction gives rise to the issuance and transfer of commercial paper so that the parties to the underlying transaction have contractual rights and obligations, which are merely suspended by the issuance or transfer of an instrument. For example, if R draws a check, payable to P, on his bank, in order to pay for goods purchased from P, R remains contractually obligated to pay P for the goods should the drawee bank refuse to honor the check. Similarly, had P negotiated the check to H, in exchange for the performance of some services, P's liability to pay H for the services is merely suspended until H receives payment of the instrument.

OUTLINE

I.   Liability of parties.

    A. Liability based on signatures.

        1. No one is liable on a negotiable instrument unless his or her signature appears thereon (Sec. 3-401(1)).

           a. A signature may be handwritten, typed, printed or some mark, such as a thumb print.

           b. A signature indicates a "present intention to authenticate a writing" (Sec. 1-201(39)).

           c. One, whose signature has been used without authorization, may ratify its use on a negotiable instrument (Sec. 3-404(2)).

           d. One, who signs another's name without authority or forges another's signature, is liable on a negotiable instrument (Sec. 3-404(1)).

           e. One, whose name is signed by another without authorization, is not liable on a negotiable instrument (Sec. 3-404(1)).

        2. A signature may be provided by an authorized representative, such as an agent (Sec. 3-403).

           a. Usually an agent gives the appropriate signature of his or her principal and signs his or her name, indicating that he or she is signing in a representative capacity, in which case only the principal is liable.

           b. An agent, who signs in his or her own name only, is personally liable on the instrument (Sec. 3-403(2)).

    c. If an agent signs for a principal and provides his or her own signature, without indicating that he or she is acting in a representative capacity, both the principal and agent are liable on the instrument (Sec. 3-403(2)).

B. Contractual liability—One, whose signature appears on a negotiable instrument, by his or her own hand or that of another authorized person, acquires either primary liability or secondary liability based on contract.

    1. Primarily liable parties.

        a. The maker of a promissory note.
           1) Maker promises to pay according to original tenor of note or according to terms as completed, if it was incomplete when issued (Sec. 3-413(1)).
           2) Maker admits the existence of the payee and his or her capacity to indorse (Sec. 3-413(3)).
           3) The underlying obligation, for which the note is given, is suspended until payment of the note. Upon dishonor, the maker can be sued either on the note or the underlying obligation (Sec. 3-802(1)).

        b. Acceptor of a draft (Sec. 3-410).
           1) No one is primarily liable on a draft when it is issued.
             a) If a draft is presented for acceptance to a drawee by a holder, the drawee becomes an acceptor upon acceptance of the draft.
             b) A drawee, who is not an acceptor, is not liable to a presenter if he, she or it fails to pay or accept a draft. A drawee's contractual liability is only to the drawer.
           2) Certification of a check is an acceptance (Sec. 3-411).
           3) Acceptor:
             a) Promises to pay according to the tenor of the instrument at the time of acceptance.
             b) Admits the existence of the drawer, the genuineness of the drawer's signature and the drawer's capacity.
             c) Admits the existence of the payee and the payee's capacity to indorse (Sec. 3-413).

    2. Secondarily liable parties.

        a. Liability of drawer, unqualified indorser and accommodation party is conditioned upon:
           1) Correct, timely presentment for payment or acceptance (Sec. 3-501).
           2) Dishonor—Refusal of payment or acceptance (Sec. 3-507(1)).
           3) Timely notice of dishonor to party, who is secondarily liable (Sec. 3-508).

        b. Rights against a secondarily liable party are preserved by complying with conditions of presentment and notice of dishonor.

        c. Presentment and notice of dishonor may be excused, delayed or waived (Sec. 3-511).

        d. Parties who are secondarily liable.
          1) Drawer engages that he or she will pay if a draft is dishonored and notice of dishonor given (Sec. 3-413(2)).
          2) Indorsers (Sec. 3-414).
            a) Unqualified indorser engages that he or she will pay according to the tenor of the instrument at the time of indorsement, if it is dishonored and notice of dishonor is given.
            b) A qualified indorser is relieved of contractual liability on an instrument.
          3) Accommodation party (Sec. 3-415).
            a) Signs for purposes of lending his or her name and credit to a party to an instrument.
            b) Obligation depends on capacity in which he or she signs.
            c) Accommodation party is not liable to the party accommodated and may obtain reimbursement for amounts paid on instrument from accommodated party.

C. Implied, unconditional warranty liability of parties.

    1. Warranties, which are made upon transfer, by one, who negotiates an instrument and receives value (Sec. 3-417).

        a. If transfer has been by indorsement and delivery, warranties apply to:
          1) Immediate transferee, and
          2) Subsequent holders, who take instrument in good faith.

        b. If transfer was by delivery alone, warranties run only to immediate transferee.

        c. Warranties of transferor.
          1) Transferor has good title or is authorized to obtain payment or acceptance on behalf of a person, who has good title.
          2) All signatures are genuine or authorized.
          3) The instrument has not been materially altered.
          4) No defense of any party is available against the transferor. A qualified indorser merely warrants that he or she has no knowledge of any such defenses.
          5) The transferor has no knowledge of insolvency proceedings instituted against the maker, acceptor or drawer of an unaccepted draft.

    2. Warranties made upon presentment by a person presenting instrument for acceptance or payment to a maker, acceptor or drawee (Sec. 3-417(1)).

        a. Good title.

        b. No knowledge that signature of maker or drawer is unauthorized.

        c. Instrument has not been materially altered.

II. Defenses—May be raised by a party, who is liable to pay on an instrument.

A. Real or universal defenses—Can be raised against all holders, including holders in due course and holders through holders in due course. Usually a void transaction is involved.

  1. Forgery or unauthorized signatures (Sec. 3-401 and 3-404).

  2. Fraud in the execution (Sec. 3-305(2)(c)).

  3. Material alteration of a completed instrument, if carelessness is not present, to the extent of the alteration (Sec. 3-407).

  4. Discharge in insolvency of bankruptcy proceedings (Sec. 3-305(2)(d)).

  5. Illegality when state statute provides that transaction is void (Sec. 305(2)(b)).

  6. Incapacity.

     a. Infancy to the extent it is a defense to a simple contract.

     b. Insanity, if state law provides that contracts are void.

  7. Extreme duress.

  8. Statute of limitations.

B. Personal or limited defenses—Can be raised against a holder but not a holder in due course or a holder through a holder in due course (Sec. 3-306).

  1. Breach of contract.

  2. Lack or failure of consideration.

  3. Lack of real assent because of fraud in the inducement, misrepresentation, mistake, undue influence or ordinary duress.

  4. Illegality and incapacity, which renders a contract voidable, rather than void.

  5. Discharge by payment or other satisfaction or cancellation of an instrument which is permitted to circulate (Secs. 3-601(1)(a) and 3-602).

  6. Unauthorized completion of an incomplete instrument (Secs. 3-304(4)(d) and 3-407).

  7. Conditional delivery or nondelivery (Sec. 3-306(c)).

III. Discharge of parties to paper—A discharge is not effective against a holder in due course, who lacks notice of the discharge, when the instrument is negotiated to him or her (Sec. 3-602).

A. Discharge by payment or other satisfaction given to holder (Secs. 3-601(1)(a) and 3-603).

    1. A party is not discharged if payment was made in bad faith or in a manner inconsistent with a restrictive indorsement.

    2. Payment by an indorser discharges payor and subsequent indorsers.

    3. Tender of payment does not discharge obligation to pay face amount, but discharges liability for interest, costs and attorney fees (Sec. 3-604).

B. Discharge by cancellation or renunciation (Sec. 3-605).

    1. Cancellation—Intentional destruction, mutilation, etc., of instrument discharges all parties. Crossing out an indorsement discharges liability of that indorser and subsequent indorsers.

    2. Renunciation—Surrender of instrument or present, absolute surrender of rights in a signed writing.

C. Discharge by material, fraudulent alteration (Secs. 3-407 and 3-601(f)).

    1. An alteration is material if it changes the obligations of a party.

    2. Parties are discharged to the extent of the alteration.

D. Discharge by impairment of the right of recourse, which is a source of reimbursement, against a party or collateral security (Secs. 3-601 and 3-606).

    1. Holder releases or agrees not to sue a party from whom an indorser can obtain reimbursement.

    2. Holder agrees to suspend the right to enforce an instrument against a party.

    3. Holder discharges prior indorsers by cancellation.

    4. Holder, without justification, impairs collateral that had been given as security that the instrument would be paid.

E. Discharge by reacquisition—When a prior holder reacquires an instrument, intervening parties are discharged (Sec. 3-601(3)(a)).

F. Discharge by an unexcused failure or delay in presentment or notice of dishonor (Secs. 3-502 and 3-601(1)(i)).

G. Discharge by any act or agreement that would discharge a simple contract for the payment of money, such as a release, accord and satisfaction, etc. (Sec. 3-601(2)).

FILL-IN QUESTIONS

1. A party to a negotiable instrument may be liable if the instrument is not paid when it is due if his or her _____ appears on the instrument. He or she may be liable based on the underlying obligation, _____
   _____ .

2. Parties, who are primarily liable based on contract, include _____
   _____ ;
   parties, who are secondarily liable, include _____
   _____ .

3. One of the purposes of giving a _____ to indorsers, following a proper presentment and dishonor, is to inform them, as secondarily liable parties, that the maker of a promissory note has failed to meet his or her obligations.

4. If a draft is presented by a holder for acceptance, the presenter warrants to the drawee/acceptor that he or she has (1) _____ ,
   (2) _____ , and
   (3) _____ .

5. A personal defense, such as _____ ,
   is one that cannot be raised against a holder in due course; a real defense is one that can be raised against _____ .

MULTIPLE CHOICE QUESTIONS

1. For breach of any of the warranties of transferors, imposed by the Uniform Commercial Code upon both qualified and unqualified indorsers, the transferor is:
   a. liable to his or her transferee and subsequent holders.
   b. never liable for unintentional acts.
   c. liable only to his or her transferee.
   d. liable only to subsequent holders.

2. Signing a note, when it is believed that only an autograph is requested, gives rise to:
   a. no defense.
   b. the defense of illegality.
   c. a personal defense.
   d. a real defense.

3. With regard to a negotiable instrument, the following is usually considered to be a personal (limited) defense:
   a. The statute of limitations.
   b. Breach of contract.
   c. Fraud in the execution.
   d. Discharge in bankruptcy.

4. With regard to a negotiable instrument, the following is usually considered to be a real (universal) defense:
    a. Fraud in the execution.
    b. Fraudulent concealment.
    c. Failure of consideration.
    d. All of the above.

5. A party, who indorses a negotiable instrument with the words, "without recourse," avoids:
    a. all liability if the instrument is not paid when due.
    b. liability, based on warranty, if the instrument is not paid when due.
    c. liability, based on the contract, which is implied in the instrument, but not liability based on an underlying contract, which gave rise to the instrument.
    d. liability, based on the contract, which is implied in the instrument, as well as liability based on an underlying contract, which gave rise to the instrument.

6. A principal is liable on a negotiable instrument, signed by his or her agent in the name of the agent:
    a. if the agent has authority to issue negotiable instruments on behalf of his or her principal.
    b. if the agent has signed only his or her own name.
    c. and in the name of the principal.
    d. only if the agent indicates that he or she is signing in his or her representative capacity.

7. Carson executed a promissory note in the amount of $4000 payable to Donaldson. On the due date, Donaldson went to Carson's place of business and told Carson, "Your note is due today but I wish to renounce all my rights in connection with it." The note is:
    a. effectively discharged by renunciation and cancellation.
    b. effectively discharged by payment or other satisfaction.
    c. not effectively discharged because Carson has not given value to Donaldson.
    d. not effectively discharged unless the note is surrendered or Donaldson's statement is contained in a signed writing.

8. Ink, in order to borrow $2000 from his local bank, asked Pencil to sign a note as an accommodation maker. Pencil agreed and both he and Ink thereupon executed the note as makers by signing the face of the instrument.
    a. Pencil is liable as an accommodation indorser.
    b. Pencil is not liable to pay if Ink tendered the $2000, plus the interest that was due to the bank when the note became due.
    c. Ink may recover from Pencil if Ink tendered the $2000, plus the interest that was due to the bank when the note became due.
    d. Ink and Pencil are completely discharged if Ink tendered the $2000, plus the interest that was due to the bank when the note became due, if the bank refused to accept the payment.

9. Martin made a contract to purchase a television set on credit from TV City Inc. She signed a negotiable promissory note for the purchase price. TV City Inc. transferred the paper to the Careful Credit Co., which paid TV City Inc. ninety percent

of the face value of the note. Martin, who was notified that Careful Credit Co. was now in possession of the note, has failed to pay Careful Credit Co. although the note is now due. Careful Credit Co. is, therefore, suing Martin, who claims (1) she has been discharged in a state insolvency proceeding and (2) the television set had not been delivered by TV City Inc. Careful Credit Co. had no notice of the existence of these defenses when it purchased the instrument.

a. Both defenses can be successfully raised against Careful Credit Co.
b. Martin can successfully raise the defense of discharge in an insolvency proceeding against Careful Credit Co. but not the defense of breach of contract.
c. Martin can successfully raise the defense of failure of consideration against Careful Credit Co. but not the defense of discharge in an insolvency proceeding.
d. Martin cannot successfully raise either defense against Careful Credit Co.

Checks and the Banking System

The most frequently used form of commercial paper is the check, a demand draft, drawn on a financial institution. The provisions of Article 3 of the Uniform Commercial Code, many of which have been discussed in the preceding chapters, apply to checks. In addition, Article 4 of the Code contains rules, pertaining to the bank deposit and collection system and the relationship between a bank customer and his or her bank, as well as other banks that may be involved in the collection process for checks and other types of commercial paper. These rules are meant to expedite the smooth flow of money, credit and business.

THINGS TO KEEP IN MIND

1. Checks are orders, issued by depositors, directing their banks to pay out funds, which the depositors have previously placed with the banks (demand deposits).

2. Often a holder of a check, who wishes to obtain cash for it or deposit it in his or her own bank account, does not use the bank upon which the check is drawn. It is, therefore, necessary that the check be forwarded through a network of intermediary banks by the holder's bank for collection and payment purposes.

OUTLINE

I. Checks.

   A. A check is a draft, drawn on a bank, ordering it to pay a stated sum certain in money on demand (Sec. 3-104(2)(b)).

   B. Usually a check is negotiable because it is signed by the drawer, contains a single, unconditional order to pay a sum certain in money on demand to the order of bearer or a named payee (Sec. 3-104(1)).

C. A postdated check is treated as a negotiable time draft.

D. A check is not an assignment of funds (Sec. 3-409). Until final payment is made, there is no effect on the depositor's account and the underlying obligation, for which the check is given, is not discharged.

E. Special kinds of checks.

1. Cashier's check—A check drawn by a bank upon itself so that it is the drawer and drawee. A cashier's check is treated as being accepted in advance.

2. Traveler's check—Check drawn by a financial institution, which requires the signature of the payee in order to be negotiable.

3. Certified check—Personal check, drawn by a depositor on his or her bank, which is accepted by the drawee bank (Sec. 3-411).

   a. The bank, which certifies, unconditionally promises that the check will be paid when presented.

   b. The bank immediately charges the depositor's (drawer's) account.

   c. If certification is obtained by the drawer, the drawer remains secondarily liable. Prior indorsers are discharged.

   d. If certification is obtained by a holder, the drawer and prior indorsers are discharged.

F. Relationship between bank and its customer.

1. A customer is a person, having an account with a bank or for whom a bank has agreed to collect items (instruments for the payment of money) (Sec. 4-104(e) and (g)).

2. Depositor is a creditor of his or her bank and a principal. The bank is a debtor and agent of its depositor.

3. Duties of bank.

   a. Honor and pay checks of customer, who has sufficient funds in his or her account.
      1) Bank is obligated to honor checks even if there are insufficient funds in the customer's account if it has agreed to honor overdrafts.
      2) Bank is not required (but may) pay stale checks—Uncertified checks presented more than six months after the date of the check (Sec. 4-404).
      3) Bank may honor checks of deceased or legally incompetent depositor, until the expiration of ten days after it receives knowledge of the death or incompetency (Sec. 4-405).

    b. Follow order from a depositor to stop payment (Sec. 4-403).
        1) Only customer may give stop payment order.
        2) Bank must receive stop payment order at time and in manner so that it has reasonable opportunity to comply.
        3) Duration—14 days if oral; six months if written. Stop payment order may be renewed.
        4) If bank fails to comply with order, it is liable to customer for the amount of actual loss incurred.

    c. Liability of bank for payment on forged signatures.
        1) Bank maintains signature cards of depositors and is required to check signatures of drawers.
        2) Bank is liable if it pays an item, on which the signature of its customer, the drawer, is forged (Sec. 3-419). Exceptions:
          a) Drawer's negligence contributed to the forgery (Sec. 3-406).
          b) Imposter situation (Sec. 3-405).
          c) Customer fails to notify bank of forgery after receipt of statement and cancelled checks (Sec. 4-406).
        3) If bank pays on a forged indorsement, it cannot rightfully charge the drawer's account, but may recover from person, who presented item for payment, because of warranties made upon presentment.

    d. Liability of bank for payment on an altered check, if drawer was not negligent.
        1) Bank may charge drawer's account for the amount of the check as originally issued.
        2) Bank bears loss to the extent of the raised amount, if it pays out on a check with a raised amount.
        3) Bank may recover from the person, who presented the check for payment, based on warranty liability.

II. Accepting deposits and the check clearing process.

  A. Definitions (Sec. 4-105).

    1. Depositary bank—First bank to receive a check or other item for purposes of collection.

    2. Payor bank—Bank, which is required to pay an item (drawee bank, upon which check is drawn).

    3. Collecting bank—Any bank, other than a payor bank, handling an item during the collection process.

    4. Intermediary bank—Any bank, other than the depositary bank or the payor bank, handling an item.

  B. Check collection between customers of the same bank, when drawer's account is sufficient.

    1. Bank charges (credits) drawer's account and debits depositor's account.

2. Considered paid on the opening of the second banking day after check was deposited (Sec. 4-213(4)(b)).

C. Check collection between customers of different banks.

1. Depositary bank arranges for presentment of check to drawee bank directly or through intermediary banks in the Federal Reserve system or a clearing house.

2. Each intermediary bank must pass the check on before midnight of the next day following its receipt (Sec. 4-202).

3. Depositor remains the owner of item until it clears. Intermediary banks are subagents of the depositor.

D. Check clearing technology in banking operations (Electronic Funds Transfer Systems).

1. Teller machines—Receive deposits, dispense funds from checking or savings accounts, make credit card advances and receive payments.

2. Point-of-sale systems—Terminal at check out counter in store verifies customer's balance at bank and debits account for amount of purchase.

3. Automated clearing houses—Entries made by electronic signals without checks.

4. Federal legislation.

a. If customer's debit card is lost, stolen or used without permission, the maximum amount that the customer can lose is $50 if he or she notifies the bank within two days of learning of its improper use.

b. Banks have to give statements and receipts for transactions through computer terminals.

FILL-IN QUESTIONS

1. A check is a demand draft, drawn on a bank or other financial institution. The bank is the drawee. The drawer of a check is termed the bank's _____. When the bank pays out on the check, it is referred to as the _____ bank.

2. Often, particularly when a person is making a large purchase, a seller is concerned that the buyer's personal check will be dishonored. In order to ensure against a dishonor, the buyer will use a cashier's check or a certified check. A _____ is a check drawn by a bank upon itself. A _____ is a personal check, drawn by the buyer on his or her own bank, which is accepted by the drawee bank.

3. If certification of a check is obtained by _____, the drawer remains secondarily liable; if certification is obtained by _____, the drawer is relieved of secondary liability. In either case _____ are discharged by certification.

4. There is a contractual relationship between a depositor and his or her bank. The bank, therefore is required to honor checks drawn on the depositor's account, unless (1) there are insufficient funds in the account and the bank has not agreed to honor overdrafts; (2) _____
    (3) _____
    (4) _____
    (5) _____ .

MULTIPLE CHOICE QUESTIONS

1. The status of a bank is such that:
    a. it is an agent of its depositor.
    b. its status varies, sometimes being classified as an agent, sometimes as a holder in its own right.
    c. it acquires its status based on the classification given it by its depositor.
    d. it is a holder.

2. In theory, a bank is liable for making a payment in all but one of the following situations. That situation is:
    a. It pays on an altered instrument, such alteration being the result of the drawer's negligence.
    b. It pays on a check on which the drawer's signature is missing.
    c. It pays after receipt of a valid stop payment order given by its depositor.
    d. It pays a check on which the signature of the drawer is forged in such a way that the forgery cannot be detected.

3. A written stop payment order is effective for:
    a. 14 days.
    b. one month.
    c. six months.
    d. one year.

4. A drawee bank is not generally obligated to pay a check, which is presented for payment more than:
    a. three months after the date of the check.
    b. six months after the date of the check.
    c. a reasonable period after the issue of the check.
    d. one year after the issue of the check.

5. If a check is presented to a drawee bank for payment, the drawee bank is under a duty to pay or dishonor such check:
    a. before the opening of business on the second banking day following the day of presentment.

    b. before the close of banking business on the day upon which the check is presented to it.

    c. within three business days.

    d. immediately upon presentment and agreement to pay.

6.   April paid a debt that she owed to May with a check upon her account with the Farmers' Bank. May took the check to the Farmer's Bank and requested and obtained certification of the check. May then indorsed the check to June, in order to pay a debt owed to June. Before June cashed the check, the Farmers' Bank became insolvent.

    a. June may receive the face amount from either April or May because, if a bank that has certified a check becomes insolvent, the drawer and indorsers remain secondarily liable.

    b. June may not recover from either April or May because the effect of certifications was to discharge their secondary liability.

    c. June may recover the face amount of the check from April because, even though the check was certified by the drawee bank, the drawer remains secondarily liable.

    d. June may recover the face amount of the check from May because the certification did not discharge the liability of an indorser who indorsed after certification.

29

Introduction

Secured transactions, which are covered by Article 9 of the Uniform Commercial Code, are credit transactions coupled with security. In a secured transaction, the buyer or borrower, referred to as the debtor, gives security rights in personal property to a seller or lender, the secured party, in addition to an assurance that an obligation will be paid or otherwise performed. If the debtor defaults by failing to carry out the underlying obligation (which is usually the payment of money), the secured party can look to the security as a substitute for the debtor's performance. Such devices are used to finance purchases made by manufacturers, retailers, other businesses and consumers.

THINGS TO KEEP IN MIND

In order for a secured transaction to be effective between the parties to it, the debtor and the secured party, the security interest must "attach" to the collateral; in order that the secured transaction be effective against third parties it must be "perfected."

OUTLINE

I.   Definitions used in secured transactions covered by Article 9.

   A. Security interest—An interest in personal property or fixtures which secures payment or performance of an obligation (Sec. 1-201(37)).

   B. Secured party—A lender or seller who obtains a security interest (Sec. 9-105 (1)(m)).

   C. Debtor—The party owing the obligation to pay money or otherwise perform (Sec. 9-105(1)(d)).

D. Security agreement—An agreement which creates or provides for a security interest (Sec. 9-105(1)(l)).

E. Collateral—Personal property subject to a security interest (Sec. 9-105(1)(c)). Classifications:

1. Goods—Things that are moveable at the time that the security interest attaches or fixtures (Sec. 9-105(1)(h)).

   a. Includes standing timber, which is to be cut and removed, growing crops and unborn young of animals.

   b. Does not include moveables that are included in other classifications of collateral.

   c. Goods are classified in accordance with their primary use (Sec. 9-109). They may be:
      1) Consumer goods—Used or bought primarily for personal, family or household use.
      2) Equipment—Used or bought primarily for business use.
      3) Farm products—Crops, livestock or supplies used or produced in farming operations or products resulting in farm operation in unmanufactured state, in the possession of the debtor.
      4) Inventory—Goods held for sale or lease, materials used or consumed in business and work in progress.

2. Chattel paper—A writing or a group of writings, evidencing a monetary obligation and a security interest in or lease of specific goods (Sec. 9-105(1)(b)).

3. Instruments—Commercial paper (negotiable and nonnegotiable), securities and writings indicating a right to receive money that is not itself a security agreement or lease (Sec. 9-105(1)(i)).

4. Documents of title—Bills of lading, dock warrants or receipts, warehouse receipts or other documents which, in the regular course of business or financing, are treated as evidencing that the person in possession is entitled to receive, hold and dispose of the document and the goods covered by the document (Secs. 1-201(15), 7-201 and 9-105(1)(f)).

5. Accounts and general intangibles (Sec. 9-106).

   a. Account—Right to payment for goods sold or leased or services performed which is not evidenced by an instrument or chattel paper.

   b. General intangible—Personal property other than goods, accounts, chattel paper, documents, instruments and money.

F. Financing statement—Document which is filed with a government office to give notice that a security interest exists in particular collateral (Sec. 9-402).

II. Creating a security interest.

    A. Transaction is one covered by Article 9 of the Code.

    B. Attachment—A security interest is enforceable between the debtor and the secured party so that the secured party is assured that certain predesignated property will be available to satisfy a debt should the debtor default, only if attachment has occurred (Sec. 9-203).

        1. Written agreement—Providing for security interest.

            a. Signed by debtor.

            b. Contains description of collateral.

            c. A writing is not necessary if the secured party is given possession of the collateral.

        2. Value is given by the secured party.

            a. Consideration sufficient to support a simple contract.

            b. Pre-existing obligation.

            c. Commitment to extend credit.

        3. Debtor has rights in the collateral.

III. Purchase-money security interest—A security interest in specific collateral is taken by a seller of the collateral or a creditor, who advances funds or incurs an obligation, enabling the debtor to acquire the collateral (Sec. 9-107).

IV. Perfecting a security interest—Legal process whereby a secured party obtains priority over other third parties having claims against the debtor. The method used for perfection is determined by the classification of collateral.

    A. By possession (Sec. 9-305).

        1. Common law pledge.

        2. Required method of perfection for instruments, other than instruments which constitute part of chattel paper (Sec. 9-304).

        3. The secured party or a bailee may be given possession.

    B. By attachment if a purchase-money security interest is created in consumer goods, other than motor vehicles and fixtures (Sec. 9-302(1)(d)).

    C. By filing a financing statement.

        1. Contents of financing statement.

a. Signature of debtor.

b. Addresses of debtor and secured party.

c. Description of collateral.

2. Required method of perfecting unless the secured party is given possession or the secured transaction involves a consumer purchase-money security interest.

3. Where to file. The code gives three alternatives. (Sec. 9-401.)

a. Central filing with state official, such as the secretary of state.

b. Local filing with official of county.

c. Combination of local filing for consumer or farm goods and central filing for other collateral.

FILL-IN QUESTIONS

1. A secured transaction is one in which a debtor, who has an obligation (usually to pay a sum of money), gives a _____ in personal property or fixtures to a lender or seller, known as the _____ .

2. The personal property, which is subject to a security interest, is called _____ .

3. Goods, which may be the subject matter of a secured transaction, are classified in accordance with the primary purpose for which they are purchased and used. If they are used primarily by the debtor for personal, family or household use, such goods are termed _____ . If they are used or consumed by a business in the manufacturing process, they are part of _____ .

4. A security interest is enforceable by a secured party against a debtor, who has defaulted, if the security interest has _____ to the collateral. The secured party, however, will only have priority over other creditors if he or she has _____ his or her security interest.

5. A security interest attaches when (1) a debtor has _____ , (2) the secured party has _____ , and (3) the parties have entered into an agreement, which is required to be in writing if the secured party does not have possession of the collateral.

MULTIPLE CHOICE QUESTIONS

1. Article 9 of the Uniform Commercial Code, dealing with secured transactions, does not apply to the creation of a security interest in:
a. personal property which has a value of $500 or less.

    b. personal property in which the debtor has no rights.

    c. personal property which is in the possession of a debtor.

    d. personal property which is in the possession of a secured party.

2. An automobile, purchased by Landau and secured by a purchase-money security interest, will be classified as inventory if:

    a. Landau is in the business of selling automobiles and the automobile in question was purchased for resale.

    b. Landau is a salesman and uses the automobile in order to call on customers.

    c. Landau purchased the automobile for his mother.

    d. Two of the above.

3. Boyne borrowed $500 from Rater and signed a writing. The writing provided that Boyne promised to repay the $500 to Rater on March 1 and gave Rater the right to take possession of and sell her fully described television set if she failed to repay the money.

    a. It is not a security agreement because the words, "security interest," are not included in the writing.

    b. A security interest has been created in the television set only if the money borrowed was used to purchase the television set.

    c. Rater is the secured party and has a security interest in the television set.

    d. A security interest did not attach to the television set because Rater did not sign the writing.

4. A security interest will attach to specified collateral, in which the debtor has an interest, if a written security agreement containing a description of the collateral is:

    a. signed by the debtor and the secured party gives value by making a commitment to extend credit.

    b. filed with the designated state or local official.

    c. signed by a secured party who lends money to a debtor.

    d. signed by a debtor and states the addresses of the debtor and the secured party.

5. A negotiable draft usually:

    a. may not be used as collateral for a secured transaction.

    b. is considered to be goods if used for a secured transaction.

    c. may be used as collateral for a secured transaction which is perfected by possession.

    d. may be used as collateral for a secured transaction which is perfected by filing.

6. Public notice of a security interest in personal property is provided by filing a:

    a. security agreement.

    b. chattel mortgage.

    c. bill of sale.

    d. financing statement.

Liens, Priorities and Remedies

The material in this chapter deals with the priorities secured parties have if they have perfected their security interests in collateral and the rights and duties of secured parties before and after a default by a debtor. Attention is given to the concept of a "floating lien," which is created by a security agreement which provides that a security interest attaches to (1) the proceeds of a sale or other disposition of covered collateral by a debtor, (2) after acquired property of a debtor, and (3) future advances to be made by a creditor, the secured party.

THINGS TO KEEP IN MIND

The objective of secured transaction devices is to protect creditors, who have extended credit, by giving them security interests in personal property which is typically in the possession of their debtors. Under the Code, lesser protection is afforded to debtors and others who may also have extended credit or otherwise dealt with the same debtors.

OUTLINE

I. Parties prevailing over a secured party who has failed to perfect his or her security interest (Sec. 9-301).

   A. Persons who have prior perfected security interests in the same collateral.

   B. Persons who have become lien creditors, including trustees in bankruptcy.

   C. Buyers in the ordinary course of business.

II. The range of perfection and the floating lien concept (Sec. 9-204).

   A. Financing statement is effective for five years. Provision is made for renewal.

B. Floating lien (Sec. 9-306).

    1. A security agreement may cover proceeds of the sale of collateral that was the subject matter of the agreement.

        a. Proceeds include whatever is received by the debtor when the collateral is sold, exchanged, collected or otherwise disposed of.

        b. Automatic perfection for ten days.

        c. May be provided for in the security agreement.

    2. A security agreement may cover advances to be made by a secured party in the future.

    3. A security agreement may cover after acquired property, personal property acquired by the debtor after the execution of the agreement.

C. Perfected security interest covers collateral that is subsequently moved to another state for the remaining perfection period or four months (whichever is shorter) (Sec. 9-103).

III. Priorities (Sec. 9-312).

A. One, whose security interest in the collateral has attached and been perfected, prevails over those who have not perfected.

B. If two or more parties have perfected security interests in the same collateral, the first to perfect has priority.

C. If two or more parties have unperfected security interests in the same collateral, the party whose security interest attached first prevails.

D. Exceptions.

    1. Buyers of goods in the ordinary course of business take free of security interests in sellers' inventory (Sec. 9-307).

    2. Second hand purchaser of consumer goods, who gives value, purchases the goods for personal or household use and lacks knowledge of the existence of a security interest in the goods, takes free of a security interest of a seller whose purchase-money security interest was automatically perfected without filing (Sec. 9-307).

    3. A subsequent purchaser of chattel paper, in the ordinary course of business, who gives value and takes possession, has priority over a secured party with a prior security interest that had been perfected by filing (Sec. 9-308).

IV. Rights and duties of parties before default or termination of a security interest when the parties have not otherwise agreed.

A. A secured party may release or assign all or part of collateral covered by a security interest (Secs. 9-405 and 9-406).

B. The financing statement can be amended (Sec. 9-402).

C. A secured party in possession of collateral must use reasonable care in preserving it; the debtor bears the expense and the risk of loss or damage (Sec. 9-207).

V. Rights and duties of parties upon default.

A. What constitutes default is usually stated in the security agreement.

B. A secured party may obtain a judgment based upon the underlying obligation or enforce the security interest (Sec. 9-501).

   1. A secured party with a security interest in collateral in the form of accounts, chattel paper and instruments may collect such obligations directly (Sec. 9-306).

   2. A secured party may take possession of collateral covered by a security agreement (Sec. 9-503).

      a. The secured party must do so without breach of the peace.

      b. The secured party must use reasonable care in the custody and preservation of collateral (Sec. 9-207).

      c. The secured party may have the debtor assemble the collateral and have it available at a mutually convenient location.

      d. If the collateral is difficult to remove, the secured party may have it rendered unusable by the debtor and dispose of it on the debtor's premises.

   3. A secured party may accept the collateral in satisfaction of the obligation and retain it (Sec. 9-505).

      a. Written notice must be given to the debtor and other secured parties, who have given written notice of claims, so that they may exercise their rights of redemption (Sec. 9-506).

      b. A secured party may not retain consumer goods if more than 60% of the price has been paid.

   4. A secured party may dispose of collateral and apply proceeds to the obligation (Sec. 9-504).

      a. Private or public sale, lease or any commercially reasonable means to produce the maximum benefit to both parties.

    b. Notice must be given to the debtor and other secured parties, who have given notice of claims, so that they may exercise their rights of redemption, unless the goods are perishables (Sec. 9-506).

    c. Effect of disposition of collateral—A purchaser or other transferee takes free of claims of the debtor and the secured party (Sec. 9-504(4)).

    d. Order of distribution of proceeds (Sec. 9-504).
       1) Expenses of sale, possessing, holding and preparing for sale, including attorney fees.
       2) Satisfaction of debt.
       3) Subordinate security interest holders who gave written notification.
       4) Usually a debtor is entitled to any surplus. (Usually a debtor is responsible for a deficiency.)

VI. Termination—When the debt is paid or other obligation satisfied, the secured party files a termination statement with the official with whom the original financing statement was filed (Sec. 9-404).

FILL-IN QUESTIONS

1. A security agreement is referred to as a floating lien if it provides that a security interest will attach to the proceeds of the sale or other disposition of specified collateral, _____ or _____ .

2. A secured party, whose security interest has attached to collateral belonging to a debtor, but has failed to perfect his interest, will not prevail over _____ _____ _____ .

3. Even if a secured party has perfected his or her security interest, he or she will not prevail over one who has a possessory lien for services and/or material furnished in repairing, storing, etc., collateral in his or her possession, or one who has purchased goods, which were part of inventory covered by a security agreement, if the purchase was made _____ .

4. If two secured parties have security interests in the same collateral and neither of them has perfected, the one _____ will have priority over the other.

5. Upon default by a debtor, a secured party may take possession of the collateral, to which his or her security interest attached, and retain the collateral or _____ _____ _____ .

MULTIPLE CHOICE QUESTIONS

1. Brennan, a manufacturer of clothing, and Carver, a producer of fabric, signed an agreement whereby Carver agreed to sell Brennan $10,000 worth of fabric, to be

paid for in six months. The agreement provided that the transaction would be secured by a security interest in Brennan's present and future inventory and that Carver agreed to provide Brennan with a continuing line of credit for a period of 18 months.

a. In order for the agreement to be binding on both Brennan and Carver, a financing statement must be filed with an appropriate government official.

b. The agreement is ineffective to give Carver a security interest in addition to Brennan's inventory, after the expiration of the six-month period.

c. The agreement provides for a valid floating lien and it is binding on Brennan and Carver.

d. If Carver advances $30,000 to Brennan 11 months later, Carver is an unsecured creditor to the extent of the $30,000.

2. TV Town Inc., a seller of television sets, maintains a large inventory of television sets which it obtains from manufacturers on credit. The manufacturers/creditors have all taken security interests in the appliances and the proceeds therefrom and have made the necessary filings in order to perfect their security interests. TV Town Inc. sells to many consumers; some pay cash and others buy on credit. TV Town Inc. takes a security interest when it makes a credit sale but does not file a financing statement.

a. The television sets in TV Town Inc.'s hands are consumer goods.

b. Since TV Town Inc. takes a purchase-money security interest in the goods it sells to customers, its security interest is perfected upon attachment.

c. The manufacturers can enforce their security interests against the television sets in the hands of the purchasers who paid cash for them.

d. A subsequent sale by one of TV Town Inc.'s customers to a purchaser for value will be subject to TV Town Inc.'s security interest.

3. C was an appliance dealer. She financed her inventory with her local bank and signed a security agreement using the inventory as security. B purchased a freezer from C. C defaulted on her payments to the bank.

a. A security agreement of this kind is illegal.

b. The bank may reclaim the freezer from B because its security interest never attached to the freezer.

c. The bank may reclaim the freezer from B because its security interest has been perfected.

d. B takes the freezer free of any security interests of C or the bank.

4. Nestler owned a candy store and was the holder of a warehouse receipt, which provided that the goods stored were to be delivered to the order of Nestler. Nestler borrowed money from Hirshy and gave Hirshy the warehouse receipt as security.

a. This is not a secured transaction because a warehouse receipt cannot be collateral in which a creditor may have a security interest.

b. Hirshy has not perfected his security interest unless a financing statement was properly filed.

c. Goodbard, who lent Nestler money before the transaction between Nestler and Hirshy, has priority over Hirshy with regard to the warehouse receipt.

d. Hirshy has perfected his security interest and has priority over other creditors of Nestler with regard to the warehouse receipt.

5. Epsilon sold Delta a CB radio for $180. Delta paid $50 immediately and agreed to pay $10 a month for thirteen months. Their agreement was reduced to writing and signed by both Epsilon and Delta. It included a provision under which Epsilon has the right to repossess the radio if Delta defaulted in his payments. Nothing else was signed, recorded or filed. The next week Epsilon and Delta had an argument. Since that time Delta has continued to use the CB but has not made any of the agreed payments.
    a. Epsilon, the debtor, and Delta, the secured party, have entered into an effective secured transaction.
    b. The security interest has attached to the CB radio and Epsilon has the right to repossess the CB and either retain the CB in satisfaction of the unpaid purchase price or sell it and apply the proceeds of the sale to the unpaid balance.
    c. If Delta's car is wrecked in an accident, in which the CB is totally destroyed, Epsilon has priority over other unsecured creditors of Delta with regard to Delta's remaining personal property.
    d. The security interest has attached to the CB radio and Epsilon has the right to repossess the CB, but will be required to sell it and apply the proceeds of the sale to the unpaid balance.

6. At a properly conducted public sale of property that was collateral for a secured transaction:
    a. the debtor is liable for any deficiency, if the sale does not produce enough to satisfy all of the incurred charges and the debt.
    b. the debtor may not purchase the collateral being sold.
    c. the secured party may not purchase the collateral being sold.
    d. junior secured parties may not participate in any excess proceeds.

Creditors' Rights and Bankruptcy

The material in this unit deals with the rights of debtors and creditors. Chapter 31 is concerned with some of the methods available to creditors for ensuring that legally owing obligations will be paid and the protection afforded to borrowers and purchasers before and after they enter credit transactions. The subject matter of Chapter 32 is the federal bankruptcy act, the purpose of which is to provide orderly procedures for discharging, rehabilitating or reorganizing debtors, who are unable to pay their debts, while providing for the equitable distribution of their assets among their creditors.

Rights of Debtors and Creditors

The law dealing with the rights of creditors to be paid obligations, which are legally owed to them, has undergone considerable change, particularly in recent years because of the expansion of consumer oriented legislation. In this chapter the authors review some of the means available to creditors to ensure payment of debts owed to them as well as recent debtor protection statutes.

THINGS TO KEEP IN MIND

A creditor, who has lent money or extended credit to others, has a contractual right to be paid when the obligation is due. You are already familiar with some methods available to a creditor to ensure payment, such as the use of commercial paper and secured transactions discussed in Unit IV. In order to have security that an obligation will be performed, a creditor may require that the debtor obtain a surety or guarantor. A creditor may obtain a lien on property, owned by a debtor, which can be sold in order to satisfy the obligation.

OUTLINE

I. Common law creditor protection based on contract—Guaranty and suretyship.

    A. Suretyship.

        1. A surety is a third party, who promises a creditor that he or she will be liable for an obligation along with the primary debtor. A surety is a joint obligor.

        2. A surety is primarily liable to a creditor. His, her or its promise need not be in writing, unless required by statute to be written.

3. If the principal debtor defaults, the creditor may make an immediate demand upon the surety for payment.

B. Guaranty.

   1. A guarantor makes a separate, collateral, secondary promise to the creditor that, if the debtor does not pay, he, she or it will pay the obligation.

   2. The guarantor is promising to answer for the debt, default or miscarriage of another (the principal debtor). The guarantor's liability is, therefore, secondary and the promise to pay must be in writing to comply with the statute of frauds.

   3. If the debtor defaults, the creditor must first make a demand on the debtor before making a demand for payment on the guarantor.

C. Defenses that may be raised by a surety or guarantor against the creditor.

   1. Material modification of the obligation owed by the principal debtor without the assent of the surety or guarantor.

   2. Discharge of the primary obligor.

   3. Tender of proper payment by the primary obligor.

   4. Surety or guarantor may raise any defense that may be asserted by the principal debtor, except minority and discharge in bankruptcy.

II. Laws assisting creditors.

A. Liens provided for by statute.

   1. Mechanic's lien on real property—If a debt arises because a property owner fails to pay for labor, services or materials furnished for purposes of making improvements on real property, the party, to whom the obligation is owed, may obtain a lien on the improved property, which may be enforced ultimately by sale of the property.

   2. Artisan's lien on personal property—Possessory lien, enforceable by a bailee, who has improved or stored another's property and not been paid for services and/or value added.

   3. Statutes provide for recording, giving notice to the debtor, foreclosure and sale.

B. Mortgage foreclosure on real property.

   1. A creditor, who lends money, secured by real property, enters into a mortgage agreement with the debtor. The creditor is the mortgagee and the debtor is the mortgagor.

2. If the mortgagor defaults, foreclosure procedures may be instituted by the mortgagee, and the property sold at a judicial sales.

    a. Proceeds are used to satisfy the cost of foreclosure and the debt.

    b. Any surplus is paid to the debtor. If there is a deficiency, a deficiency judgment can be thereafter obtained by the creditor.

C. Procedure if a creditor is not paid.

    1. A lawsuit, instituted by a creditor, results in a judgment against a debtor for the amount of the debt plus interest and costs.

    2. If the judgment is not paid, the creditor can obtain a writ of execution, a court order directed to the sheriff to seize specified property of the debtor, sell it and give the proceeds to the judgment creditor.

    3. In some states by complying with statutes, a creditor may get an order for attachment of a specified property of a debtor, before obtaining a judgment.

    4. By complying with statutes, a judgment creditor can reach property of a debtor in the hands of a third party, such as wages due to an employee (the debtor), in a garnishment proceeding.

D. Bulk sales law—Article 6 of the U.C.C.—See Chapter 18.

III. Protection of the debtor.

A. Statutory exemptions.

    1. Real property—Homestead exemption. If the family home is sold in order to satisfy a judgment, a specific amount of the sale price must be reserved for the debtor so that he or she can provide shelter for his or her family.

    2. Personal property—Usually a specified dollar amount of household furnishings, clothing, personal possessions, pensions received from the government based on military service and a proportion of disposable income are exempt from satisfaction for debts.

B. Consumer Credit Protection Act (The Truth-in-Lending Act).

    1. A lender or seller, who is extending credit, must disclose the loan or credit terms, including finance charges.

    2. C.C.P.A. applies to creditors, who, in the ordinary course of business, lend money, extend credit or arrange for the extension of credit to natural persons for purchases for personal, family, household or agricultural use, if the price is less than $25,000.

    3. The Fair Credit Billing Act, which amends the C.C.P.A., relates to credit reports and collection procedures.

C. Uniform Consumer Credit Code.

   1. Adopted in a few states.

   2. Similar to the federal Truth-in-Lending Act.

   3. Alters the holder in due course rule.

D. Debt collection—Federal and state statutes have been enacted to prevent the use of abusive practices.

E. Real estate transactions—Federal legislation includes the Interstate Sales Full Disclosure Act, designed to prevent fraudulent land sales, and the Real Estate Settlement Procedures Act.

FILL-IN QUESTIONS

1. A _____ is one who is primarily liable because he or she joins an obligor in promising to pay a debt to a creditor; a _____ is secondarily liable because his or her promise to pay an obligation is conditioned on the failure of the primary obligor to pay a debt to a creditor.

2. If a debt is incurred, but not paid, by the owner of real property for services rendered or materials furnished, in order to improve the property, the creditor, who furnished the services or supplied the materials may obtain a _____ lien, which will be enforceable by the sale of the real property.

3. A bailee in possession of personal property, which he or she has stored, cared for and/or repaired has an _____ lien, if the charges for storage and/or improvements are not paid.

4. If a judgment creditor has not been paid the amount of the judgment, he or she may apply for a writ of execution, which is a court order _____
_____.

5. _____ is a procedure whereby a court order is obtained, directing the sheriff to reach specified property of a debtor in the hands of a third person so that it can be applied to reduce the amount of a judgment.

6. Following the foreclosure of mortgaged real property, if the proceeds of the judicial sale are inadequate to satisfy the cost of foreclosure and the debt, the _____ is liable for any deficiency.

7. Statutes provide that certain property of a debtor cannot be reached in order to satisfy his or her debts. Usually such property includes a specific amount of the sale price realized on the sale of _____
as well as clothing and personal possessions. Certain income is also exempt because a creditor cannot reach _____
_____.

MULTIPLE CHOICE QUESTIONS

1. David owed Goliath a $1000 debt, due November 1. On October 15, for considera-
tion, Rocke promised in writing that he would pay Goliath the $1000 if David failed
to pay it. On November 1, David failed to pay Goliath.
   a. Rocke is a surety and is, therefore, primarily liable to Goliath.
   b. Rocke is a guarantor and is, therefore, primarily liable to Goliath.
   c. Rocke is a surety and is, therefore, secondarily liable to Goliath.
   d. Rocke is a guarantor and is, therefore, secondarily liable to Goliath.

2. Beta owed Kappa a $400 debt due December 1. On November 15, Xi for considera-
tion promised Kappa orally that he would pay the $400 if Beta did not pay. On
December 1, Beta failed to pay Kappa. Kappa demanded that Xi pay the $400 but
Xi refused, saying that his promise was not legally enforceable.
   a. Xi's promise to act as surety is unenforceable because it is not in writing.
   b. Xi's promise to act as a guarantor is unenforceable because it is not in writing.
   c. Xi is a surety and, therefore, Kappa must proceed against Beta before demanding payment from Xi.
   d. Xi is a guarantor and, therefore, Kappa need not proceed against Beta before
demanding payment from Xi.

3. Deb loaned Mollie $10,000 for one year. Mollie obtained a bond from the Sue-Us
Bonding Company, which guaranteed payment of the $10,000 to Deb. Mollie did not
pay Deb, and Deb is suing the bonding company for payment.
   a. The guarantee made by Sue-Us Bonding Company did not have to be in writing
in order to be enforceable.
   b. If Mollie was a minor, spent the money and disaffirmed her promise to repay the
loan, Deb may not recover from the bonding company.
   c. If Mollie had given Deb a promissory note for $20,000 in exchange for the
$10,000 loan, the defense of usury can be successfully raised by the Sue-Us
Bonding Company.
   d. Sue-Us Bonding Company can successfully raise the defense of bankruptcy, if
Mollie has been discharged in bankruptcy.

4. Pine supplied lumber to Holmes for the construction of a barn on Holmes' land.
Carpenter was employed by Holmes to build the barn. Neither Pine nor Carpenter
have been paid by Holmes. By complying with state statutes, requiring recording
and notice to a debtor, Pine and Carpenter may obtain and enforce:
   a. mechanic's liens on Holmes' real property.
   b. mechanic's liens on Holmes' personal property.
   c. artisan's liens on Holmes' real property.
   d. artisan's liens on Holmes' personal property.

*Questions 5 and 6 are based on the following fact situation: Dunstone owns no real
property but she owns an automobile worth $4000, a television set worth $300 and
miscellaneous personal property worth $5000. She is employed at a salary of $400 per
week. Dunstone owes a local bank $2000 for a loan that is past due.*

5. The bank can obtain:
   a. a writ of execution for the immediate seizure of Dunstone's automobile.

    b. an order for garnishment immediately of a proportion of Dunstone's salary.

    c. a lien on Dunstone's television set and/or her automobile by recording its lien and notifying Dunstone.

    d. a writ of execution for the seizure of Dunstone's television set, after obtaining a judgment against Dunstone.

6.   If the bank obtains a judgment against Dunstone and an appropriate court order:

    a. a proportion of Dunstone's salary cannot be reached through garnishment.

    b. for the seizure and sale of Dunstone's property, a specific amount of the sale price must be set aside so that Dunstone can provide shelter for her family.

    c. the bank will have liens on Dunstone's property, which may then be foreclosed.

    d. the bank will not be able to recover from any of Dunstone's assets because of statutory exemptions.

7.   The Truth-in-Lending Act:

    a. applies to any lender or seller who, in the ordinary course of business, lends money or extends credit to others, if the amount lent or the amount of credit given is less than $25,000.

    b. applies to any lender or seller who, in the ordinary course of business, lends money or extends credit to natural persons for purchases, not exceeding $25,000, for personal, household or business use.

    c. establishes a maximum percentage amount that can be charged for extending credit.

    d. is a disclosure statute, requiring lenders and sellers to disclose the cost of credit.

Bankruptcies and Reorganization

The Bankruptcy Reform Act, which became effective October 1, 1979, substantially changed and modernized the federal law relating to bankruptcy.

The goals of bankruptcy law are to provide relief for an honest debtor from the oppressive burden of indebtedness and for the fair, ratable distribution of a debtor's assets among creditors. As with the prior bankruptcy law, provision is made (but simplified in the present act) for alternative debtor rehabilitation solutions in the form of reorganization.

THINGS TO KEEP IN MIND

1. In addition to the federal bankruptcy law, other methods are available for insuring a fair distribution of the assets of an insolvent debtor among his, her or its creditors, so that the debtor has an opportunity to financially rehabilitate himself, herself or itself. State insolvency statutes, which do not conflict with the U.S. Constitution (by impairing the obligations of contracts) or the federal bankruptcy statutes and effect only property within the state, may be utilized. Other solutions, based upon principles of contracts, trusts and/or equity, such as compositions and/or extensions, assignments for the benefit of creditors and equitable receivership, may also be used.

2. Definitions of insolvency.

   Bankruptcy meaning, unless otherwise specified in the bankruptcy act—Liabilities exceed assets.

   Equity meaning—Current liabilities exceed current assets so that debtor cannot pay debts as they mature.

OUTLINE

I.   The Bankruptcy Reform Act of 1978.

   A. Establishes bankruptcy courts with jurisdiction over all controversies affecting the debtor or his, her or its estate.

   B. Provides procedures for:

      1. Voluntary and involuntary liquidation (bankruptcy) of natural persons, firms or corporations (Chapter 7).

      2. Reorganization of persons, firms and corporations (Chapter 11).

      3. Adjustment of debts of individuals with regular income (Chapter 13).

II. Liquidation—Ordinary or straight bankruptcy.

   A. Voluntary liquidation.

      1. Commenced by any natural person, firm, association or corporation, except railroad, banking, insurance or municipal corporation or building and loan association (to which other chapters of the act apply).

      2. Petitioning debtor need not be insolvent, unless it is a partnership.

      3. Debtor will be granted an order for relief if petition is proper and debtor had not been discharged in bankruptcy within the past six years.

   B. Involuntary liquidation.

      1. Commenced against any debtor, except railroad, banking, insurance or municipal corporation, building and loan association, charitable organization or farmer.

      2. Creditors having noncontingent, unsecured claims amounting to $5,000 or more petition court.

         a. If there are 12 or more creditors, three of them must join in the petition.

         b. If there are less than 12 creditors, one or more may sign the petition.

         c. If a party so requests, a temporary trustee may be appointed to take possession of the debtor's property in order to prevent loss.

      3. The court will grant an order for relief if the debtor fails to file an answer or, if debtor files an answer, creditors prove that:

         a. The debtor is not paying debts as they become due, or

         b. A custodian was appointed or took possession of the debtor's property within 120 days preceding the filing of the petition.

C. Debtor must file:

1. A list of creditors with their addresses and the amounts owed.

2. A schedule of assets.

3. A statement of financial affairs.

4. A schedule of exempt property, if debtor wishes to claim exemptions. Debtor has option of taking exemptions provided by either the law of the state in which he, she or it is domiciled or the federal bankruptcy act, which provides for the following exemptions:

    a. Equity in home and burial plot, not exceeding $7,500.

    b. Interest in one motor vehicle, up to $1,200.

    c. Interest in personal household goods, clothing, books, animals, etc., up to $200 for any single item.

    d. Interest in jewelry, up to $500.

    e. Other property, worth up to $400, plus any unused part of the $7,500 homestead exemption.

    f. Items used in trade or business, up to $750.

    g. Interests in life insurance policies.

    h. Professionally prescribed health aids.

    i. Federal and state benefits, such as social security, veterans' disability, unemployment benefits.

    j. Alimony and child support, pensions and annuities.

D. First meeting of creditors. After the order for relief, the court calls the first meeting of creditors, which is attended by the debtor and at which a trustee is elected.

E. Claims of creditors.

1. Filed within six months of the first meeting of creditors.

2. Claims, which arose before the filing of the petition, are allowed, unless objected to or unenforceable or excluded:

    a. Claims for interest accruing after petition was filed.

    b. Certain claims of landlords or employees, based on breach of lease or contract.

F. The trustee.

   1. The trustee takes title to all the debtor's property, exempt and nonexempt.

      a. All the legal and equitable interests which the debtor owned at the time the petition was filed.

      b. All property, inherited within 180 days after the filing of the petition; property acquired in a settlement with a spouse or as a beneficiary of life insurance.

   2. Duties of trustee—Trustee administers the estate of the debtor, by collecting assets, reducing them to cash and approving claims.

      a. Trustee may assume or reject executory contracts.

      b. Trustee may bring actions to avoid transfers of the debtor's assets, which the debtor or a judgment, lien or unsecured creditor would have had a right to avoid under state law or the bankruptcy act.

      c. Trustee is empowered to avoid transfers of property interests that were not perfected when the petition was filed.

      d. Trustee may avoid preferential transfers—A transfer of property or a payment that favors one creditor over other creditors. With some exceptions, any transfer made:
        1) When the debtor was insolvent.
        2) To or for the benefit of a creditor for or on account of an antecedent debt.
        3) During the 90 days before the petition was filed.
        4) Resulting in the receipt by the creditor of a greater percentage of payment than would be made under the provisions of the bankruptcy act.

      e. Fraudulent conveyances are voidable by the trustee.
        1) Transfer made in order to hinder, delay or defraud creditors or for less than reasonable consideration when the debtor was insolvent or, as a result of the transfer, becomes insolvent.
        2) Trustee has the power to avoid conveyances made within one year before the filing of the petition or the state statutory period, which is usually two to five years.

G. Priorities of payment of claims upon distribution.

   1. Secured creditors, having valid liens or security interests in property, are entitled to their security.

   2. Costs and expenses of preserving and administering the debtor's estate.

   3. Claims arising in the ordinary course of business, after the commencement of the action but before the election of the trustee.

4. Claims of wage earners, not exceeding $2,000 per claim, for wages earned within 90 days before filing of the petition.

5. Claims, not exceeding $2,000 per employee, for employee benefit plan contributions, arising within 180 days before filing of the petition.

6. Claims for deposits made for consumer purchases, up to $900 per claim.

7. Taxes legally due and owing within three years before filing of the petition.

8. Claims of general creditors on a pro rata basis.

9. Any balance is returned to the debtor.

H. Discharge of debtor from debts.

1. Claims that are not discharged.

   a. Back taxes (three years), which are not paid in full.

   b. Those based upon fraud, embezzlement, misappropriation or defalcation against the debtor, acting in a fiduciary capacity.

   c. Alimony and support.

   d. Intentional tort claims.

   e. Property or money obtained because of false pretenses or fraudulent representations.

   f. Student loans obtained within five years.

   g. Claims from prior bankruptcy action in which the debtor was denied a discharge for a reason other than the six year limitation.

2. Denial of discharge of a debtor.

   a. Assets are distributed, but debtor remains liable for unpaid portion of the claims.

   b. Discharge will not be granted if the debtor:
      1) Waives the right to discharge.
      2) Failed to appear at the first meeting of creditors or to participate in proceedings, involving objections raised to the application for discharge.
      3) Committed a bankruptcy crime.
      4) Unjustifiably failed to keep records from which his, her or its financial and business conditions could be ascertained.
      5) Refused to obey an order or answer material questions of the court.
      6) Concealed, transferred, etc., property.

III. Reorganization.

    A. Chapter 11 applies to individuals, business firms and corporations.

    B. A voluntary or involuntary petition may be filed.

    C. Plans for settling claims and/or extending time for payment in order to avoid liquidation are approved by the court.

    D. Debtor may file a plan within 120 days after the order for relief. If debtor does not do so or if the plan is not approved, the trustee, creditors or shareholders committee, appointed by the court, or any party in interest, may file a plan within 180 days after the order for relief.

    E. Plan must be approved by two-thirds of each class of creditors and shareholders, whose claims and interests will be impaired.

    F. Although not accepted by a class of creditors or shareholders, if the court finds that the plan is fair and confirms it, the plan is binding on all parties.

    G. Provision is made for the conversion of a reorganization into a liquidation proceeding.

IV. Adjustment of debts of an individual with regular income (Chapter 13).

    A. A debtor, who is a wage earner or engaged in business, may voluntarily file a petition and submit a plan providing for additional time within which to pay his or her debts.

    B. A reasonable plan, made in good faith, will be confirmed by the court. In most instances, the plan will have to be approved by all the secured creditors. Approval by unsecured creditors is not necessary.

    C. A Chapter 13 proceeding may be converted into a Chapter 7 liquidation or Chapter 11 reorganization.

FILL-IN QUESTIONS

1. If the total liabilities of a debtor exceed his or her assets, the debtor is insolvent in the _____ sense. If only his or her current liabilities exceed his or her current assets, the debtor is insolvent in the _____ sense.

2. A debtor, who is a natural person, _____, other than a railroad, banking, insurance or municipal corporation or building and loan association, may voluntarily petition for liquidation under Chapter 7 of the federal bankruptcy statute. If such a debtor owes more than $_____, his, her or its creditors may file a petition for _____, provided that the debtor is not a farmer or charitable organization.

3. In a liquidation proceeding instituted under the federal bankruptcy law, usually the creditors elect the trustee for the debtor's estate at the first meeting of the creditors, which is called by _____. Creditors have _____ from the date of the meeting within which to file their claims.

4. The trustee may avoid transfers of the debtor's property if _____ _____ or a judgment, lien or unsecured creditor would have had the right to avoid the transfer under state law or the federal bankruptcy act.

5. A preferential transfer by a debtor is one in which the debtor transferred money or property to one creditor which resulted in _____ and may be avoided by _____.

6. Either debtors or their creditors may commence liquidation proceedings (under Chapter 7) or _____ proceedings (under Chapter 11) but only a debtor may apply for _____ (under Chapter 13).

MULTIPLE CHOICE QUESTIONS

1. A debtor, who is in financial difficulty and transfers all of his property to another, in trust, for distribution among his creditors, has:
    a. entered into a composition.
    b. agreed to an extension.
    c. made an assignment for the benefit of creditors.
    d. made a voidable fraudulent conveyance.

2. An insolvent debtor owes many creditors and has filed a petition for voluntary liquidation. If he had transferred title to his automobile to one creditor a month before filing the petition, he has made a voidable:
    a. fraudulent conveyance.
    b. assignment for the benefit of creditor.
    c. admission of debt.
    d. preferential transfer.

3. Organizations that may be subjected to involuntary liquidation under the federal bankruptcy statute include:
    a. manufacturing corporations.
    b. banking corporations.
    c. insurance corporations.
    d. charitable associations.

4. Spendthrift is in financial difficulty. She is insolvent in the bankruptcy sense but has not filed a petition for voluntary liquidation. A few of her creditors are threatening to force her into liquidation.
    a. If she makes an assignment of her property to a third person, as custodian, for the benefit of her creditors, the bankruptcy court will grant an order for relief following the filing of a petition for involuntary liquidation.
    b. If she has ten creditors, whose claims are not contingent as to liability and amount to more than $5,000, a petition for involuntary liquidation must be signed by at least three of them.

    c. As long as she is able to meet current obligations, there is no basis for creditors to file a petition for involuntary liquidation.

    d. She cannot file a voluntary petition for liquidation without the approval of her creditors.

5. Environmental Heat Inc. is a medium sized corporation that has been having some difficulty paying current bills. For example, checks issued by it have not been honored by its bank because of insufficient funds. The principal creditors have held a meeting in order to consider possible alternative courses of action. At the meeting they have learned that Environmental Heat Inc. has sufficient assets to meet liabilities in the event of liquidation and that potentially the corporation will be profitable in the next five years.

    a. The best action that the creditors can take is to file a petition for involuntary liquidation.

    b. The bankruptcy court will not grant an order for relief if the creditors file a petition for involuntary liquidation because Environmental Heat Inc. is not insolvent in the bankruptcy sense.

    c. If the creditors file a petition for involuntary reorganization, Environmental Heat Inc. will have to submit a plan for reorganization and all creditors will have an opportunity to vote on the plan.

    d. If the creditors file a petition for involuntary reorganization, the bankruptcy court may confirm a plan for reorganization, submitted by the shareholders, even if the plan was not accepted by two-thirds of one class of creditors.

UNIT VI

Agency and Employment

The efficient operation of a business, whether it is a sole proprietorship or a large corporation, depends upon employing other people, some of whom are considered to be agents. How agency relationships are created and terminated are discussed in Chapter 33. If an agency relationship exists, the agent and the person employing him or her, the principal, owe certain duties to each other (the subject matter of Chapter 34), and acts committed by an authorized agent will be treated as being the acts of the principal. As a result, a principal will be liable in contract to third parties, with whom the agent has dealt, and in tort to those who have been injured by an agent, acting within the scope of his or her authority. The extent of contractual and tort liability is explored in Chapter 35.

Creation and Termination
of Agency Relationship

An agency is a representative relationship which arises when one person, the agent, represents or acts for and in the place of another person, the principal. It is a consensual relationship. In most cases, consent of the parties to the creation (and the termination) of an agency relationship is, in fact, given. In other instances, the parties may be treated as having consented because of their conduct. In this chapter the authors discuss the nature of the agency relationship and the ways in which it is created and terminated.

THINGS TO KEEP IN MIND

It is sometimes necessary to distinguish agency relationships from those of employment or independent contractors. Although there are no hard and fast rules for doing so, usually the issue is resolved by examining the relative amount of independent discretion given and the amount of control exercised by the principal/employer.

OUTLINE

I.   The nature of agency.

    A. By using a representative or agent, one person may conduct multiple business operations.

    B. A corporation can function only by using agents.

II. Agency distinguished from other relationships.

    A. Principal — Agent.

    1. An agent acts on behalf of and instead of a principal in engaging in business transactions.

    2. An agent may bind his or her principal in contract with a third person.

    3. An agent has a degree of independent discretion.

B. Master (Employer) — Servant (Employee).

    1. In order to determine if a relationship is one of employment, a court will examine surrounding circumstances.

        a. Employer controls or has right to control the employee in the performance of physical tasks.

        b. Employees have little or no independent discretion.

        c. Employees are paid for time rather than results.

    2. The rights and duties of an employee differ from those of an agent. Today the distinction is important for purposes of applicability of legislation, such as tax statutes and workmen's compensation acts.

C. Independent contractor.

    1. An independent contractor engages to bring about some end result.

    2. The person employing an independent contractor does not exercise control over the details of the performance.

    3. An independent contractor cannot bind the person employing him or her in a contract with a third party.

    4. An independent contractor usually uses his or her own materials, equipment and employees.

III. Formation of agency relationship.

A. In general.

    1. An agency may be formed for any legal purpose.

    2. An agency is a consensual relationship.

    3. Generally, no special formalities are required in order to create an agency.

        a. Unless required by the statute of frauds or other statute, a writing is not necessary.

        b. If the appointment of an agent is in a writing, the writing is called a "power of attorney."

4. Capacity.

    a. A principal must have legal capacity because contracts, entered into by his or her agent, are treated as contracts of the principal. If a principal lacks capacity, such contracts are voidable by the principal but not the third party.

    b. An agent need not have capacity in order to act as agent, but the contract of agency may be avoided by the agent, who lacks capacity (but not the principal).

B. Agency created by agreement.

1. The agent and principal affirmatively indicate that they consent to the formation of the agency.

2. The agreement may be an express one or implied from the conduct of the parties.

C. Agency created by ratification.

1. The principal's consent to the agency is given after the purported agent acted on behalf of the principal.

2. Ratification may be express or implied.

3. Ratification related back to the time the agent acted without authorization.

D. Agency created by estoppel. A person may be estopped to deny the existence of an agency if he or she caused a third party to reasonably believe that a person was his or her agent.

E. Agency created by operation of law.

1. A court may find an agency in order to carry out a social policy. (Purchases of necessaries by family members.)

2. Statutes provide that a state official will be treated as having been appointed as an agent to receive service of process under certain circumstances.

IV. Types of agencies.

A. Gratuitous agencies or agencies for hire.

B. Agency coupled with an interest.

1. Agency may be created for the benefit of the agent or a third person.

2. Agent has a beneficial interest in the subject matter of the agency.

V.   Termination of agency.

    A. Termination by act of the parties.

        1. Lapse of time.

            a. Agency expires at the end of a specified time if one is stated.

            b. Agency terminates after the expiration of a reasonable period of time if no term has been specified.

        2. Purpose accomplished. Agency is terminated when the objective for which it was created has been achieved.

        3. Occurrence of specific event. An agency ends upon the happening of a particular event if its formation had been so conditioned.

        4. Mutual agreement. The parties may consent to the termination of an agency.

        5. Termination by one party.

            a. A principal may revoke the authority of an agent or an agent may renounce his or her appointment as an agent.

            b. Either party may have the power but not necessarily the right to terminate an agency.
               1) If an agency is an agency at will (not for a stated term or for a particular purpose), either party has the power and right to terminate the agency.
               2) If an agency is not an agency at will, a party may have the power but not the right to terminate the agency and is, therefore, liable to the other party for the wrongful termination, which is a breach of contract.

            c. An agency may be terminated for cause.

            d. A principal does not have the power nor the right to terminate an agency coupled with an interest.

    B. Termination by operation of law.

        1. Death or insanity terminates an agency.

            a. Knowledge of the death or insanity is not required.

            b. An agency coupled with an interest is not automatically terminated.

            c. Statutory exceptions exist.

        2. Bankruptcy of the principal terminates the agency.

      a. Insolvency does not terminate the relationship.

      b. Bankruptcy of the agent does not necessarily terminate the agency relationship.

  3. Impossibility.

      a. Destruction of the subject matter of the agency.

      b. Outbreak of war.

      c. Change in law making further conduct of the agency illegal.

  4. Unforeseen change in circumstances.

C. Notice required for termination.

  1. If termination is by act of a party, the agency continues between the principal and agent until notice is given.

  2. Notice must be given to third persons.

      a. Actual notice must be given to third persons who dealt with the agent.

      b. Constructive notice must be given to those who knew of the agency by publication in a newspaper, posting a sign, etc.

  3. The party terminating the agency or another person may give the notice.

  4. Notice generally is not required if the agency is terminated by operation of law. (See Chapter 28 herein regarding Uniform Commercial Code, Sec. 4-405.)

FILL-IN QUESTIONS

1. A person who agrees to work for another, subject to his or her control and directions, for an agreed hourly rate, would most likely be considered an _____ rather than an _____.

2. A person who agrees to construct a house for another, furnishes the materials, supplies and employees and is to be paid a lump sum upon completion of the house would most likely be considered to be an _____.

3. An agency may be created by agreement of the parties, _____ _____ or _____.

4. Most agencies are created for the benefit of the principal. An agency _____ _____, however, is created for the benefit of the agent or a third person.

5. A principal may terminate an agency by _____ the authority of his or her agent, without liability to the agent, if _____
    _____.

6. An agency is terminated by operation of law upon the death or insanity of either the principal or agent, _____ or _____.

MULTIPLE CHOICE QUESTIONS

1. Creation of an agency relationship does not require:
    a. consent of the agent.
    b. contractual capacity on the part of the principal.
    c. consideration.
    d. any of the above.

2. An agency relationship:
    a. must be evidenced by a writing.
    b. creates a power of attorney.
    c. may be terminated only by the principal.
    d. may be created by estoppel.

3. Parmer sends Anders a letter requesting that Anders act as his agent to sell an acre of land which he owns. Anders accepts by signing a carbon copy of the letter and returning it to Parmer. This is an example of:
    a. an agency created by express agreement of the parties.
    b. an agency created by implied agreement of the parties.
    c. a formal contract of ratification.
    d. an illegal power of attorney.

4. As to third parties, an agency by estoppel:
    a. is the same thing as an agency created by operation of law.
    b. is the same thing as an agency created by ratification.
    c. can be imposed upon the principal even though there is, in fact, no agency relationship created by agreement.
    d. will be found to exist if a third party sold goods to a minor or did not pay for them even though they were necessaries.

5. Pearson, a minor, entered into a contract of agency with Argyle, an adult. Argyle made a contract with Yeager, while acting as agent for Pearson. The contract:
    a. of agency is voidable by Argyle.
    b. of agency is voidable by Pearson.
    c. with Yeager is voidable by Argyle.
    d. with Yeager is voidable by Yeager.

6. Prince, an adult, enters into a contract of agency with Queen, a minor. Queen made a contract with Zephir, while acting as agent for Prince.
    a. The contract of agency is not binding on Prince.
    b. The contract of agency is not binding on Queen.
    c. The contract with Zephir is not binding on Prince.
    d. The contract with Zephir is not binding on Zephir.

7. A lender is given, as security, authority to collect rents due to a borrower and to apply these rents to the payment of a debt owed to the lender.
   a. This does not create an agency.
   b. The agency is created by operation of law.
   c. This is an agency coupled with an interest.
   d. The agency is terminated by the death of the borrower.

8. April was an agent of Primmer. April died last month. The agency is, therefore, terminated by:
   a. mutual assent.
   b. revocation of authority.
   c. implied agreement of the parties.
   d. operation of law.

9. Marple has been authorized to act as Christie's agent until December 31, 1982. The agency will be terminated without liability to either Marple or Christie:
   a. on December 31, 1982, only.
   b. upon the insolvency of Christie, before December 31, 1982.
   c. upon the death of Marple, before December 31, 1982.
   d. upon the dismissal, without cause, of Marple by Christie.

10. In order to terminate the authority of an agent to bind his or her principal, actual notice to creditors who dealt with the agent or extended credit to the principal through the agent, must be given:
    a. if the principal is bankrupt.
    b. to the attorney general of the state in which the principal resides.
    c. if a change in law makes the further continuation of the agency illegal.
    d. if the principal revokes the authority of the agent.

Duties of Agents and Principals

Parties to an agency relationship owe each other those duties which are specified in their agreement and other duties, which are implicit because of the agency relationship. Some of these duties are based on the fact that an agency relationship is a fiduciary one founded upon trust and confidence. As a result, agents and principals are required to act with good faith, honesty and loyalty toward each other.

THINGS TO KEEP IN MIND

Duties, owed by principals and agents, may arise out of the fact that the agency relationship is usually a contractually created one. Generally, actions based on a failure of either party to perform or an agent to account or a principal to compensate an agent are founded on contract. Actions based upon a breach of the fiduciary duty (competing with one's principal, acting for a third person's benefit, failing to reveal material information or making a secret profit) are founded on tort and do not require a showing of fraud or actual, measurable damages.

OUTLINE

I. Agent's duties to principal.

A. Some of the duties of an agent are specified in the agency agreement, others are implied from the agency relationship.

B. Duty to perform—An agent is required to follow instructions, use reasonable skill and diligence in carrying out agency obligations and to use special skills, which he or she possesses, if they are applicable.

C. Duty to notify principal of material information, relating to the subject matter of the agency.

D. Duty of loyalty.

    1. An agent may neither compete with his or her principal nor act for another principal, unless full disclosure is made to the principal and the principal consents.

    2. After termination of an agency, the agent may not disclose trade secrets, confidential information, customer lists, etc., acquired in the course of his or her employment.

    3. Conflicts of interest—Any secret profits or benefits, received by an agent, acting adversely to his or her principal, belong to the principal, who may recover them from the agent. (A court will impose a constructive trust.)

E. Duty to account—An agent must account to his or her principal for any moneys or property, rightfully belonging to the principal, which have come into the agent's hands. An agent should not commingle such property with his or her own property or that of others.

F. Remedies available to principal for breach of duty by agent.

    1. Principal's right to indemnification—If a principal is required to pay damages to an injured party for an agent's tortious conduct or, as a result of an agent's violation of the principal's instructions, incurs a loss, the principal may recover the amount of resulting damages from the agent.

    2. A principal may seek remedies based on breach of contractual duties or in tort, based on a breach of the fiduciary duty.

    3. Transactions between a principal and agent, which violate the fiduciary duty, are voidable.

    4. A court will impose a constructive trust on property, received by an agent, who has used his or her agency position in conflict with those of his or her principal, so that the property (or the proceeds of its sale) is treated as held for the benefit of the principal.

II. Principal's duties to agent.

A. Some of the duties of a principal are specified in the agency agreement; others are implied from the agency relationship.

B. A principal has an obligation to perform in accordance with his or her contract with an agent.

C. Duty to compensate and reimburse.

    1. A principal is required to pay any agreed compensation to his or her agent.

2. If no compensation is specified, a principal is required to pay expenses, losses and reasonable compensation for services rendered by the agent, unless the agency is a gratuitous one or there are circumstances, such as a family relationship, indicating that compensation had not been intended.

3. There is no duty to pay compensation to an agent, who has breached his or her duties.

D. Duty of cooperation—A principal is required to assist an agent in performing his or her duties and to do nothing to prevent such performance.

E. Duty to provide safe working conditions.

F. Agent's remedies against principal.

1. Indemnification—A principal may be required to indemnify an agent for payments or liabilities, incurred in executing his or her obligations, and losses, caused by the failure of the principal to perform his or her duties.

2. An agent may obtain a lien against his or her principal's property.

3. An agent may sue for breach of contract or counterclaim if sued by his or her principal.

4. An agent may bring an action for accounting.

5. An agent may withhold further performance.

FILL-IN QUESTIONS

1. An agent is contractually obligated to his or her principal to perform in accordance with their agency agreement. This means that an agent is required to _____
    _____
    _____ .

2. An agent is a fiduciary. As a result, an agent must act _____
    _____ . He or she
    must reveal information, relating to the subject matter of the agency to his or her principal, and will have to account to his or her principal for any secret profit or benefit obtained, while acting for the principal. If an agent breaches the fiduciary duties, the contract of agency is _____ by the principal.

3. A principal is obligated to pay his or her agent _____
    unless the agency agreement or other circumstances clearly indicate that such services were to be rendered gratuitously.

4. A principal has a right to _____ if, as a result of the failure of his or her agent to carry out instructions, he or she incurs a loss. An agent has a similar right

of _____ for payments made or liabilities incurred in executing his or her agency duties.

MULTIPLE CHOICE QUESTIONS

1. An agent owes a duty of loyalty to his or her principal:
    a. because the agent occupies a fiduciary relation with the principal.
    b. which is breached if the agent acts in a negligent manner.
    c. and if this duty is violated, the agent is liable only for actual losses incurred by the principal as a result of the breach.
    d. but this duty prohibits an agent from making a secret profit while representing the principal only if the interests of the principal are adversely affected.

2. An agent, employed by both the buyer and seller of certain personal property, will be considered as violating his fiduciary duty:
    a. although both the buyer and seller know of his dual position and consent thereto.
    b. although no actual monetary damage can be shown.
    c. but is entitled to retain compensation paid for his services by the seller.
    d. but neither the buyer nor the seller can rescind an executory contract made on his behalf by the agent.

3. J. P. Metty hired Leopard as his agent for purposes of finding a building contractor and supervising the construction of a new mansion for Metty. It was anticipated that the cost would be at least $500,000. For his services Leopard would receive a fee of $30,000. Leopard contacted Castle Construction Co., which agreed to construct the stately manor house for Metty for $500,000 and an addition to Leopard's house at no charge. The Metty mansion and the addition to Leopard's house have been completed and Metty has paid the $500,000 to Castle Construction Co. Leopard is liable to Metty because:
    a. he failed to inform Metty that the mansion could be constructed for less than $500,000.
    b. he acted disloyally by failing to obtain the most favorable terms for Metty.
    c. he failed to account for a benefit he received as a result of the agency.
    d. all of the above.

4. Paul appointed Fred as his agent to purchase 500 shares of ETT Co. stock for $18 per share. Unknown to Paul, Fred owned 500 shares of ETT Co. stock. Fred sold his own shares to Paul at $18 per share.
    a. Paul must carry out his duty of compensating Fred for the services performed.
    b. A court will impose a constructive trust on the 500 shares of ETT Co. stock now held by Paul.
    c. The contract of sale is voidable by Paul so that he can return the 500 shares of stock to Fred and recover the $9,000 paid therefor.
    d. If the value of the stock increases to $24 per share, Paul has no basis for suing Fred.

5. A principal engages an agent for three months as its exclusive agent to sell its product in a three state area.
    a. The contract creating the agency must be in writing.

b. If the principal sells its product in the three state area through another agent, it will be liable for damages to the first agent.

c. The principal does not have the power to terminate the agency because it is an agency coupled with an interest.

d. The principal can disaffirm contracts made by the agent when it is discovered that the agent is a minor.

6. M's agent, Q, had access to a secret formula which M developed and used for the manufacture of a substance that absorbs snow causing it to disappear. Q sold the trade secret to S.

a. M cannot discharge Q without liability.

b. M can recover the consideration paid by S to Q although the sale of the trade secret occurred after Q left M's employ.

c. M can recover the consideration paid by S to Q or recover in tort for the breach of Q's fiduciary duty, but not both.

d. There is no basis for a suit by M against S.

Liability of Agents and Principals

A named principal is liable as a party to an act or transaction engaged in or conducted by his or her agent. As a result, a principal may be liable in contract or tort to a third party. The third party in such case will have to establish that there was an agency relationship and that the agent was acting within the scope of his or her actual or apparent authority or that the act of the agent was later ratified by the principal. In this chapter the authors discuss the nature of the liability of employers as well as the rights and liabilities of principals and agents with regard to third parties.

THINGS TO KEEP IN MIND

An agent's authority to do a particular thing may have been expressly or impliedly conferred by his or her principal, in which case the agent has actual authority. An agent may lack the actual power to perform a particular act but may possess apparent authority if, because of his or her principal's words or conduct, a third party reasonably and justifiably believed that the agent had the necessary authority.

OUTLINE

I. Liability of principals to third parties based on contract.

A. A principal is liable as a party to a lawful contract made for and on his or her behalf by his or her agent, while acting within the scope of his or her actual or apparent authority, or subsequently ratified by the principal.

B. Third party must show that:

1. The agency relationship existed, and

2. The agent acted within the scope of his or her authority.

C. Authority of agent.

   1. Actual—Conferred by principal upon the agent in order to accomplish the purpose of the agency.

      a. Express actual authority.
        1) May be given orally or in a writing.
        2) "Equal dignity" statutes may provide that, if a contract being executed by an agent is required to be in writing, the agent's authorization must also be in writing.

      b. Implied actual authority.
        1) Inferred because of conduct of principal.
        2) Conferred because of custom.
        3) Reasonably necessary to carry out express authority.
        4) Arising because of an emergency which necessitates action by the agent to protect or preserve the property or rights of the principal.
        5) An agent has limited power to delegate performance of his or her duties to subagents.

   2. Apparent authority.

      a. The principal manifests to a third person that his or her agent has authority and the third person reasonably relies upon the principal's statement or conduct, deals with the agent and is injured.

      b. Apparent authority cannot be based upon declarations or conduct of the agent.

      c. Apparent authority may arise if a principal gives possession and evidence of ownership of his or her property to a purported agent.

      d. The principal is estopped from asserting that the agent lacked authority.

D. Ratification—The affirmation by a principal of a previously unauthorized contract or act.

   1. The principal must have knowledge of all material facts surrounding the transaction.

      a. If the principal lacks complete knowledge, he or she may repudiate the ratification, unless the third person has changed his or her position in reliance on the ratification.

      b. It does not matter that the lack of knowledge results from the agent's wrongful conduct or a mistake.

   2. The effect of ratification is to bind the principal as if the act or contract had been originally authorized.

   3. The entire transaction must be ratified.

4. The agent must have held himself or herself out as acting for the person who subsequently ratifies.

5. The principal must have had capacity at the time the act was performed and at the time it was ratified.

6. Ratification may be express.

7. Ratification may be implied.

    a. Acceptance of benefits.

    b. Failure to repudiate.

8. Death, insanity or withdrawal of third party before ratification prevents principal from effectively ratifying.

II. Contract liability of agent to third party.

  A. An agent is not liable in contract, if the contract is made in the principal's name and authorized, because the parties to the contract are the principal and the third party.

  B. If a contract is made in the name of a principal by the agent, lacking authority, and the contract has not been ratified by the principal, the agent is not liable as a party, but is liable to the third party based upon breach of implied warranty of authority.

  C. An agent is liable to a third party if he or she expressly obligates himself or herself or guarantees performance by his or her principal.

III. Liability when principal is undisclosed.

  A. An undisclosed principal is one whose existence and identity are not disclosed to a third party with whom an agent deals.

  B. The agent is a party to the contract and is liable as such.

  C. If the agent had authority:

    1. The agent is entitled to indemnification from the principal.

    2. The third party can recover from the principal, unless:

      a. The third party elected to look only to the agent.

      b. Liability is based upon a negotiable instrument, because the principal's signature does not appear thereon.

    3. The third party can recover from either the principal or the agent but not both.

D. The principal can enforce the contract against the third party, if it was entered on his or her behalf by an authorized agent, unless:

  1. Liability is based upon a negotiable instrument and the principal did not acquire rights thereto.

  2. The third party was being defrauded by the principal.

  3. The contract was for the performance of personal services by the agent.

E. The principal bears the loss if his or her agent acted dishonestly.

F. Partially disclosed principal.

  1. Third party knows of principal's existence but not identity.

  2. The principal and the agent may both be treated as parties to the contract.

IV. Liability to third party for torts.

A. An agent is personally liable for his or her torts, even if they were authorized.

B. A superior, such as an employer or principal, is vicariously liable for torts committed by a subordinate, such as an employee or an agent, if the subordinate was acting within the scope of his or her employment or agency, in furtherance of the superior's business.

  1. The principal/employer cannot normally disclaim vicarious liability for subordinate's torts.

  2. The principal is liable for tortious acts of employees and subagents hired by an agent, who had authority to hire.

  3. An employer, who has the right to control employees who are "borrowed," is liable to third parties.

  4. One employing an independent contractor is not liable for torts of the independent contract or those of his or her employees.

C. A superior is not liable if a subordinate substantially deviates from his or her required duties and goes on a "frolic of his or her own."

D. A principal is liable for the intentional tort of fraud or misrepresentation, if his or her agent had the authority to make representations concerning the subject matter with which he or she dealt on behalf of the principal.

E. The one in a superior position, having the right to control the activities of his or her subordinate, is liable for the subordinate's negligence and intentional torts and has a duty to restrain subordinates from engaging in reckless acts.

F. Notice of material facts, relating to a principal's or employer's business, received by an agent or employee, will be imputed to the principal or employer.

V. Liability of superior (an employer or principal) for injuries to subordinates.

    A. Employers are absolutely liable for injuries sustained by employees during the course of their employment under workmen's compensation statutes.

    B. Common law defenses, such as the fellow servant rule, assumption of the risk and contributory (or comparative) negligence, are eliminated by workmen's compensation statutes.

    C. If a workmen's compensation statute is inapplicable, the common law defenses may be raised by the superior.

FILL-IN QUESTIONS

1. The extent of an agent's power to engage in transactions on behalf of his or her principal is referred to as the agent's _____.

2. Actual authority may be _____, if a principal uses words to confer authority upon an agent, or implied, because such authority is incidental to and clearly necessary or logically inferred from the express powers granted or based upon _____.

3. A principal is liable on a contract made in his or her name by an agent, acting within the scope of his or her authority or subsequently _____ by the principal. In such case, the agent is _____ liable to the other contracting party as a party to the contract. If the agent lacked authority, he or she is liable to the other contracting party based upon the _____.

4. The doctrine of *respondeat superior* results in one in a superior position being vicariously liable without actual fault for _____ committed by his or her subordinates, while acting within _____
_____.

MULTIPLE CHOICE QUESTIONS

1. An agent is liable for performance of a contract to the third party, with whom he or she deals, on a contract that he or she has entered on behalf of his or her principal:
   a. whenever the agent exceeds his or her authority.
   b. whenever the agent acts in behalf of a nonexistent principal.
   c. whenever the agent acts in behalf of a principal, who did not have contractual capacity at the time of the transaction.
   d. only if the agent expressly assumes liability and thus becomes a party to the contract.

2. An agent is thought of as possessing the same authority as is possessed by other agents in similar positions. Such authority is normally:
   a. express actual authority.
   b. express apparent authority.

    c. implied actual authority.

    d. implied express authority.

3.   If a principal leads a third party to believe that he or she has conferred authority on his or her agent, although he or she has not conferred such authority on the agent in fact, the agent will be considered as having:

    a. express actual authority.

    b. implied actual authority.

    c. apparent authority.

    d. no authority.

4.   Arnold is the manager of a snow clearing service. Although not expressly authorized to do so, Arnold would have:

    a. implied authority to discharge an employee who has refused to lift a shovel and has thrown snowballs at customers.

    b. implied authority to borrow money to purchase twenty snowblowers.

    c. apparent authority to borrow money to purchase twenty snowblowers.

    d. actual authority to cancel an order for snow plows, placed by the purchasing agent of the snow clearing service.

5.   Cramer, chief clerk for Morris, is asked by Morris to assume management of his store, while Morris is on special undercover assignment for the CIB. If Morris cannot be reached for advice, Cramer is justified in:

    a. discharging an incompetent employee.

    b. borrowing money in Morris's name for purposes of enlarging the store.

    c. lending Egger, an employee in the store, $9,000.

    d. all of the above.

6.   If a principal accepts the benefits of a contract, entered into by his agent, acting without the scope of his authority, the principal will be considered to have ratified the contract:

    a. in its entirety.

    b. although he lacked actual knowledge of some of the material terms of the agreement.

    c. although the other party to the contract has withdrawn.

    d. retroactive to the date upon which it was entered, although at that time the principal was incompetent.

7.   Paul has authorized Arthur to purchase a television set from Exeter on his (Paul's) behalf. Instead of purchasing a television set, Arthur, fully disclosing the agency relationship, purchased a CB radio. Paul used the CB radio for one month but neither he nor Arthur paid Exeter therefor.

    a. Only Arthur is liable for the purchase price of the CB radio.

    b. Paul is liable for the purchase price of the radio because he ratified the transaction by accepting the benefits.

    c. Paul is liable for the purchase price of the radio because Arthur had actual authority to purchase it.

    d. Paul is not liable for the purchase price of the radio because he made no implied warranty as to his capacity.

8. An agent, who has been appointed by a principal to move lumber that is obstructing a road which the principal is required to keep clear:
    a. is liable to a third person, who is injured while trying to climb over the lumber, which the agent failed to remove.
    b. is not liable to a third person, who is injured by a falling two by four, because the agent has moved the lumber but stacked it in a negligent manner.
    c. is liable to a third person, with whom he gets into a dispute while in the process of moving the wood and hits him with a two by four.
    d. is not liable to a third person if his principal, under the doctrine of *respondeat superior*, is liable for the tort committed by the agent.

9. Watson was an employee of the H and M Contracting Corp. Watson was specially trained in procedures to be used in blasting operations with particular emphasis on safety precautions. H and M Contracting Corp. had contracted to construct a factory. In order to put in the foundation, it was necessary to do some blasting and Watson's services were used. Watson disregarded a number of safety precautions. As a result, neighboring buildings were damaged and Watson incurred personal injuries.
    a. H and M Contracting Corp. is liable to the owners of the damaged buildings, despite the fact that Watson disregarded the precautions and the fact that it exercised reasonable care.
    b. H and M Contracting Corp. is not liable to the owners of the damaged buildings because Watson disregarded safety precautions and it exercised reasonable care.
    c. H and M Contracting Corp. is not liable to Watson under the workmen's compensation statutes.
    d. Watson is not liable for the damage to the neighboring buildings because he was acting on behalf of his employer.

10. Workmen's compensation laws are:
    a. governed by federal regulation.
    b. designed to eliminate some common law defenses, such as the fellow servant rule, when an employee is injured.
    c. not applicable if an employee's negligence contributed to his own injury.
    d. applicable to all employees and agents.

UNIT VII
Business Organizations

As indicated in Chapter 36, various forms of organization may be utilized in order to engage in a business enterprise, the most common of which are the sole proprietorship, the partnership and the corporation. The formation, termination, management and rights and liabilities of partnerships and corporations and those associated with them are explored in the chapters in this unit.

Note that the law of contracts and agency form a foundation for your understanding of the material in this unit.

Forms of Business
Organization

In this chapter the authors briefly explain and compare the basic and some less frequently used forms of business organizations.

THINGS TO KEEP IN MIND

The choice, as to which form of organization is most appropriate for a particular business enterprise, depends upon a number of considerations, some of which, such as capital needs, liability of participants and tax advantages, are referred to in this text. The type of organization selected in each case is a matter for sound business judgment, based in part upon knowledge of legal implications.

OUTLINE

I. Basic forms of business organization.

A. Sole proprietorship—A business owned by an individual, who is personally liable for the obligations of the business.

B. Partnership.

1. An association of two or more persons, who jointly control and carry on a business as co-owners for the purpose of making a profit. (Covered substantially by the Uniform Partnership Act—See Appendix C.)

2. A limited partnership is one in which at least one partner is a general partner and at least one other, who, as a limited partner, does not participate in management and has limited liability. (See the Uniform

Limited Partnership Act in Appendix D and the Revised Uniform Limited Partnership Act in Appendix E.)

C. Business corporation.

1. A separate legal entity, created by the state.

2. The owners, the shareholders, have limited liability.

3. Many states have adopted the Model Business Corporation Act. (See Appendix F.)

II. Other forms of business organization.

A. Joint venture—A special type of association, formed to carry out a single transaction or a series of similar transactions, which for tax purposes is treated in the same manner as a partnership.

B. Syndicate or investment group—A number of persons agree to pool their resources in order to finance a business venture.

C. Joint stock company—An association, structurally resembling a corporation, but often treated as a partnership.

D. Business trust—Arises if a number of people turn over management and legal title to property to one or more trustees, who distribute the profits to the participants (the beneficiaries of the trust).

III. Comparisons between different forms of organization.

A. Advantages and disadvantages of a sole proprietorship.

1. Advantages.

a. Receive all profits.

b. Easier and less costly to initiate than other forms of organization.

c. Possible tax benefits.

d. Sole proprietor is his or her "own boss."

2. Disadvantages.

a. Bears entire risk of loss (unlimited liability).

b. Difficult to raise large amounts of capital.

c. Possible tax disadvantages.

B. Liability of owners.

1. Sole proprietorship—Unlimited.

2. Partnership—Usually unlimited.

3. Corporation—Usually limited.

C. Ability to raise capital—Usually increases as organization changes from a sole proprietorship to partnership to corporation.

D. Comparison of partnership to corporate form of organization. See Exhibit 36-1 in text.

E. Tax considerations. See Exhibit 36-2 in text.

Creation and Termination

of A PARTNERSHIP.

Much of the law relating to partnerships is codified in the Uniform Partnership Act, which defines a partnership as being "an association of two or more persons to carry on as co-owners a business for profit" (Sec. 6). Persons means natural persons, other partnerships, associations and corporations (Sec. 2). Business includes trades, occupations and professions (Sec. 2).

THINGS TO KEEP IN MIND

Partnership law is based upon the law of agency so that each partner is treated as an agent of his or her co-partners. As a result, as shall be seen in Chapter 38, each partner may be liable as a principal to third persons if a partnership relationship existed.

OUTLINE

I. Characteristics of a partnership.

   A. A partnership is treated as an entity, separate and apart from its individual members for limited purposes.

      1. The capacity of a partnership to sue and be sued in the name of the partnership varies from state to state.

      2. Judgments entered against a partnership in its partnership name may be collected from partnership property.

      3. Under the federal bankruptcy laws, a liquidation proceeding is effected against only the partnership itself if the petition specified the partnership in the firm name.

4. With variation among the states, ownership to personal and real property may be transferred by and to a partnership in its firm name.

B. A partnership may be treated as an aggregate of the individual members.

1. This is so under the law in some states.

2. Under the federal tax laws, a partnership is treated as an aggregate.

II. Formation of a partnership.

A. No special formality is ordinarily necessary in order to create a partnership.

B. A partnership may be expressly created by contract.

1. Partnership agreement may be oral or in writing.

   a. Because of the statute of frauds, a partnership agreement must be in writing in order to be enforceable, if it authorizes partners to deal in transfers of real property.

   b. If a partnership is formed for a term of more than one year but the agreement is oral, it will be treated as a partnership at will, which may be terminated by any party without liability, unlike a partnership for term, which requires the assent of all the partners for dissolution.

   c. Usual contents of articles of partnership.
      1) Name—State law may restrict use of certain names and/or words.
      2) Nature of business and duration.
      3) Contributions to be made by individual partners.
      4) Manner of dividing profits and losses—Unless otherwise specified, partners share profits equally; if no provision is made for the manner of sharing losses, losses are shared in the same proportion as are profits.
      5) Salaries and drawing accounts, if any.
      6) Restrictions on the authority of any partners.
      7) Conditions for withdrawal from partnership and provisions for the continuation of the business if the partnership is dissolved.

2. Capacity of partners.

   a. Minors—Partnership agreement is voidable by a minor but, if rights of creditors are involved, the minor cannot withdraw his or her original investment in the partnership.

   b. If a partner is adjudicated insane after the partnership is formed, the partnership is not automatically dissolved.

   c. Corporations—State laws vary.

      1) Traditionally a corporation could not be a partner.

      2) If corporation's charter (certificate or articles of incorporation) so provides, it may be a partner.

      3) The Model Business Corporation Act provides that a corporation may be a partner.

  3. Consent to formation of partnership by all partners is necessary.

C. Partnership may be implied if parties intended to be co-owners of a business.

  1. Factors to be considered are holding property together, contributing capital or investing jointly and sharing profits.

  2. It does not, however, necessarily mean that a group of people have formed a partnership if they are co-owners of property or share gross income (U.P.A. Sec. 7).

  3. A person will not be treated as a partner merely because he or she receives a share of profits in payment of a debt, wages, interest on a loan, an annuity to a widow or representative of a deceased partner, or consideration for the sale of good will or other property.

D. Partnership by estoppel.

  1. A party, who is in fact not a partner, will be estopped from denying that he or she is a partner and, therefore, held liable as a partner to third persons, who reasonably relied and dealt with or advanced credit to the partnership if:

    a. He or she held himself or herself out as being a member of a partnership, or

    b. Consented to a misrepresentation of an alleged partnership relationship by another.

  2. The purported partner does not become a partner, although he or she may be liable as one to third persons.

III. Partnership property includes:

A. Real and personal property contributed by individual partners, at the time of formation of the partnership or subsequently, for the permanent use of the partnership.

B. Property acquired subsequently with partnership funds on account of the partnership.

C. Any realized appreciation in the value of partnership property.

IV. Rights of partners.

A. Right with respect to specific partnership property (U.P.A. Sec. 25).

1. Partners are tenants in partnership—Co-owners of partnership property with the right to possession for partnership purposes.

2. Upon the death of a partner, his or her rights in specific partnership property vest in the remaining partners.

   is placed in the possession or discretion of

3. A partner may not assign rights to specific partnership property nor subject it to dower, attachment or execution by his or her individual creditors, etc.

B. Rights to an interest in the partnership.

   1. Each partner has a right to his or her share of the profits and surplus, which is considered to be personal property (U.P.A. Sec. 26).

   2. A partner's interest in the partnership is subject to assignment, attachment and other charging orders. An assignment does not dissolve the partnership or permit an assignee to interfere with management. (U.P.A. Secs. 27 and 28).

C. Right to participate in management. See Chapter 38.

V. Termination of partnership—Occurs following the dissolution and winding up (liquidation) of a partnership.

   A. Dissolution—Occurs when a partner ceases to be associated with the partnership business, resulting in a change in the relations of the partners (U.P.A. Sec. 29).

   1. By acts of the parties (U.P.A. Sec. 31).

      a. If the partnership agreement provided for a partnership for term and the term has elapsed or the purpose for which it was formed has been accomplished, the partnership is dissolved.

      b. Partners may mutually agree to dissolution.

      c. If the partnership is a partnership at will, a partner's good faith withdrawal or expulsion dissolves the partnership without liability.

      d. If the partnership was for a specified term, withdrawal of a partner, without cause, will subject withdrawing partner to liability; expulsion, without cause, subjects other partners to liability.

      e. Admission of a new partner results in dissolution of the former partnership and the creation of a new one, which is liable for the obligations of the old partnership (U.P.A. Sec. 41).

   2. Dissolution by operation of law.

      a. Death of a partner.

      b. Bankruptcy of the partnership or a partner (in most cases).

c. Illegality, which makes it illegal to continue the business or to do so with one of the partners.

3. Dissolution by judicial decree (U.P.A. Sec. 32).

   a. Upon application of a partner.
     1) A partner has been judicially declared insane.
     2) A partner is permanently incapable of participating in management.
     3) The business of the partnership can only be operated at a loss.
     4) Improper conduct of a partner.
     5) Serious personal dissension among partners.

   b. Upon application of a third party.
     1) Assignee of a partner, if it was a partnership at will.
     2) Judgment creditor of a partner, who obtained a charge on the interest of his or her debtor in the partnership.

B. Notice of dissolution—Failure to give required notice results in liability.

1. A withdrawing partner must give notice to his or her co-partners.

2. Personal notice must be given to those who extended credit to the partnership and public notice must be given to those who dealt with the firm on a cash basis, if dissolution occurs because of acts of the parties or by operation of law, except for illegality or bankruptcy (U.P.A. Sec. 35).

C. Winding up.

1. Dissolution terminates the authority of partners, except the authority to complete unfinished business and that which is necessary to winding up, including collecting, preserving and selling partnership assets, discharging liabilities, collecting debts owed to the partnership and accounting to each other for the value of their interests in the partnership.

2. Distribution of assets.

   a. Distribution is made out of partnership assets and any additional "contributions" by partners necessary to pay liabilities of the partnership.

   b. Order of payment.
     1) Payment to outside creditors.
     2) Payment to partners who have made advances or incurred liabilities on behalf of the partnership.
     3) Return of capital contributions.
     4) Payment of any surplus to partners in accordance with ratios fixed by agreement or, if none, equally.

   c. Concept of marshalling of assets arises when the partnership and/or an individual partner is insolvent.

1) Partnership is insolvent—Partnership creditors have priority over individual partner's creditors with respect to partnership assets and may then look to partners' assets.
2) If a partner is insolvent, the order of payment is:
   a) His or her individual creditors.
   b) Partnership creditors.
   c) Other partners, who may be entitled to contribution.

FILL-IN QUESTIONS

1. A partnership may be treated by state law as having the capacity to sue and be sued and to transfer property in its firm name, in which case it is considered to be _____. In other instances, such as the federal tax laws, it is treated as _____.

2. A partnership is usually created by an _____ of those participating in it. A partnership may also be formed by the implied assent of its members, who agree to be co-owners of a business for profit and _____ _____.

3. In a partnership, each partner has the right to _____, to have an interest in the partnership and to participate in management.

4. Partners' ownership rights with regard to specific partnership property are those of _____.

5. A partnership is dissolved by _____ if the partners mutually agree to its dissolution or the partnership agreement provides that the partnership will exist for a limited period and the period has expired.

6. A partnership is dissolved by operation of law upon the _____ _____.

7. A partnership will be terminated following dissolution and the completion of _____ _____.

MULTIPLE CHOICE QUESTIONS

1. A and B, doing business as Able Co., a partnership, hold out to the public that C is also a partner and C, in his relations with third parties, acts as though he is a partner. Z enters into a contract with Able Co. through C. Able Co. now denies that C is, in fact, a partner.
   a. C is personally liable on the contract with Z.
   b. The partnership is not liable on the contract with Z.
   c. C is, in fact, a partner of A and B.
   d. C is a member of the partnership by operation of law.

2.   Murray and Norton conduct a business in the name of Norton and Murray Associates. Their relationship was informal and neither one considered himself to be a partner of the other; stationery was printed with the name of Norton and Murray Associates. Loon loaned Murray $400 for and on behalf of the business. Murray informed Norton of this but Norton stated to Murray, "That's your responsibility. I've had nothing to do with it." Murray failed to pay the loan back and Loon seeks to hold both Murray and Norton liable on the debt. Under these circumstances:
   a.   Loon cannot recover from Norton because Norton's statement to Murray was effective against Loon.
   b.   Norton and Murray are partners by estoppel.
   c.   since there was no signed, written partnership agreement, Loon cannot recover from Norton.
   d.   the fact that neither Murray nor Norton considered their relationship to be a partnership precludes recovery against Norton.

3.   A partnership is dissolved by operation of law when:
   a.   one of the partners is bankrupt.
   b.   one of the partners is imprisoned for a year.
   c.   the purpose for which it was formed has been accomplished.
   d.   a court enters a decree of dissolution.

Questions 4, 5 and 6 are based on the following fact situation: The partnership of Parnell and Quincy is being dissolved. The firm has assets of $100,000 and liabilities of $145,000, all owed to outside creditors. Parnell's total capital contribution was $10,000 and Quincy's was $5,000. The partnership agreement did not provide for sharing of profits or losses. The partnership and the two partners have all filed for voluntary liquidation. Parnell has personal assets of $200,000 and personal liabilities of $150,000. Quincy has personal assets of $85,000 and personal liabilities of $80,000. Neither is entitled to any exemptions.

4.   The total amount due to be distributed from the partnership is:
   a. $100,000.
   b. $145,000.
   c. $160,000.
   d.   none of the above.

5.   The outside creditors of the firm will receive:
   a. $145,000.
   b. $135,000.
   c. $130,000.
   d. $100,000.

6.   Parnell's share of the total firm deficiency is:
   a. $30,000, but the actual amount to be paid to firm creditors from his personal assets is $40,000.
   b. $30,000, but the actual amount to be paid to firm creditors from his personal assets is $20,000.
   c. $30,000, but the actual amount to be paid to firm creditors from his personal assets is $10,000.

d. $40,000, but the partnership creditors cannot obtain anything from his personal assets.

7. R, S and T were equal partners in a partnership that engaged in the business of buying and selling real property for profit. Title to all property, purchased with partnership funds, was taken in the name of R. R died with partnership real estate and personal property standing in his name, valued at $100,000 and $10,000 respectively. The partnership had no debts. R's wife claims a dower right in the real property. R's children, to whom he had bequeathed all his personal property, claim a statutory right to one-third of the personal property. Under the circumstances:
   a. R's wife has a valid dower right to all the real property held in her deceased husband's name.
   b. R's children are entitled to one-third of the personal property standing in their deceased father's name.
   c. R's wife is entitled to R's share of undistributed partnership profits.
   d. R's estate is entitled to settlement for the value of R's partnership interest, which is considered to be personal property.

8. Y and Z formed a partnership. Y contributed $1,000 and Z contributed $500. The firm has been dissolved and its creditors have been paid. There is $2,100 left.
   a. Y gets $1,300 and Z gets $800.
   b. Y gets $1,050 and Z gets $1,050.
   c. If Y had lent the firm an additional $1,000, he would get $2,000 and Z would get $100.
   d. Unless one of the partners died or became bankrupt, the partnership cannot be dissolved.

9. A, B and C, partners, have decided to call it a day and to dissolve their partnership, which has assets of $50,000 (all cash) and owes outside creditors $75,000. A has made a $5,000 loan to the partnership, which has not been repaid, and owns personal property worth $10,000. B has no assets but is a member of another partnership. The value of his interest in that partnership is $3,000. C has no personal assets. The capital balance of A, B and C in the partnership is $10,000 each.
   a. Creditors can receive no more than $50,000 of the partnership property and $10,000 from A.
   b. Creditors can only receive $50,000 of the partnership property.
   c. Creditors can receive no more than $50,000 of the partnership property, $10,000 from A and $3,000 from B.
   d. Creditors can receive no more than $45,000 of the partnership property and A can receive $5,000 or partnership property.

10. Kincaid, a member of the Joker Co., a partnership, wishes to retire as a partner. He, therefore, assigns his interest in the partnership to Lensing for $50,000 and assigns all his rights, title and interest in the partnership to Lensing, who he names as his successor partner in Joker Co.
   a. Absent any limitation, regarding the assignment of a partner's interest in the partnership agreement, Kincaid is free to assign it at his will.

b. The assignment to Lensing effectively dissolves the partnership.
c. Lensing is entitled to an equal voice in the management of the partnership.
d. Although Lensing does not have the status of a partner, she can, upon proper demand, inspect the partnership books.

Operation and Duties

Partners usually have rights and duties to participate in the management of the affairs and business of the partnership and to share in the profits thereof. As each partner is an agent for his or her co-partners, a partner owes fiduciary duties to his or her partners as well as a duty to account. In addition, each partner may incur liability, as a principal, for contracts entered into and torts committed by co-partners, acting within the scope of their authority, or subsequently ratified.   Knowledge received by one partner will be imputed to the other members of the partnership and representations, made by a partner, will be treated as having been made by all the partners.

THINGS TO KEEP IN MIND

Normally, partners include explicit provisions, relating to their respective rights and duties, in the partnership agreement, which provisions will be enforced as long as they are lawful. If the partners have not done so, the provisions of the Uniform Partnership Act will be controlling in those states which have adopted it.

OUTLINE

I.   Rights and duties of partners.

    A. As indicated in Chapter 37, each partner has rights:

        1. As a tenant in partnership, with regard to partnership property.

        2. To an interest in the partnership to the extent of his or her share in profits and a return of capital upon termination of the partnership.

B. Each partner has a right and a duty to share in the management of the partnership (U.P.A. Sec. 18). Unless otherwise provided in the partnership agreement:

   1. Each partner has one vote, regardless of his interest in the firm.

   2. In connection with ordinary business decisions, majority vote controls.

   3. Unanimous consent is required for changing the partnership agreement, the scope of the business or the capital structure and in matters significantly affecting the nature liability or existence of the partnership (U.P.A. Sec. 9).

   4. Each partner is expected to devote full time and exclusive service to the partnership, absent a contrary agreement.

   5. Unless otherwise agreed, partners are not remunerated for their partnership services, except that surviving partners are entitled to reasonable compensation for services rendered in winding up the affairs of a dissolved partnership.

   6. Each partner has the right to examine the books and records of the partnership, which should be maintained at the place of business of the firm, and has the right to information concerning the partnership's business from his or her co-partners (U.P.A. Secs. 19 and 20).

C. Accounting.

   1. The purpose of accounting is to determine the value of each partner's proportionate share in the partnership.

   2. An accounting may be rendered voluntarily.

   3. A partner may bring an equitable action for an accounting.

      a. Usually accounting occurs in connection with dissolution proceedings.

      b. Accounting is available if the partnership agreement so provides, a partner has been wrongfully excluded from the business, a partner is wrongfully withholding profits in violation of the fiduciary duties or other circumstances "render it just and reasonable" (U.P.A. Sec. 22).

D. Fiduciary duties.

   1. Each partner is an agent for his or her co-partners and is, therefore, accountable as a fiduciary (U.P.A. Sec. 21).

   2. A partner must act in good faith with loyalty and honesty for the benefit of the partnership and make full disclosure to his or her co-partners of matters relating to the partnership.

   3. A partner will be liable for any personal gain or profits, derived from using the partnership property or the exercise of power as a partner.

II.   Relationship between partners and third persons.

A. In dealing with third persons, on behalf of the partnership, each partner acts as an agent for the partnership and its members (U.P.A. Sec. 9).

B. A partner's authority to bind the partnership contractually may be based upon:

1. Express actual authority, provided for in the partnership agreement.

2. Implied actual authority.

a. Necessary for the conduct or the ordinary business of the partnership.

b. Usually partners have broad implied authority, which will vary with the nature of the particular business of each partnership, unless limited by agreement.
1) A partner of a trading partnership has authority to buy and sell commodities of the type in which the firm regularly deals, give warranties, borrow money and issue and indorse a negotiable instrument.
2) A partner has the power to pay and collect debts, hire and discharge employees, give a security interest in personal property and lease or purchase property needed in the usual operation of the firm's business.
3) Restrictions on partners' implied authority—Unanimous consent is required in order to:
a) Convey or mortgage real property, other than in the ordinary course of the partnership's business.
b) Make an assignment of property.
c) Dispose of the firm's goodwill.
d) Confess judgment or submit a controversy to arbitration.
e) Do any act, which would make it impossible to continue the business of the partnership (U.P.A. Sec. 9).

3. Apparent authority.

a. A third person, who deals with a partner, may assume that the partner has authority to bind the firm in a transaction relating to the usual business of the firm.

b. Unless the third person knows that the partner lacks authority, the partnership and co-partners will be liable to him or her for any damage.

4. Partners may ratify unauthorized acts of a partner.

C. Admissions and representations concerning partnership affairs, made by an authorized partner, bind the partnership, if made while conducting the ordinary business of the partnership (U.P.A. Sec. 11).

D. Knowledge of or notice to a partner of facts, concerning matters relevant to the partnership's affairs, will be imputed to the partnership and other partners (U.P.A. Sec. 12).

E. The partnership and the co-partners are liable for breaches of trust and torts committed by a partner or employee, acting within the scope of his or her authority in the ordinary course of the business of the partnership.

F. Liability of partner to third persons.

  1. Partners are jointly liable in contract. Any action based on contract must be brought against all the partners jointly (together).

  2. Partners are jointly and severally liable for torts and breaches of trust. A third person may sue all the partners together or any one or more of them separately.

FILL-IN QUESTIONS

1. Unless the partnership agreement provides otherwise, partners are presumed to have equal rights to possess partnership property for partnership purposes, to share in partnership profits and to _____.

2. Majority vote will be effective in connection with ordinary business decisions of a partnership. Unanimity is necessary, however, in order to _____ _____.

3. If a partner makes a contract on behalf of the partnership, the co-partners will be liable if he or she acted within the scope of his or her _____ _____.

4. In addition to the usual implied actual authority of a partner, one, who is a partner in a trading partnership, has power to _____ _____.

5. Partners are _____ liable for a contract of the partnership, entered by an authorized partner, and must, therefore, all be included in a lawsuit based upon the contract. They are _____ liable for torts and may, therefore, be sued separately or together.

MULTIPLE CHOICE QUESTIONS

1. Able and Baker, doing business as Aber Co., a partnership, hold out to the public that Charlie is also a partner, and Charlie, in his relations with third persons, acts as though he were a partner. Frank enters into a contract with the firm through Charlie. Aber Co. now denies that Charlie is a partner.
   a. Charlie is not personally liable as a partner on the contract with Frank.
   b. The partnership of Aber Co. is liable on the contract with Frank.
   c. Charlie is, in fact, a partner of Aber Co.
   d. Charlie is, in fact, not a partner of Aber Co. but has some of the rights of a partner.

2. Unanimous consent is not required in order to:
   a. enlarge the scope of the business of a partnership.
   b. admit new partners.
   c. sell equipment of the partnership used in the ordinary operation of its business.
   d. purchase personal property needed in the ordinary operation of the business of the partnership.

3. Orange, Plum and Quince were general partners in the marmalade manufacturing business. Orange managed the partnership, Plum contributed her name and Quince contributed his capital. Absent an agreement to the contrary:
   a. Quince has the majority vote in respect to new business.
   b. Quince has assumed the responsibility of paying Plum's debts upon the insolvency of the partnership.
   c. Orange, Plum and Quince share profits and losses equally.
   d. Orange is entitled to a reasonable salary for his services.

Questions 4 and 5 are based on the following fact situation: M, N and O operated a pizza restaurant as a partnership. All three partners worked in the restaurant. The partnership agreement provided that only M had authority to order beverages.

4. O ordered 100 cases of soda from the salesman for a bottling company. The salesman knew that O was a partner but did not know that he was not the soda purchaser for the partnership.
   a. Only O is liable for the 100 cases of soda.
   b. O had apparent authority to make the purchase of soda.
   c. O had actual and apparent authority to make the purchase of soda.
   d. M, N and O are jointly and severally liable for the purchase of soda.

5. One day N was mopping the floor, but he failed to clean up some anchovies that had fallen on the floor. H, a customer, slipped on the anchovies and broke a leg. H's damages total $5,000.
   a. H may sue each of the partners in separate actions for tort.
   b. H will have to sue the partnership in order to recover for his injury.
   c. H may sue and recover only from N.
   d. H may sue M, N and O in separate actions and recover $5,000 from each of them.

6. D, a partner of the D E F partnership, engaged in the retail grocery business, gave X, a personal creditor (of D) a security interest in the inventory owned by the partnership. E also gave Y, a wholesaler, who supplied the firm with canned goods, a similar security interest in the inventory to secure the payment of the purchase price of canned goods delivered to the store.
   a. Y has no rights with respect to his security interest in the inventory.
   b. X has no rights with respect to his security interest in the inventory.
   c. E, and neither D nor F, will be personally liable for the purchase price of the canned goods purchased from Y.
   d. D, E and F are jointly and severally liable for the purchase price of the canned goods.

Limited Partnerships

A limited partnership is formed by complying with state statutory requirements, and consists of at least one general partner, who potentially has personal liability for all debts of the partnership, and one or more limited partners. A limited partner contributes capital, in the form of money or other property, owns an interest in the firm and shares in the profits of the partnership, but does not participate in management and is not personally liable for partnership obligations beyond the amount of his or her investment. This form of organization enables an investor to limit his or her liability and, in some instances, take advantage of certain tax benefits available to high risk enterprises.

THINGS TO KEEP IN MIND

If a limited partnership fails to comply with the statutory requirements or if a limited partner participates in management, the partnership will be treated as a general partnership and the limited partner will be liable as a general partner.

OUTLINE

I.   Formation.

A. Certificate, setting forth the firm name, nature and duration of business, location of principal place of business, names and addresses of members, capital contributions of limited partners, share of profits or other compensation that limited partners are entitled to receive, methods for changes in membership and subsequent continuation of the business, is signed by the partners.

B. Certificate is filed with a designated state or county official.

II.   Liability of limited partner to creditors.

   A. A limited partner is liable to creditors only to the extent of his or her contributed or promised capital.

   B. A limited partner will be liable as a general partner if:

       1. The surname of the limited partner is included in the partnership name.

       2. The limited partner participates in management.

       3. The limited partner learns that the firm is defectively formed and fails to withdraw from the partnership.

III. Rights of limited partner.

   A. A limited partner (member) has no authority to bind the partnership.

   B. A limited partner has the same rights as do partners in a general partnership with respect to suing, examining books, accounting, the return of his or her capital contribution, the assignments of rights to his or her interest, etc.

IV.   Dissolution.

   A. By acts of parties.

       1. Expiration of term for which the partnership was formed.

       2. If the partnership is not formed for a specified term, the will of a general partner.

       3. Withdrawal or expulsion of a general partner, unless otherwise provided in the certificate or unless members consent to continuation.

   B. By operation of law.

       1. Death or insanity of a general partner, if the business cannot be continued in accordance with certificate or consent of other members.

       2. Illegality.

       3. Bankruptcy of firm or a general partner.

   C. Limited partner's withdrawal, death, assignment of his or her interest or bankruptcy (unless it causes the bankruptcy of the firm) does not result in the dissolution of the firm.

   D. Winding up and liquidation procedure, following dissolution, is the same as that for a general partnership, except for the priorities in distribution.

1. The Uniform Limited Partnership Act specifies the following order:

    a. Outside creditors.

    b. Limited partners' shares of profit and any other compensation.

    c. Limited partners' return of capital contributions.

    d. Advances, loans, etc., made by general partners.

    e. General partners' share of profits.

    f. General partners' return of capital contributions.

2. The Revised Uniform Limited Partnership Act changes the order by including claims of partners, who are creditors, with outside creditors and combining limited and general partners together.

FILL-IN QUESTIONS

1. In order to form a limited partnership, compliance with certain statutory requirements is necessary, including the filing of a certificate, stating _____ _____ _____ _____ _____.
The certificate must also be _____
and _____ with the appropriate governmental official.

2. If the state limited partnership act is complied with in all respects, a limited partner is not liable to firm creditors except to the extent of _____.

3. A limited partner will be liable to a creditor if the firm was defectively organized and he or she failed to withdraw after receiving knowledge of the defect or if _____.

4. Assume that a limited partnership was formed for a term of ten years. Prior to the expiration of the ten-year period, the partnership may be dissolved if a general partner _____ _____
or if the continuation of the firm will be illegal or if the firm is bankrupt. _____
of a limited partner does not result in the dissolution of the firm.

MULTIPLE CHOICE QUESTIONS

1. Angus is a limited partner in the Digby, Ernst and Friendly Ltd. partnership. Angus' existence and name is not disclosed to the public. Angus' liability will not be

limited to the amount of his capital contribution because:
a. his surname is not included in the name of the firm.
b. his capital contribution is less than that of the general partners.
c. he participates in decisions concerning the operation of the business.
d. the government official with whom the partnership certificate was filed is not notified of Angus' change of address.

2. P, Q and R are active members of P Q R Plumbing Co., a partnership. O is a limited partner thereof. P installed the plumbing system in G's new $150,000 home. G moved in and turned on the water, only to learn that the water lines had been negligently installed. The pipes burst and the entire house was flooded. Damage has been extensive.
a. If G bases an action on tort, he must sue all the partners jointly.
b. If G bases an action on contract, he may sue all the partners separately.
c. G will not be able to recover from O if his action is based on contract.
d. G will not be able to recover from P, Q or R if he sues them jointly but does not include O as a party.

3. The G H Limited Partnership, the partnership agreement of which provides for sharing of profits equally, is insolvent. F was a limited partner and is now solvent. G and H were general partners. G is now insolvent. He has no non-exempt property but owes $2,000 to personal creditors. H has a truck worth $1,000 and an interest in the H and R Co., another partnership, valued at $2,000. He has no individual debts. F's net worth is $500,000. The liabilities of the G H Limited Partnership amount to $3,000 all owed to V. No financial adjustments among the partners are necessary.
a. Assume that F participated in management. V may collect only from F.
b. Assume that F did not participate in management. V may collect only from H by attaching H's car and H's interest in the H and R partnership.
c. Assume that F did not participate in management. V may collect only from F.
d. Assume that F did not participate in management. V may collect $1,500 from F and $1,500 from H.

Questions 4 and 5 are based on the following fact situation: A certificate of limited partnership has been properly filed by a partnership, the books of which indicate the following:

The partnership consists of three partners, Manfred, Norstad and Oops, who share profits equally. The partnership agreement is silent as to the manner of sharing losses.

Manfred loaned the partnership $10,000, without interest, and made a capital contribution of $20,000; Norstad made a capital contribution of $10,000; Oops made no capital contribution but has devoted all his time to the partnership. Manfred, a general partner, and Norstad, a limited partner, have devoted no time to the management of the partnership.

4. Which of the following statements is false?
a. Norstad will be liable as a general partner, if the name of the partnership is Manfred, Norstad and Oops, Ltd.

b. Norstad will be liable as a general partner for willful, intentional torts, committed by Oops, while acting within the scope of his authority.

c. The partnership will not be dissolved upon Norstad's death.

d. The partnership will be dissolved upon the bankruptcy of Oops.

5. The partners have agreed to dissolve the partnership. Outside creditors are owed $50,000. The firm and each of the partners are solvent. Under the Uniform Limited Partnership Act, the order of distribution is:

a. outside creditors ($50,000); Norstad for his share of the profits and capital contribution of $10,000; Manfred $10,000 for his loan; Manfred and Oops for their shares of the profits; Manfred $20,000 for his capital contribution.

b. outside creditors ($50,000); Manfred $10,000 for his loan; Norstad $10,000 for his capital contribution; Manfred $20,000 for his capital contribution; Manfred, Norstad and Oops then share profits.

c. the same as that of a general partnership.

d. the same as that under the Revised Uniform Limited Partnership Act.

Nature and Formation

A corporation is a legal entity, created by the state, under the terms of a general corporation statute. Important characteristics of a corporation include perpetual existence, centralized management, ease of transferability of ownership interests and limited liability for owners.

THINGS TO KEEP IN MIND

The formation, operation and rights and duties of corporations and those associated with them are regulated by state statutes which, with varying degrees, closely resemble the Model Business Corporation Act, which is referred to herein as MBCA. (See Appendix F in the text.)

Note: The document prepared for purposes of incorporation may be referred to as a charter or articles of incorporation or certificate of incorporation or another similar word or phrase. The terms are used interchangeably in this book. For reasons of brevity only, the term, charter, is used more frequently.

OUTLINE

I.   Nature of corporations.

    A. Business corporations are artificial, legal entities whose creation and operations are controlled by state statutes.

    B. Corporations are regarded as "persons," separate from the shareholders, the owners of interests in corporations, for most purposes under federal and state constitutions and statutes, when application thereof is not restricted to natural persons.

1. U.S. Constitution.

   a. A corporation is treated as a person under the due process clause of the Fifth Amendment and the equal protection clause of the Fourteenth.
      1) Corporation may sue and be sued; corporation is protected against unreasonable searches and seizures and double jeopardy.
      2) Corporation is not protected against self incrimination.

   b. A corporation is regarded as a citizen of the state in which it was incorporated for purposes of jurisdiction, but not necessarily entitled to all the privileges and immunities of citizens. (The states may impose burdens on corporations, incorporated in sister states, wishing to do intrastate business.)

2. Criminal liability—A corporation may be prosecuted for a crime for which the penalty includes a fine.

3. Licensing statutes—Corporations are excluded from some professions, which require personal qualifications.

C. Shareholders—As a general rule:

   1. Holders of ownership interests in corporation, which are freely transferable.

   2. Death of a shareholder does not dissolve or otherwise affect the corporation.

   3. Shareholders are not personally liable for the debts of the corporation. Their liability is limited to their investments.

   4. Shareholders have equitable interests in but not legal title to corporate property.

   5. Shareholders do not represent the corporation, but vote for the board of directors, which determines corporate policy and appoints officers, who represent the corporation.

   6. Shareholders may sue and be sued by the corporation, and may deal with the corporation, in an arm's length transaction.

D. Tax considerations ("double taxation of profits").

   1. The profits of a corporation are taxed by the United States and the several states at special corporate rates.

   2. Distributions of profits, in the form of dividends, are treated and taxed as income to the recipient, the shareholder.

   3. Profits that are retained and invested by the corporation may result in capital gains. If a shareholder sells his or her shares, he or she is taxed but at a rate lower than the rate imposed on income.

II. Classifications of corporations.

   A. Based on location.

      1. Domestic corporation—In state in which the corporation is incorporated.

      2. Foreign corporation—In other states.

   B. Based on sources of funds (or revenue), function and ownership arrangements.

      1. Public corporation—Formed by legislature for governmental purposes.

      2. Private corporation—Created for private benefit.

         a. Issues shares of stock.

         b. May be close corporation—Shares of stock are held by one individual or by a small group.

      3. Nonprofit corporation—Organized for charitable, religious, educational, social, etc., purpose, under special state statute.

      4. Professional corporation—Private corporation, the members of which engage in a profession, organized to gain advantages relating to taxes, pension and insurance plans, etc.

III. Formation of a corporation.

   A. Promoters' activities before corporation comes into existence.

      1. Analyze economic feasibility, find investors, assemble necessary personnel, property and capital, take preliminary steps for organization and incorporation.

      2. Promoters are generally personally liable on pre-incorporation agreements.

         a. Liability during the promotion period.
           1) A promoter is a party to a contract and, therefore, bound as a party.
           2) The corporation is not in existence and, therefore, not liable as a party to a contract.

         b. Liability after incorporation.
           1) Promoter remains liable to other contracting party, unless:
              a) Released by the contracting party.
              b) Contracting parties clearly indicated that the promoter would not be personally liable.
              c) Corporation is substituted as a party to the contract in a novation.
           2) Corporation becomes liable after incorporation if:
              a) It enters a novation.
              b) It adopts or becomes an assignee of the rights of the promoter, who remains secondarily liable.

3. Subscribers and subscriptions.

    a. A subscription is an agreement to purchase unissued shares of stock in a corporation that has not yet been formed.

    b. Subscription may be treated as:
       1) A continuing offer by the subscriber, which may be accepted by the corporation following incorporation.
       2) A contract among subscribers and, therefore, irrevocable.
       3) An irrevocable offer for the period specified in the statute, unless all subscribers consent to revocation (MBCA Sec. 17).

B. Incorporation procedure.

    1. Charter, articles of incorporation or certificate of incorporation—Contents (MBCA Sec. 54).

       a. Corporate name.
         1) Must use word "corporation" or "incorporated" or abbreviation, such as "co.," "corp." or "inc."
         2) Name cannot be misleading or subject to confusion with the name of another organization.

       b. General nature and purpose.

       c. Duration—Usually perpetual.

       d. Capital structure.

       e. Internal organization—May be described in articles or in by-laws.

       f. Location of principal office and agent to receive services of process within the state.

       g. Names, addresses and signatures of incorporators.
         1) Usually incorporators need not have any interest in the corporation, nor be subscribers.
         2) Number varies from one to three; statute may provide that incorporations need not be natural persons (MBCA Sec. 53).

    2. Articles of incorporation are filed with the appropriate state official (typically the secretary of state), necessary fees are paid and notice of the filing given (MBCA Sec. 55).

    3. Organizational meeting.

       a. Incorporators elect the board of directors, adopt by-laws, authorize the board to issue stock, etc.

       b. Board of directors adopts minutes of meeting of incorporators (if one was required), adopts pre-incorporation contracts, seal, form for stock certificate, accepts subscriptions, etc. (MBCA Sec. 57).

    c. By-laws—Internal rules for governing and regulating the conduct of corporate affairs. By-laws cannot conflict with articles of incorporation or statutes (MBCA Sec. 27).

C. Improper incorporation.

  1. *De jure* corporation—Corporation organized in accordance with required mandatory conditions precedent to incorporation. Its existence cannot be attacked.

  2. *De facto* corporation—Operates as a corporation but failed to comply with some statutory mandate so that the state may challenge its existence. Element:

    a. Statute exists, under which it could be validly incorporated.

    b. Good faith attempt to comply with the statute.

    c. Some exercise of the functions of a corporation.

  3. Corporation by estoppel.

    a. Corporation has neither *de jure* nor *de facto* status.

    b. Associates (alleged shareholders, directors), who participated in holding the association out as a corporation, are precluded from denying that it was a corporation against third parties, who, in reliance upon the holding out, changed their positions and were injured.

    c. Parties, who dealt with the association and contracted believing only the corporation would be liable, may be estopped from denying that it was a corporation.

    d. If a corporation by estoppel cannot be established, in general, associates, who took an active part in management, will be liable as partners.

IV. Disregarding the corporate entity.

A. In unusual situations, a court may ignore the legal fiction of the corporation as an entity (pierce the corporate veil) when it is used to perpetuate fraud, circumvent law, accomplish an illegal purpose or otherwise evade law.

B. Courts will disregard the corporate entity, even though technically a corporation exists, and hold directors, officers or shareholders personally liable for the transactions conducted in the corporate name.

C. Courts will disregard corporate entity if a corporation is not maintained as an entity, separate from its shareholders, in order to prevent abuse of corporate privilege for personal benefit.

1. Records and funds have been commingled and enterprise has not been established on an adequate financial basis.

2. This arises occasionally in the case of a close corporation with only one or a few shareholders or in the case of parent-subsidiary corporations.

FILL-IN QUESTIONS

1. A corporation is considered to be a "person" when the use of the word "person" in a statute _____.

2. A shareholder of a corporation may be distinguished from a partner in a general partnership because, unlike a partner, he or she _____
_____.

3. A municipality (city) may have a charter and be created by statute for governmental purposes. It is a _____ rather than a _____ corporation.

4. A corporation, which has complied with all statutory requirements relating to incorporation, is considered to be a _____. A _____ corporation is one, which believed that it was properly organized, but whose organization was defective. The existence of such a corporation may normally only be challenged by _____.

MULTIPLE CHOICE QUESTIONS

1. Piper, the promoter of the Atlas Corporation, made a contract for and on behalf of the Atlas Corporation with World Copy Inc. for the purchase of a copying machine. Piper failed to disclose that the corporation had not been created. Thereafter, the corporation was duly organized.
   a. Piper will not be liable on the contract if the corporation, after coming into existence, rejects the contract.
   b. Piper will not be liable on the contract if the corporation, after coming into existence, adopts the contract.
   c. Piper will not be liable on the contract, if the corporation, World Copy Inc. and Piper enter into a novation regarding the contract.
   d. Piper will not be liable on the contract if the corporation does not come into existence.

2. A written subscription, signed by a subscriber, to purchase shares of stock in a corporation to be formed in a state which has adopted the Model Business Corporation Act, is:
   a. unenforceable by the corporation when it comes into existence.
   b. revocable until the corporation comes into existence.
   c. irrevocable for six months after the corporation comes into existence.
   d. irrevocable for six months after it is signed by the subscriber.

3. Martin has determined that there is a large market for copper widgets. She, there-fore, engaged in promotion activities for the purpose of organizing the Winking Widget Co. Before filing articles of incorporation, she ordered a large quantity of copper from KK Koper Co. and leased office space in the name of the corporation. The copper was shipped to and used by Winking Widget Co. after its organization, but payment therefor has not been made. At the first meeting of the board of directors, the following action was taken:
   a. refused to accept the contract with KK Koper Co. It will be required to pay for the copper.
   b. declined to accept the lease of office space. It will be liable for breach of contract.
   c. accepted all the subscriptions for stock that Martin had obtained. It may later revoke some of its acceptances.
   d. refused to accept some of the subscriptions that Martin had obtained. It will be obligated to all the subscribers.

4. Under the Model Business Corporation Act, incorporators must:
   a. be natural persons.
   b. be residents of the state of incorporation.
   c. subscribe to at least one share of stock.
   d. none of the above.

5. U, V and W did business as Z Corporation but made no effort to incorporate. They never filed any documents with any state official. Arcus entered into a contract with Z Corporation to supply stationery to the corporation but did not know it had not been formally incorporated. U, V and W breached the contract with Arcus by failing to pay for the stationery. Arcus is now suing Z Corporation and U, V and W jointly.
   a. U, V and W are liable to Arcus as general partners, unless they are estopped from denying the existence of Z Corporation.
   b. Z Corporation is a *de facto* corporation and, therefore, Arcus cannot dispute its existence.
   c. U, V and W are liable to Arcus because the Z Corporation is a *de jure* corpora-tion.
   d. U, V and W are liable to Arcus because they are principals with relation to each other.

6. A, B and C represented to F that they are shareholders and directors of a corpora-tion and persuade F to purchase stock in the corporation. There is, in fact, no corporation but A, B and C have been engaging in a business together. A, B and C manage the business and F participates in no way.
   a. F will not be liable to a third party on a contract entered by B in the name of the corporation.
   b. A, B and C will be estopped to deny the existence of the corporation.
   c. A third party, with whom the purported corporation contracted, will be estopped to deny the corporate existence because, when he or she contracted with the "association," his or her expectation was that only the corporation would have liability.
   d. All of the above.

Corporate Powers and Management

Corporations have only those powers which are granted them by the state of incorporation. Corporate powers are expressly provided in statutes and corporate charters (articles or certificates of incorporation) and, generally, are quite broad. In addition, corporations have implied power to do those things that are necessary to execute their purposes and express powers.

A corporation is, in theory, owned by and for the benefit of its shareholders. Managerial policies are determined, however, by the board of directors, elected by the shareholders. Actual operation of a corporation is normally performed by officers, appointed and supervised by the directors.

THINGS TO KEEP IN MIND

Corporations usually are empowered to do almost anything, unless it is criminal or tortious, so that today it is rare that a corporation is found to exceed its powers.

OUTLINE

I.   Corporate purpose—Defines the nature of the business in which the corporation engages. The purpose must be legal and may be broadly stated in the charter (MBCA Sec. 3).

II. Corporate powers—Necessary to accomplish purpose.

   A. Statutory, general powers apply to all corporations, organized under the state business corporation law, and usually include the power to have perpetual existence; to enter into contract; to sue and be sued; to lend and borrow money;

to buy, hold, lease, receive, dispose of and sell real and personal property; etc. (MBCA Sec. 4).

B. Express powers are those specifically enumerated in the corporate charter.

C. Implied powers are those which are incidental or necessary in order to carry out the corporation's purpose and express powers.

D. *Ultra vires* acts—Corporate exercise of power which it does not possess.

   1. Corporate director(s) or officer(s) does something that corporation is not authorized to do, because it is not in furtherance of the corporation's purpose.

   2. Illegal acts are *ultra vires.*

   3. An *ultra vires* act may be ratified by the shareholders.

      a. Act was one that could have been authorized by the shareholders when it was originally done.

      b. Unanimous ratification is necessary if there has been a gift or wasting of corporate assets.

   4. Judicial treatment of *ultra vires*—Approaches taken.

      a. Corporation has no capacity to perform the *ultra vires* act. An *ultra vires* contract that is executory or partially or completely executed is therefore void.

      b. An agent (corporate officer), acting without authority, does not bind his or her principal (the corporation).

      c. The defense of *ultra vires* can be raised in order to prevent enforcement of an executory contract, but not all courts allow the defense if the contract has been executed.

   5. Modern judicial and statutory approach (MBCA Sec. 7).

      a. The defense of *ultra vires* may not be raised in an action to enforce a contract (even if the contract is executory) by the corporation or the party with whom it contracted.

      b. The issue of *ultra vires* may only be asserted in an action brought by:
         1) Shareholders, to enjoin the carrying out of the act.
         2) The corporation (or shareholders in a derivative action), to recover from officers or directors, who made an *ultra vires* contract or carried out the unauthorized act.
         3) The state attorney general, to enjoin the *ultra vires* act or to dissolve the corporation.

E. Corporate liability for wrongful acts.

   1. Torts—A corporation is liable for torts committed by its officers, directors, other agents and employees, acting within the scope of their authority in furtherance of the corporation's business.

   2. Crimes—A corporation is liable for the commission of a nonviolent crime. An element of a crime may be intent. A corporation cannot have intent, but intent may be imputed to a corporation, and a fine imposed as punishment.

III. Relationship of shareholders to corporation.

   A. Shareholders' position in the corporation—Shareholders have limited powers.

      1. The shareholders' approval is necessary to make fundamental changes affecting the corporation, such as amending the charter, merging with another corporation or dissolving.

      2. The shareholders have power to elect and remove members of the board of directors for cause.

      3. With some limitations, the shareholders have the right to inspect books, records and shareholders' lists.

      4. The shareholders do not participate in the management of the corporation.

   B. Meetings of the shareholders.

      1. Annual meeting (MBCA Sec. 28).

         a. Usually the date and place is fixed in the by-laws.

         b. Written notice must be given within the specified statutory period of time, but may be waived (MBCA Sec. 29).

      2. Special meetings may be called (MBCA Sec. 28).

      3. Quorum (minimum number of shares that must be represented at a meeting) —Fixed in charter within specified statutory range.

      4. Voting.

         a. List of record owners of shares as of a cutoff date is prepared by corporation (MBCA Secs. 30 and 31).

         b. Unless otherwise specified by statute or charter (MBCA Sec. 32), usual vote required for shareholder action:
            1) Election of members of board of directors—Plurality of those shares represented at meeting.
            2) Other non-extraordinary matters—Majority of those shares represented at meeting.

   3) Extraordinary matters.
      a) Statute or charter may require a specified proportion of all shares.
      b) Usually a greater than majority vote is required.

   c. Methods of voting (MBCA Sec. 33).
      1) Straight voting—One vote per share standing in the name of a record holder.
      2) Cumulative voting for election of directors.
         a) May be provided for in charter.
         b) In some states, cumulative voting is mandatory.
         c) Shareholder's vote = number of shares owned multiplied by number of directors to be elected.
      3) Proxy voting.
         a) Shareholder may vote in person or by proxy.
         b) Written, revocable authorization to an agent to cast the vote of the shareholder.
      4) Voting agreements—Shareholders may agree to pool votes by casting them in a prescribed manner (MBCA Sec. 34).
      5) Voting trusts—Legal title to shares is transferred to a trustee, who then votes the shares, for the benefit of shareholders, who retain the right to receive dividends and receive a voting trust certificate.

IV. Board of directors.

   A. Qualifications, election and tenure.

      1. There are few statutory requirements for qualification as a director (MBCA Sec. 35).

      2. The number of directors is specified in the charter or by-laws (MBCA Sec. 36).

      3. The initial board of directors is named in the charter or elected by the incorporators, and subsequent directors are elected by the shareholders (MBCA Sec. 36).

      4. Term of a director is usually one year but may be longer; directors may be divided into classes with staggered terms (MBCA Sec. 37).

      5. Provisions in the charter and/or statute determine method of filling vacancies (MBCA Sec. 38).

      6. Shareholders have power to remove directors, with or without cause, in accordance with the charter or by-laws. Directors may have power to remove a director for cause (MBCA Sec. 39).

   B. Functions of board of directors—Responsible for the management of the corporation.

      1. The board must act as a body at a meeting (MBCA Sec. 43). The MBCA

(Sec. 44) does, however, provide for signed, written unanimous consent in lieu of a meeting.

    a. Regular meetings are provided for in the by-laws. Notice is not necessary.

    b. Special meetings may be called, but notice is required.

    c. Quorum requirements vary from state to state (usually a majority) and are established by the by-laws (MBCA Sec. 40).

    d. Directors may not vote by proxy.

    e. Ordinarily a majority vote is necessary for board action.

2. Management responsibilities—Corporate powers are exercised by the board of directors (MBCA Sec. 35).

    a. Declares dividends.

    b. Makes policy decisions concerning the scope of business, initiates major changes in corporate financing, structure, etc.

    c. Appoints, supervises and removes officers.

    d. Fixes compensation of officers and directors.

3. Delegation of powers of board of directors.

    a. Functions, relating to ordinary, interim managerial decisions, may be delegated to an executive committee (MBCA Sec. 42).

    b. Functions relating to daily operations are normally delegated to officers, who as agents carry out the transactions on behalf of the corporation.

C. Liability of directors (MBCA Secs. 35 and 41).

1. The fiduciary duty of directors runs to the corporation. Directors must act in good faith, honestly and with loyalty and are to exercise reasonable care, judgment, skill and diligence.

2. Directors do not insure the business success of the corporation.

3. Directors are liable to the corporation (or the shareholders in a derivative suit only or a representative of the corporation, such as a trustee) for *ultra vires* acts, improper stock issues or dividends, breaches of fiduciary and supervisory duties, fraud and misrepresentation and for violations of statutes.

See also Chapter 44 herein.

FILL-IN QUESTIONS

1. _____ powers are those possessed by all corporations formed within a particular state. An example of such a power would be _____

   _____.

2. Corporations are empowered by corporation statutes to purchase real property but, if a corporation is not organized for the purpose of purchasing and selling real estate, it commits an _____ act if it buys land purely for speculative purposes. In most states today, however, the corporation _____ the defense that it lacked the power or capacity to make such a purchase in a lawsuit brought by the seller of the land for the unpaid purchase price.

3. A voting trustee is given _____ title to the shares of shareholders participating in a voting trust. The shareholders are considered to be the _____ owners of the shares.

4. _____ but not _____ may vote by proxy at their respective meetings.

5. Directors of a corporation are agents of and, therefore, owe a fiduciary duty to the _____.

MULTIPLE CHOICE QUESTIONS

1. The articles of incorporation of the Careful Chew Corporation state that it is formed for the purpose of manufacturing chewing gum. Even if there is no express authorization in the articles of incorporation to do so, the corporation has the implied power to:
   a. purchase gum base, sugar and artificial flavoring.
   b. purchase 50 acres of land which the board of directors, in good faith, believe will triple in value in one year.
   c. manufacture razor blades.
   d. purchase and use a factory in a state in which it is not incorporated without qualifying to do business in that state.

2. On March 2 an explosion and fire destroyed the Rubber Products Co. plant. The corporation filed an insurance claim with its insurer promptly. On April 15, the corporation, the president and two others were charged with arson (the intentional burning of any structure, punishable by imprisonment for up to 50 years) in connection with the March 2 fire. It was alleged that the president of the corporation paid $50,000 out of corporate funds to an "arson squad" which started the fire. Which of the following statements is false?
   a. The corporation can escape criminal liability for the fire.
   b. The president is liable for breach of duties owed to the shareholders.
   c. The shareholders may bring a derivative action against the president for the *ultra vires* act.
   d. The defense of *ultra vires* cannot be raised in a lawsuit instituted by the corporation against the insurer which refused to pay the claim.

3. The shareholders of the Unispol Corp. are to elect five directors. If there is cumulative voting, a shareholder with 100 shares may cast a maximum of:
    a. five votes for one person.
    b. 100 votes for one nominee.
    c. 500 votes for one person.
    d. 500 votes for one person and 500 in connection with other matters that are voted on at the meeting.

4. At a meeting of shareholders:
    a. in order to amend the Certificate of Incorporation, notice thereof must be given and a majority of the shareholders present must approve the amendment.
    b. shares of a deceased shareholder may be voted only if the shares are transferred to and registered in the name of the representative of the decedent.
    c. shareholders have the right to elect directors and to vote on any other business that may properly come before the meeting by cumulative voting.
    d. a shareholder may vote by proxy only if he gives an irrevocable proxy.

5. The following is prohibited by statute:
    a. A voting pool.
    b. A voting trust.
    c. The sale of a proxy.
    d. The sale of property by a shareholder to the corporation in which he owns stock.

6. M and O Co. is incorporated in a state that has adopted the Model Business Corporation Act. It has a board of directors composed of nine people. Its charter and by-laws contain no provisions relative to quorum requirements for meetings of the board or the conduct of such meetings. The charter provides for cumulative voting by shareholders. Six members of the board of directors attended a meeting that had been called after due notice to ratify an important contract. Prior to the annual shareholders' meeting, P, a holder of 200 shares, gave A a proxy to vote her shares.
    a. The board can ratify the contract by a vote of four to two.
    b. The board can unanimously ratify the contract if two directors leave the meeting before the board acts on the contract.
    c. A may not cast 1,800 votes for a single director.
    d. A may vote P's shares if, on the day before the meeting, P gives her proxy to Z.

Special Corporate Forms
and Benefits of
Incorporating

The authors discuss Subchapter S, closely held, nonprofit and professional corporations and some tax benefits that can be received by incorporating in this chapter. Those students to whom these topics are of particular importance will, no doubt, read the text with care. No materials, dealing with these topics is, therefore, included herein.

OUTLINE

I. Domestic corporation—One doing business in the state of its incorporation. See other chapters in this part of Unit VII.

II. Foreign corporation—One conducting business outside of the state of its incorporation.

    A. If a foreign corporation does intrastate (as contrasted with interstate) business in a state, it must comply with the laws of that state.

        1. Normally it must apply for and obtain a certificate to do business from a state official, such as the secretary of state (MBCA Secs. 106, 110 and 111) and will thereafter enjoy the same rights as domestic corporations (MBCA Secs. 107 and 112).

        2. It must maintain a local registered office and agent (MBCA Sec. 113), upon whom service of process may be made. If such service cannot be effected, the secretary of state will be an agent for this purpose (MBCA Sec. 115).

    B. Doing business within a state—Interpreted to mean some minimum contact, such as maintaining an office or factory, or conducting systematic commerce. It does not include holding meetings, maintaining or defending legal action, maintaining bank accounts, transfer agents, soliciting orders which are accepted outside the state, etc. (MBCA Sec. 106).

FILL-IN QUESTIONS

1. A corporation, incorporated in one state but desiring to engage in business in another state, is required to obtain _____ in the other state and will have to maintain a _____ in that state. The purpose of this requirement is to protect residents of the state so that a state court can obtain jurisdiction over the corporation.

2. If a foreign corporation has complied with statutes relating to qualifying to do business and has received a _____ from the appropriate state official, it is empowered to do anything that a domestic corporation may do and those things which it is authorized to do in the state of its incorporation.

MULTIPLE CHOICE QUESTIONS

1. A California corporation sells goods to residents of Illinois by mail, but has no employees or offices in Illinois.
   a. The California corporation is required to register or qualify as a foreign corporation in Illinois.
   b. The California corporation will not be able to sue an Illinois resident in Illinois, if the resident fails to pay for merchandise purchased from the California corporation.
   c. The California corporation will be required to qualify to do business in Illinois if it establishes a shipping office in Chicago, employing 40 people, and solicits and enters contracts from that office.
   d. An Illinois resident who has been injured by merchandise, purchased from the California corporation, can sue the corporation in Illinois by serving it with a complaint in California.

2. The certificate of incorporation of the Green and Red Corp., a New York corporation, states that it is formed for the purpose of manufacturing Christmas decorations in Rhode Island, where it maintains a plant and office.
   a. The corporation must qualify to do business in New York.
   b. The corporation must qualify to do business in Rhode Island.
   c. The corporation must qualify to do business in Utah, if it sends a traveling salesman there to solicit orders.
   d. The corporation must qualify to do business in Delaware, if it maintains a transfer agent there.
   e. All of the above.

Corporate Financing and
Securities Regulation

In order to finance their operations, corporations issue securities, such as debt securities, as evidences of obligations to pay money (bonds and debentures) and equity securities, representing ownership interests (shares of stock). The issuance and sale of such corporate securities are extensively regulated by the Securities Act of 1933 and the Securities Exchange Act of 1934, relevant provisions of which are explained in this chapter.

THINGS TO KEEP IN MIND

As indicated in the text, the area of law relating to the issuance and regulation of securities is most complex. Should the occasion arise, consult an expert.

OUTLINE

I.   Debt securities.

   A. In general, bonds are evidences of obligations to pay money. The term, "bond," is often used, although technically a particular obligation may be a debenture.

      1. Bonds—Secured by a lien or other security interest in assets.

      2. Debentures—Secured by the general credit of the borrower, rather than specific property.

      3. Issued by business firms, governments and others to investors, from whom they are borrowing funds, with a designated maturity date when the principal or face amount is to be paid.

4. Bonds provide fixed income because interest is paid at specified times and at specified rates.

5. Discount—Bonds may be sold for less than their face value.

6. Premium—Bonds may be sold for more than their face value.

B. Corporate bonds—Agreement is termed the bond indenture. Bondholders do not participate in corporate affairs.

   1. Debentures are unsecured obligations. If the issuing corporation defaults, holders can look only to assets in which other creditors or bondholders have no security interests.

   2. Mortgage bonds—Secured by real property.

   3. Equipment trust bonds—Secured by equipment, legal title to which is vested in a trustee.

   4. Collateral trust bonds—Secured by intangible corporate property, such as shares of stock in other corporations or accounts receivable.

   5. Convertible bonds—Bonds that may be exchanged for other bonds or stock at a specified rate.

   6. Callable bonds—The issuing corporation has the right to repay prior to maturity.

II. Equity securities—Every corporation issues common stock and may be authorized to issue preferred stock.

A. Preferred stock—Holders of preferred stock have a preference that usually is in rights to receive dividends or distribution upon liquidation of the corporation. Corporations may issue different classes and/or series of preferred stock.

   1. Cumulative preferred—If the corporation fails to pay a dividend, the dividend is carried over and paid in a subsequent year, before the holders of common stock receive dividends.

   2. Participating preferred—Preferred shareholders share in distribution of additional dividends after payment of dividends to preferred and common if there are additional distributions of corporate profits.

   3. Convertible preferred—Preferred shares may be exchanged for common stock or other preferred stock at a specified rate.

   4. Redeemable (callable) preferred—Corporation has the right to purchase, reacquire and cancel shares at a specified price.

B. Common stock.

1. The owners of common stock are entitled to a pro rata share of properly declared dividends out of corporate profits, without any preferences and after payment of taxes, interest to lenders and bondholders, etc., and any specified dividends required to be paid to preferred shareholders, if any preferred stock has been issued.

2. Common stock shareholders have right to vote.

3. Common stock shareholders have rights to ultimate distribution of assets of corporation upon dissolution.

C. Dividends—Declared by the board of directors, which has discretion.

1. Distributions of property to shareholders in proportion to their respective numbers of shares or interest in the corporation.

2. May be cash or other property, including stock.

3. Payable to record holders on specified record date.

4. Limitations on issuance of dividends.

a. Dividends may only be paid out of legally available funds of a corporation, in accordance with state law.

b. Dividends cannot be declared if it will result in insolvency of the corporation or impair its capital. Directors may be liable to the corporation and/or shareholders for improper issuance of dividends, especially if they acted in bad faith.

III. Federal securities regulation—Legislation is based on the power of Congress to regulate interstate commerce and the use of the mails.

A. Federal regulation is administered by the Securities and Exchange Commission.

B. Securities Act of 1933.

1. Requires full disclosure of material information, which is relevant to investment decisions, and prohibits fraud and misstatements when securities are offered to the public through the mail and/or interstate commerce.

2. Registration statement is filed with the SEC, containing a thorough description of the securities, the financial structure, condition and management personnel of the issuing corporation.

3. Prospectus, based on the information in the registration statement, must be given to any prospective investor and purchaser.

4. Intrastate and nonpublic offerings are exempt, as are those of banking and

common carrier corporations (which are covered by other legislation), nonprofit corporations and governmental bodies.

5. Regulation A—Less demanding disclosure and registration are required for small issues (under $500,000).

6. Issuer may solicit revocable offers from prospective purchasers after filing registration statement but may not sell securities until the effective date of the statement.

7. Civil liability for failure to register and for misstatements and omissions in a registration statement.

   a. Imposed upon the issuing corporation, its directors and anyone who signed or provided information that was incorporated in the registration statement and underwriters.

   b. Liable to persons acquiring shares.

C. Securities Exchange Act of 1934.

   1. Regulates securities exchanges, those engaged in the markets in which securities are traded and corporations having assets of more than one million dollars and 500 shareholders.

   2. Insider trading (Sec. 10(b) and SEC Rule 10b-5).

      a. Liability is imposed upon directors and others, who, because of their positions, have access to information (not available to the public) which may affect the future market value of the corporation's securities.

      b. Liable for misleading or deceptive omission or misrepresentation of material facts in connection with the purchase or sale of a security.

      c. SEC, purchaser or seller of securities, who has been damaged, may bring action.

   3. Insider reporting and trading (Sec. 16(b))—Officers, directors and large shareholders are required to file reports with the SEC and may be liable to corporation for gains made in trading in securities.

   4. Proxy statements (Sec. 14(a))—Full disclosure is required of those soliciting proxies from shareholders.

IV. Blue Sky Laws—State securities laws also regulate the offering and sale of securities in intrastate commerce.

   A. Anti-fraud provisions similar to federal laws.

   B. Regulation of brokers and dealers in securities.

C. Registration and disclosure are required before securities can be offered for sale.

D. Some state statutes impose standards of "fairness."

FILL-IN QUESTIONS

1. Corporations obtain funds for their operations by issuing equity securities, or _____, and debt securities, such as _____, and by retaining some of their earnings and profits, rather than distributing them in the form of _____ to shareholders.

2. Debt securities include _____, which are secured by liens or other security interests in assets of a corporation, and _____, which are backed only by the general credit of a borrowing corporation.

3. Preferred stock refers to shares having some measure of preference in respect to priority rights associated with _____ or _____ or, in some instances, voting.

4. The regulation of securities is covered concurrently by state statutes, often termed _____, and federal legislation under the _____ and _____, administered by the _____. The basis for federal regulation is the power of Congress to regulate _____ and the use of the U.S. _____.

MULTIPLE CHOICE QUESTIONS

1. Jones paid $900 for a document that provided that ten years from the date of its issue the ABC Corporation promised to pay the holder $1000, and until that date the corporation promised to pay the holder $40 on the first day of every March and September.
   a. Jones is a shareholder of the ABC Corporation.
   b. Jones has purchased a bond at a discount.
   c. Jones has a right to cumulative dividends.
   d. Jones has the right to vote at the annual shareholders' meeting.

Questions 2, 3 and 4 are based on the following fact situation: A corporation has issued 20,000 shares of common stock, 10,000 shares of nonparticipating, nonconvertible, redeemable, cumulative preferred stock.

2. Which of the following statements is correct?
   a. A preferred shareholder has a right to exchange his or her shares of preferred stock for common stock.
   b. A shareholder holding common stock has a right to exchange his or her shares for preferred stock.
   c. The corporation has the right to purchase, reacquire and cancel the preferred shares at a specified price.

    d. The corporation has the right to purchase and reacquire the preferred shares at a specified price and reissue the shares.

3.   An owner of:
    a. common stock is entitled to vote at the annual meeting of the shareholders.
    b. common stock is entitled to receive a pro rata share of dividends before payment of dividends to preferred shareholders.
    c. either common or preferred stock is entitled to vote at the annual meeting of the shareholders, even though this right is not indicated on his or her share certificate.
    d. preferred stock has a right to share in the distribution of additional dividends, after payment of dividends to common shareholders.

4.   If the corporation is dissolved and all taxes and other obligations are paid:
    a. the preferred shareholders must be paid the face amount of their respective shares before any distribution is made to common stock shareholders.
    b. each preferred and common shareholder shares pro rata in the distribution of remaining assets.
    c. the remaining assets are distributed as a dividend.
    d. only the common shareholders share in the distribution of the corporate assets.

5.   The Z Corporation is planning to sell $2,000 worth of corporate debentures, which will mature in 25 years from the date of issue, to the public in the United States. The issue need not be registered with the SEC because:
    a. the federal securities acts apply only to the issuance of equity securities.
    b. bonds of this nature are not considered to be securities.
    c. Z Corporation is a municipal corporation.
    d. the amount of the issue is less than $5,000,000.

6.   A corporation, which desires to issue $1,000,000 worth of preferred shares, has complied with the appropriate state Blue Sky Laws and filed a registration statement with the SEC, but has omitted a material fact regarding the corporation's financing.
    a. An accountant, who certified a financial statement, made in conjunction with the registration statement, is liable to a purchaser of the new issue.
    b. The underwriter of the new issue is liable to a purchaser of the shares.
    c. A director of the corporation issuing the shares is liable to any person who acquires the shares of the new issue.
    d. All of the above.

Rights and Duties of
Directors, Managers and
Shareholders

In a corporation, the overall managerial responsibility rests with the board of directors, elected by the shareholders. The actual operation of a corporation is conducted by officers, elected or appointed and supervised the board, other managers, agents and employees. The rights and duties of directors and officers and their potential liability to the corporation are discussed in the first part of this chapter.

Ultimately the risks and benefits of incorporation inure to the shareholders, the investors, who provide the funds which initially finance the corporate operations. Generally, they exercise no control over policies adopted by the corporation after participating in the election of the board of directors. Their rights and liabilities are treated in the latter section of the chapter.

THINGS TO KEEP IN MIND

Directors and officers are fiduciaries and have obligations to act in good faith, honestly and loyally. The trend has been to expand the nature and extent of their responsibilities to the corporation.

OUTLINE

I.   Role of directors and officers.

    A. Directors manage the corporation and establish general policies and the scope of the business within the purposes and powers stated in the corporate charter (MBCA Sec. 35).

       1. Directors may not act individually; they must act convened as a board.

2. The board of directors has power to authorize actions which are legal exercises of the corporation's powers.

3. The board supervises and selects officers, defines their duties and authority and fixes their compensation, if not otherwise provided for in the by-laws.

4. Dividends are declared by the board of directors.

B. Rights of directors.

1. Participate in meetings of the board of directors; notice of special meetings must be given (MBCA Sec. 43).

2. Inspect books and records of the corporation.

3. Indemnification for expenses, judgments, fines, costs, etc., incurred in corporate related criminal or civil actions, other than actions brought by or on behalf of the corporation (MBCA Sec. 5).

4. Compensation may be fixed in charter or by the board of directors (MBCA Sec. 35).

C. Officers—Deal with third persons as agents of and on behalf of corporation (MBCA Sec. 50).

1. Usually officers include a president, one or more vice presidents, secretary and treasurer, selected by the board of directors.

2. The board may also select other officers and agents.

3. Law of agency and employment applies. The authority of officers, other agents and employees may be express (in charter, by-laws or resolutions of board of directors) or implied (customary and incidental power of such officers) actual authority or apparent authority (because the corporation holds out that its officers have the usual power of similar officers of other corporations) or the board may ratify acts of its officers.

D. Duties of directors and officers—If the duties are breached, directors and officers are liable to the corporation.

1. Directors are fiduciaries and are required to perform their duties in good faith, acting in the best interests of the corporation "and with such care as an ordinary prudent person in a like position would use under similar circumstances" (MBCA Sec. 35).

    a. Directors are required to be honest and loyal and to exercise reasonable diligence, care and skill.

    b. Business judgment rule—Directors are not normally liable for poor business judgment or honest mistakes. They are not insurers of business success.

    c. Directors are expected to be informed and attend meetings.
      1) If a director is present at a meeting, he or she is presumed to assent to action taken, unless he or she files a written dissent or has his or her dissent entered in the minutes (MBCA Sec. 35).
      2) A director, having a personal interest in a matter being considered by the board, should not vote thereon.

    d. Directors should not use their positions to secure personal advantages.

    e. Directors, who deal with the corporation, must make full disclosure.

2. Directors are liable to the corporation if they:

    a. Compete with the corporation.

    b. Usurp a corporate opportunity.

    c. Fail to disclose an interest conflicting with that of the corporation.

    d. Engage in insider trading in buying or selling shares, by using confidential information that they possess because of their position.
      1) Liable to shareholder to whom they sold or from whom they purchased stock.
      2) See Chapter 43 herein with regard to liability under the securities laws.

    e. Improperly issue a dividend.

    f. Make an improper stock issue.
      1) Shares may be issued for money, property or services actually performed.
      2) Par value shares cannot be issued for less than par value, unless bonus or discount issues are permitted by statute.
      3) No par shares can be issued for less than the consideration fixed by the board of directors or the shareholders, if so empowered by the charter.
      4) Directors are also liable if they overvalue the consideration (property or services) received for shares.

    g. Fail to comply with provisions of law, charter or by-laws of the corporation.

3. Contracts between a corporation and a director of a corporation, having one or more common directors, are scrutinized by the courts.

4. Officers have fiduciary duties similar to those of directors.

5. In some cases, majority shareholders are treated as also owing a fiduciary duty to the corporation and minority shareholders.

II. Shareholder rights.

A. Right to have a stock certificate, evidencing rights of an owner of a proportionate interest in the corporation according to the total number of shares issued.

1. Intangible personal property.

2. Shareholder, whose ownership interest is recorded, has right to:

   a. Receive notice of meetings and participate in meetings.

   b. Dividends when declared.

   c. Participate in distribution of assets upon dissolution.

   d. Receive operational and financial reports.

3. Certifies that the named person is the owner of the stated number of fully paid and nonassessable shares.

B. Right to transfer shares. (See UCC, Article 8.)

1. Stock certificate is usually transferred by negotiation.

   a. Physical delivery and indorsement on the certificate itself, so that a good faith purchaser for value is the owner of the shares represented by the certificate, free of adverse claims and entitled to be registered as a shareholder and to receive a new certificate.

   b. Until the corporation is notified of the transfer, it recognizes the record holder (transferor) as entitled to all shareholder rights.

2. Restrictions on transferability are enforceable if noted on the certificate. Such limitations are usually provided for in the case of a small closely held corporation, in order to maintain ownership within the group.

   a. Consent of group is necessary in order to transfer shares, or

   b. Corporation or shareholders have the right of first refusal.

C. Preemptive rights.

1. The right of current shareholders to purchase or subscribe to newly issued stock in proportion to the amount of stock currently owned before it is offered to the public.

2. Preserve prior relative power of each shareholder.

3. Statutes vary.

   a. Right is denied, unless provided for in charter (MBCA Sec. 26).

b. Right is granted, unless denied in charter, but does not apply to certain issues (MBCA 26 Alternate).

4. Stock purchase warrants are issued to the shareholders of record so that they can purchase the shares in accordance with their preemptive rights.

D. Dividend rights (MBCA 45).

1. Shareholders do not have rights to dividends (distributions of profits) until declared by the board of directors.

a. Cash—Once declared, dividends are corporate debts and cannot be rescinded.

b. Stock—May be revoked before actually issued to shareholders.

2. Statutes impose restrictions on issuance of dividends which will result in the corporation's insolvency or in impairment of its capital.

3. Directors must act diligently, prudently and in good faith and may be liable civilly and criminally for improperly or illegally declaring dividends.

4. Ordinarily directors are not required to declare dividends unless a refusal to do so is an abuse of discretion.

E. Right to vote. (See Chapter 43.) Normally common and preferred shareholders have the right to vote, unless denied in the charter (MBCA Sec. 33).

F. Right to inspect (MBCA Sec. 52).

1. A shareholder has a right to obtain information and may examine and copy relevant books, records and minutes for proper purposes in person or by an agent, attorney, etc.

2. A shareholder for more than six months or of more than five percent of the outstanding shares may so inspect.

3. Written demand, stating the purpose, must be given.

4. Shareholder must act in good faith and for a proper purpose.

G. Rights upon dissolution or an extraordinary change in the corporation. (See Chapter 45 herein.)

III. Shareholder liabilities—Shareholders are not normally personally liable to creditors of the corporation. They may, however, be liable in the following situations:

A. See Chapter 40 herein with regard to disregarding the corporate entity.

B. A shareholder is liable for illegally or improperly paid dividends if he or she had knowledge they were improper.

C. A shareholder is liable if he or she received shares that were issued for no consideration or consideration that did not satisfy the statutory requirements.

D. A shareholder is liable for any unpaid stock subscriptions.

FILL-IN QUESTIONS

1. The directors of a corporation establish general policy for the corporation. In order to participate in meetings at which the board takes action, a director has a right to _____.
Action taken by the board of directors must be taken by _____.

2. A director is not liable to the corporation for action taken by the board of directors if _____
or for losses caused by honest mistakes or _____
and may have a right of indemnification for costs, expenses and judgments incurred as a result of defending in a lawsuit in an action _____.

3. In general shareholders of a corporation are not liable for corporate indebtedness. They are, however, liable to creditors for the amounts of _____
_____.

4. Payment for stock subscriptions may be made in money _____ or _____.

5. Shareholders' _____ refers to the right to subscribe to newly issued stock in a corporation in proportion to the amount of stock currently owned before it is offered to the public.

MULTIPLE CHOICE QUESTIONS

1. John was president and a director of the M Company, a manufacturing corporation. John learned that the corporation could probably obtain adequate, inexpensive electric power in the town of Electra, located near a nuclear power plant, due to be completed and operational in two years. John represented this information to the board of directors and recommended moving the corporation's operations to Electra. The board agreed and a new factory was constructed in Electra. Before operations were begun the Electra Power Co., a public utility, advised M Company that it would be unable to provide electricity to the factory because its plant was denied a license to begin its operations by the Nuclear Regulatory Commission. As a result the corporation has sustained a considerable loss.
    a. As John was a director of the corporation, he could not also serve as an officer.
    b. John owed a fiduciary duty to the corporation, which he breached by recommending the move.
    c. The directors are liable to the shareholders for the loss.
    d. John is not liable for any loss sustained by the corporation.

2. Shares of stock may be issued without par value for such consideration as may be fixed by:
    a. a corporation's board of directors.
    b. a corporation's officers.
    c. the by-laws of the corporation.
    d. the statutes of the state of incorporation.

3. The Sell Wrong Corp. issued 1,000 shares of its $1 par value common stock to Mr. Rite, its vice president, for a price of $1,000. In consideration therefor, he gave the corporation $100 in cash, a note for $200, cancelled $400 salary owed to him for services rendered to the corporation in the past month and promised to render $300 worth of services in the following month. His shares are:
    a. paid in full.
    b. 70% paid for.
    c. 50% paid for.
    d. completely unpaid for.

4. An owner of common stock in a corporation, incorporated in a state in which the Model Business Corporation Act has been adopted, will not have liability beyond actual investment, even though he:
    a. purchased treasury shares for less than par value.
    b. paid less than par value for stock purchased in connection with an original issue of shares.
    c. failed to pay the full amount owed on a subscription contract.
    d. was the sole shareholder and treated the corporation as a personally owned proprietorship.

5. DEF Corporation is authorized to issue 1,000 shares of $10 par value common stock and 1,000 shares of no par preferred stock. It has issued 1,200 shares of the common stock and 300 shares of the preferred stock at $10 per share. UCC Sec. 8-104 provides that:
    a. the recipients of the 200 shares, representing an over-issue, are entitled to receive 200 shares of the preferred stock.
    b. the recipients of the 200 shares, representing an over-issue, are entitled to the same rights of shareholders as the recipients of the 1,000 shares of properly issued common shares.
    c. with regard to the preferred stock, stated capital would include the 300 authorized and issued shares only.
    d. the preferred shares are considered to be a form of debt security.

6. Under the provisions of the UCC, a transfer of a share certificate in registered form may:
    a. not be made.
    b. be made by delivery alone.
    c. be made by delivery alone if indorsed in blank.
    d. be made by delivery if indorsed by an appropriate person.

7. A dividend that may be revoked, unless actually distributed, is:
    a. a cash dividend.

    b. a stock dividend.

    c. a liquidating dividend.

    d. all of the above.

Merger, Consolidation and Termination

A corporation, making a fundamental change in its structure or the nature of its busines or terminating its existence, is required to comply with the laws of the state of incorporation. This may be accomplished by a merger or consolidation with another corporation or by the purchase or other acquisition of assets or stock of another corporation or by dissolution and termination, all of which are discussed in this chapter.

THINGS TO KEEP IN MIND

A corporation cannot avoid compliance with statutory procedures, which are meant to safeguard the rights of corporate shareholders and creditors, by camouflaging an extraordinary fundamental corporate change as something else.

OUTLINE

I.   Merger and consolidation—Exchange of shares of stock in one corporation for stock in another corporation.

    A. Merger—One corporation (the surviving corporation) acquires the assets of one or more other corporations (the merged or disappearing corporations).

       A Corporation ————————————— A Corporation (surviving corporation)

       B Corporation
       (merged or disappearing corporation)

       1. The surviving corporation assumes the obligations and debts of the disappearing corporation and the existence of that corporation ceases.

    2. The shareholders of the disappearing corporation become the shareholders of the surviving corporation.

        a. The surviving corporation exchanges its stock for the assets of the disappearing corporation, which distributes the stock to its shareholders, or

        b. The surviving corporation exchanges its stock directly with the shareholders of the disappearing corporation.

B. Consolidation—Two or more corporations combine so that each of them ceases to exist and a new corporation comes into existence. The new corporation acquires the assets and assumes the obligations and debts of the consolidated (disappearing) corporations.

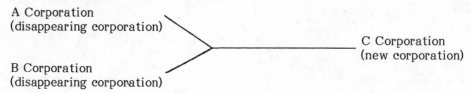

A Corporation
(disappearing corporation)

B Corporation
(disappearing corporation)

C Corporation
(new corporation)

C. Applicable legal principles, effect and procedure are basically the same for either merger or consolidation.

D. Procedure.

    1. Board of directors of each corporation adopts a plan.

        a. Names of constituent merging or consolidating corporations and that of the surviving or new corporation.

        b. Terms of the merger or consolidation.

        c. Manner of converting shares of stock of constituent corporations into securities of the surviving or new corporation.

        d. In the case of merger, the changes in the charter of the surviving corporation, and in the case of consolidation, the appropriate provisions for the charter of the new corporation (MBCA Sec. 71 and 72).

    2. Shareholder approval after notice to all (voting and nonvoting) shareholders of all corporations—Usually a two-thirds vote of voting shares is required (MBCA Sec. 73).

    3. Filing of Articles of Merger or Consolidation, which includes the plan, with the appropriate state official, who issues a certificate, and any local officials as required (MBCA Sec. 74).

E. If one or more of the corporations is a foreign corporation and the laws of each state permit merger or consolidation, each corporation complies with the laws of the state of its incorporation (MBCA Sec. 77).

F. Surviving corporation, in case of merger, or new corporation, in case of consolidation, acquires the assets, rights, liabilities and debts of the disappearing corporations (MBCA Sec. 76).

G. Short form (parent-subsidiary) merger—When the surviving (parent) corporation owns more than a stated proportion, such as 90% or 95%, of the outstanding shares of each class of stock of the disappearing (subsidiary) corporation, formal shareholder consent is not required (MBCA Sec. 75).

II. Acquisition of all or substantially all of the assets of another corporation, other than in the regular course of business (MBCA Sec. 79).

A. Acquisition may be by purchase, lease or other disposition.

B. Acquiring corporation may pay cash, property or stock.

C. Each corporation remains in existence but the character of its assets and business change.

D. Procedure for corporation disposing of assets includes giving notice to all shareholders and vote of some prescribed proportion thereof.

E. Approval of shareholders of the acquiring corporation is not necessary unless payment is to be made in shares which are unauthorized or unavailable or if required by a stock exchange, upon which one or more of the corporations is listed.

III. Dissenting shareholders' rights to fair market value of shares.

A. Normally, if a shareholder disagrees with corporate policy or decisions, his or her recourse is to sell the stock.

B. A dissenting shareholder may have appraisal rights in cases of:

1. Disposition of all or substantially all of the assets of the corporation.

2. Consolidation and merger, including short form merger in some states (MBCA Sec. 80).

3. In some states only:

a. Amendments of charter, affecting classifications of shares, when shareholders are adversely affected and not otherwise protected by preemptive rights.

b. Acquisition of securities, to be distributed to shareholders, when disposing of assets of a dissolving corporation.

C. Dissenting shareholder must strictly adhere to statutory procedure (MBCA Sec. 81).

1. Vote against particular corporate action.

2. Give notice to corporation, which then makes offer to purchase shares.

3. Apply for appraisal of fair market value of shares by an appropriate court if offer of corporation is not accepted.

IV. Purchase of stock directly from shareholders by an "acquiring" corporation to acquire voting control of another (the "target") corporation.

   A. "Tender offer" is publicly made and may be to exchange shares for cash or securities. Often the offer price is higher than the market value of the shares.

   B. Today this method of gaining control is regulated by federal and state laws.

V. Termination—Dissolution and liquidation.

   A. Nonjudicial dissolution.

      1. Act of the legislature in the state of incorporation.

      2. Expiration of duration provided for in charter, if not perpetual.

      3. Voluntary.

         a. By incorporators (MBCA Sec. 82).

         b. By unanimous action of all the shareholders (MBCA Sec. 83).

         c. By act of the corporation, after adoption of resolution by the board of directors and its approval by shareholders (MBCA Sec. 84).

      4. Procedure for liquidation and winding up (MBCA Secs. 86 and 87).

         a. Cease conducting new business, notify creditors, pay debts and liabilities, including taxes, fulfill existing contracts, collect and sell assets.

         b. Distribute remaining assets among shareholders, according to their respective interests and preferences.

         c. Make any filings required by state law (MBCA Secs. 85, 92 and 93).

   B. Involuntary judicial dissolution.

      1. Upon application of attorney general of state of incorporation for failure to comply with statutory, administrative or tax requirements, obtaining charter through fraud, abuse of corporate powers (see Chapter 41 herein), violation of state law or failure to commence or abandonment of business operations (MBCA Secs. 94, 95 and 96).

      2. In some states, petition for dissolution may be made by:

    a. Creditors (MBCA Sec. 97).

    b. Corporation, requesting court supervision of liquidation (MBCA Sec. 97).

    c. Majority of directors, if corporation is insolvent or if it will benefit shareholders.

  3. Upon application of shareholders, if directors or shareholders are deadlocked, or directors are acting illegally, oppressively, fraudulently or wasting or misapplying assets (MBCA Sec. 97).

FILL-IN QUESTIONS

1. A, B and C Corporations are planning to merge. Upon completion of the statutory requirements, C Corporation will continue to exist. A and B Corporations will _____ and C Corporation will acquire _____ and assume _____. The shareholders of A and B Corporations will receive _____.

2. E and F Corporations are planning to consolidate. Upon completion of the statutory requirements, E and F Corporations will _____. Their assets will be acquired and their liabilities assumed by G Corporation, _____ _____.

3. State corporation laws require _____ if a corporation is selling, leasing or otherwise disposing of all or substantially all of its assets, other than in the ordinary course of its business, even though the corporation's existence will _____ because it results in a fundamental change in _____ _____.

4. The objective of statutory provisions requiring shareholder approval for plans resulting in fundamental changes in the nature and structure of a corporation and filing with a state official is to protect the rights of _____. A corporation _____ avoid compliance with the statutory procedures by characterizing or disguising a transaction in such a way as not to require such approval or filing.

5. A shareholder, who has voted against a merger, consolidation or disposition of all or substantially all of the assets of a corporation, may dissent. If so the shareholder has a right to be paid _____ by the corporation and, by adhering to the statutory provisions, may apply to an appropriate court for _____.

MULTIPLE CHOICE QUESTIONS

1. Which of the following statements is incorrect?
   a. The surviving corporation in a merger assumes the liabilities of the corporation which merged into it.

    b. Assets of all consolidating corporations are acquired by the surviving corporation after consolidation.

    c. A shareholder, who dissents from a lease of all the assets of a corporation, is entitled to the fair market value of her shares.

    d. Bondholders have rights to corporate assets upon dissolution, superior to those of common shareholders.

2.   C Co. was merged into D Co. C Co. had only issued common stock. Under the terms of the plan of merger, each share of common stock of C Co. received one share of 8% cumulative, nonvoting D Co. preferred stock. The directors and the required proportion of shareholders of both corporations voted in favor of the merger. The holders of 10% of the common stock of C Co. voted against the plan and have demanded that the corporation purchase their shares rather than give them D Co. stock.

    a. Creditors of C Co. are not entitled to payment from D Co. if D Co. did not agree to assume C Co.'s obligations.

    b. The merger is ineffective because the shareholders of C Co. are to receive nonvoting shares in exchange for their voting shares.

    c. Dissenting shareholders of C Co. are entitled to the fair market value of their shares.

    d. If the corporation refuses to pay the dissenting shareholders a price that they believe is adequate, a court will not substitute its judgment for that of the directors.

Questions 3 and 4 are based on the following fact situation: The ABD Land Corp. has sold 98.3% of its assets, all of which is real property, to the FGH Land Corp.

3.   Which of the following statements is correct?

    a. The board of directors of ABD may authorize the sale, if it is in the regular course of business.

    b. The sale must be approved by the shareholders of ABD, if it is in the regular course of business.

    c. The sale must be approved by the shareholders of FGH, if it is not in the regular course of business.

    d. The ABD Corp. will be dissolved by operation of law following the transfer of its assets to FGH.

4.   If the sale is not in the regular course of business of ABD Land Corp:

    a. the sale must be approved by all the shareholders of ABD, including those without voting rights.

    b. the sale need not be approved by the shareholders of ABD, if the directors unanimously approved it.

    c. a dissenting shareholder of ABD has a right to be paid the fair market value of her shares, if she promptly notified and made a demand on the corporation.

    d. a dissenting shareholder of FGH has a right to be paid the fair market value of his shares, if he promptly notified and made a demand on the corporation.

5.   A majority of the shareholders of a corporation may petition for dissolution, if the:

    a. assets of the corporation are insufficient to meet its liabilities.

    b. directors have failed to declare a dividend.

    c. directors are deadlocked in the management of the corporation.

    d. never.

6.   A corporation's existence terminates when:

    a. the sole owner/shareholder dies.

    b. it becomes insolvent.

    c. all of its shares are purchased by another corporation.

    d. it legally consolidates with another corporation.

Private Franchises

A franchise is an agreement or arrangement, in which the franchisor, the owner of a trademark, trade name, copyright or similar interest, grants the right to use the mark, name or other interest to another, the franchisee, in connection with selling, marketing or supplying goods and/or services.

The relationship between the franchisee and the franchisor may be one of agency, especially if the franchisor may exercise considerable control over the activities of the franchisee and derives substantial benefit from them. In other instances, the franchisee has a great deal of discretion and is subject to little control by the franchisor, in which case, the franchisee will be treated as an independent contractor. As you will recall from Unit VI, the nature of a relationship determines the respective liability of the parties.

THINGS TO KEEP IN MIND

There is considerable disparity in bargaining power in many franchise relationships. For this reason, a number of states have enacted statutes protecting franchisees, and courts have refused to enforce grossly unfair termination provisions in franchise agreements and have prevented franchisors from unconscionably refusing to renew franchise licenses without good cause.

OUTLINE

I. The law of franchising.

    A. Approximately 15 states have enacted statutes dealing with franchising.

    B. The courts tend to apply general common law principles in cases involving franchising.

II.   Types of franchises.

    A.   Distributorship—A manufacturer licenses a dealer to sell its product.

    B.   Chain-style business—A franchisee operates under a franchisor's name and is identified as a member of the group engaged in the franchisor's business.

    C.   Manufacturing or processing plant arrangement—The franchisor furnishes ingredients or formula for making or processing a particular product and marketing it in accordance with the franchisor's standards.

III. Advantages.

    A.   Franchisor.

        1.   Furnishes aid, protection, goodwill, supportive services and customer acceptance.

        2.   Gains rapid market expansion with minimal outlays of capital.

    B.   Franchisee.

        1.   The franchise system provides opportunities to individuals to own their own businesses.

        2.   A legally independent business unit furnishes capital but is economically dependent upon the franchisor.

IV.   The franchise agreement—Usually prepared by the franchisor.

    A.   Payment for franchise—Initial fee for franchise license, a percentage of sales or profits and sometimes payment of a proportion of the franchisor's costs and expenses.

    B.   Control by the franchisor over the business location, organization and decisions.

        1.   Franchisee may be required to lease or own the premises and/or supply equipment. In some cases, the franchisor supplies equipment and leases the premises.

        2.   The franchisor may impose standards for the form of business organization, its capital structure, the operations, training of personnel and the quality of products or services.

        3.   The franchisor may require that the franchisee purchase supplies and products at an established price, but may only suggest retail prices.

        4.   Usually the agreement contains exclusive dealings provisions.

    C.   Termination of the franchise arrangement.

1. Initial duration may be limited to one year.

2. May be terminated by the franchisor for cause—Death, disability or insolvency of the franchise, breach of the agreement or failure to meet sales quota.

3. Notice of termination is generally necessary.

4. Courts have read good faith and commercial reasonableness into franchise contracts and will not enforce unconscionable provisions.

D. Legislation.

1. Federal Automobile Dealers' Day in Court Act.

2. State statutes may be subject to constitutional challenges.

V. Regulation of the franchising industry.

A. State statutes and case law are not uniform.

1. It is often difficult to prove the existence of the elements of fraud in the inducement and, even if proven, the remedies afforded by common law for fraud may be inadequate.

2. Some states have enacted franchise disclosure acts, which afford some protection to potential franchisees.

3. Some courts have attempted to apply state Blue Sky Laws to franchise agreements.

B. Federal regulation.

1. Franchise agreements have been held not to be securities, subject to regulation under the Securities Act of 1933.

2. Remedies available for mail fraud are generally unsatisfactory.

3. The FTC has power to prevent unfair or deceptive advertising and practices in interstate commerce.

4. The FTC has begun investigating abusive practices used in franchising.

5. The FTC franchise rule imposes disclosure requirements to enable prospective franchisees to make informed decisions before entering into franchise arrangements.

6. See also Chapters 50 and 51, dealing with antitrust and trade regulation.

_____UNIT VIII

Government Regulation

Government, at the federal, state and local level, has played an increasing role in regulating activities of individuals and businesses. The power to do so and to legislate in this area is derived, in general, from a governmental unit's power to protect and provide for the common defense, safety, health and welfare ("the police power") and, in the case of the federal government, Congress's authority to pass laws regulating interstate and foreign commerce (U.S. Constitution, Article I, Section 8). Evidence of regulation has been referred to in the preceding and subsequent units of the text and this material.

Chapter 47 provides an overview of such regulation and the agencies created to oversee them. Chapters 48 and 49 focus on consumer and environmental protection, areas in which each student, because of his or her own individual bias, will be personally interested in one or more particulars. For this reason, extensive materials concerning these matters has been omitted.

Chapters 50 and 51 deal with governmental efforts to regulate the economy in order to maintain the free private enterprise system.

Regulation and
Administrative Agencies

The objective of this chapter is to acquaint you with the regulatory process as well as explore the general scope of regulatory activities. In the United States, a trend appears to be a movement away from market and common law or legislative controls, interpreted by the courts, to increasing regulation by administrative governmental agencies, some of which have been given broad discretionary executive, legislative and judicial powers.

THINGS TO KEEP IN MIND

The emphasis in the chapter is on federal agencies and their powers, but remember that regulatory agencies (sometimes termed boards, departments, commissions, authorities, etc.) exist at all levels of government.

OUTLINE

I.   Regulatory powers and procedures—Congress has delegated judicial, executive and legislative power to government agencies, whose decisions may be reviewed by the courts. In general, a court will enforce an agency's decision and overturn its action only if it is clearly arbitrary, not supported by the record or contrary to law.

   A. Ministerial powers—Grant licenses in accordance with rules and guidelines fixed by Congress and/or formulated by the agency.

   B. Investigatory powers—Necessary in order to obtain information.

   C. Hear and rule on complaints initiated by private parties or the administrative agency.

D. Rulemaking powers—Following compilation of information, obtained after exercise of investigatory power, hearings may be held (after notification) and rules promulgated.

E. Compliance and enforcement powers—Failure to comply with an order of an agency may result in the imposition of a civil remedy, such as damages or an injunction, or criminal penalties.

F. Adjudicative powers—Decisions are usually made after extensive presentation of evidence at hearings. The courts will generally be bound by the findings of facts by an agency.

II. Scope of activities subject to regulation.

A. Profits may be controlled directly through taxation or indirectly, because of a regulatory board's power over rate making, particularly in industries in which participants have been given exclusive rights to produce a commodity or provide a service.

B. Price regulation in the form of establishment of a maximum, minimum or uniform price.

C. Advertising—Policy is to favor truthful disclosure. Prohibitions against advertising are becoming rarer.

D. Quotas and duties—Restrict levels of production, imports or sales.

E. Licensing and allocating rights—Entry into an economic activity may be restricted.

F. Standard setting in order to protect health or to provide information to consumers.

G. Disclosure of information requirements.

H. Restrictions imposed upon contents of private contracts.

I. Restrictions on materials and processes used in production.

J. Imposition of taxes and granting of subsidies in order to alter economic behavior.

III. Regulated activities—Virtually every economic activity is regulated to some extent. Often multiple agencies have regulatory power affecting an activity.

A. Transportation is regulated chiefly by the Interstate Commerce Commission, which has extensive rate making power.

B. Utilities, which are granted monopolies, are chiefly regulated at the state and local levels.

C. Communications—Licensing is used in order to allocate limited air waves and air space.

D. Consumer products—Direct regulation is imposed to protect the health and safety of the public.

E. Health and safety—A major area of federal regulation was created by the Occupational Safety and Health Act, authorizing the Department of Labor to establish and enforce standards for most industries.

F. Industrial production.

G. Employment—Areas regulated by federal and state government agencies include minimum wage and maximum hours of work; terms and conditions of employment; child labor; pensions, retirement, unemployment and disability income; discriminatory practices and labor-management relations.

H. Energy—Regulated by the Department of Energy and some independent agencies.

I. Innovation and investment in new products and methods of production.

J. Patents and copyrights—Limited monopolies are given to inventors for 17 years in order to encourage innovation, development and production of goods and services, and to authors and their estates for life plus 50 years.

K. Trademarks—A merchant/user of words or symbols may register the mark and prevent its infringement by others.

L. Financing—Extensive regulation of banking, securities and other financial activities exists at the federal and state levels.

FILL-IN QUESTIONS

1. In recent years, regulation by government agencies with specialized knowledge and functions has, to some extent, been substituted for common law and _____ _____.

2. A decision or ruling made by a specialized regulatory body will be upheld by a reviewing court, unless it is _____.

3. An agency, authorized to grant licenses, has _____ power; one authorized to establish standards, with which firms must comply, has _____ power in order to obtain information, and _____.

4. Entry into a particular industry or business may be affected by a government agency through its power to regulate price, _____ _____ and to restrict private contracting rights and _____ as well as by taxation and subsidies.

5. The power of government to protect the health and safety of its citizens is the basis for regulation in the areas of _____.

6. Although our economic system is based on free competition, monopolies are granted to _____ in order to carry out the strong public policies.

MULTIPLE CHOICE QUESTIONS

1. The Interstate Commerce Commission:
    a. regulates railroads, the trucking industry but not air carriers.
    b. may permit a merger of two railroads even if it is contrary to the objectives of the antitrust laws.
    c. has extensive rate making power.
    d. all of the above.

2. Regulations regarding safety, emissions, controls and fuel economy of automobiles is regulated by:
    a. the Department of Energy.
    b. the Department of Transportation.
    c. the National Highway Traffic Safety Administration.
    d. the Department of Transportation and the National Highway Traffic Safety Administration.

Questions 3 and 4 are based on the following fact situation: The ABC Co. is a medium sized manufacturing firm. Its only factory is located in Pennsylvania, where it employs 100, including eight women above the age of 16 and five children, who are 15 years of age. All employees work a minimum of 38 hours per week and are paid a minimum of $2.10 per hour. Sales of its product in Pennsylvania account for 90% of its business.

3. Under the general rules of the Federal Fair Labors Standards Act, ABC Co.:
    a. violated the statute because it employed children under the age of 16.
    b. violated the statute because its employees worked less than 40 hours a week.
    c. did not violate the statute by employing children if the work they did was non-hazardous.
    d. did not violate the statute because it paid more than the minimum wage.

4. ABC Co.:
    a. is exempt from the Federal Occupational Safety and Health Act because all of its employees are working in the state of Pennsylvania.
    b. is exempt from the Federal Occupational Safety and Health Act only if Pennsylvania has equivalent legislation.
    c. is subject to the Federal Equal Opportunity Act because it engages in interstate commerce.
    d. is not subject to the Federal Equal Pay Act if it pays its female workers less than it pays its male workers because less than 10% of its work force is female.

Consumer Protection

The distinct trend away from the *caveat emptor* (let the buyer beware) philosophy can be observed in judicial decisions, statutes and regulations issued by administrative agencies. The focus of this chapter is upon protection afforded to consumers engaging in sales and financing (credit) transactions. The emphasis of protective legislation and regulation has been upon preventing deceptive practices and assuring full disclosure of material information relating to sales of personal property, real property and services and credit transactions.

The concept of consumer protection overlaps other areas of the law, with which you are already familiar. Recall, for example, discussions dealing with: torts (Ch. 3), illegal bargains (Ch. 9), fraud and misrepresentation (Ch. 10), written agreements (Ch. 11), product warranties, safety and liability (Chs. 20 and 21), rights of debtors and creditors (Chs. 31 and 32), secured transactions (Ch. 30) and securities regulation (Ch. 43). See also material dealing with environmental protection (Ch. 49), regulation and the FTC (Chs. 47 and 51) and real property transactions (Chs. 52 and 53).

THINGS TO KEEP IN MIND

A consumer is usually considered to be a natural person, who obtains or tries to obtain personal property, real property, services, money or credit for personal, household or family use. In some cases too, small businesses and farmers or farm units are also afforded protection under legislation and regulation dealing with consumers.

OUTLINE

I.   Sources of consumer protection.

A. Common law.

1. Procedures have been simplified and costs of maintaining a lawsuit reduced.

2. See also Chapters 3, 9, 11 and 31.

B. Federal, state and local legislation.

1. Statutes have codified, simplified and often expanded the protection afforded by the common law.

2. The UCC, which is incorporated into state laws, is limited to transactions involving personal property. Other state statutes, which may not be uniform, provide protection to consumers in all types of transactions, involving personal and real property, services, financing, etc.

3. See chapters dealing with the sale of goods, commercial paper, secured transactions, regulation, etc.

C. Administrative agencies, carrying on consumer protection activities, include the FTC (with regard to unfair and deceptive practices) and the Department of Housing and Urban Development (which enforces the National Mobile Home Construction and Safety Standards Act and the Interstate Land Sales Full Disclosure Act).

D. Nongovernmental organizations—Better Business Bureaus and local Chambers of Commerce.

II. Activities and practices giving rise to consumer grievances and means of consumer protection.

A. False and deceptive advertising.

1. Limited redress is afforded under common laws rules relating to fraud.

2. Section 5 of the Federal Trade Commission Act, as amended, authorizes the FTC to prevent "unfair or deceptive acts or practices in commerce."

3. Deceptive advertising refers to intentional misrepresentations of facts, which are material factors in inducing purchasers' decisions to buy advertised products.

4. A determination, as to whether or not a particular advertisement is deceptive, is delegated to the FTC and the courts have not been prone to overruling determinations made by the FTC.

5. "Bait and switch" advertising.

a. Advertisement relates to one item, which is offered at a low price. When a consumer tries to purchase the item, a sales person tries to get the consumer to buy a more expensive item.

b. FTC guidelines are designed to prevent the practice.

6. The FTC may require that one, who engaged in deceptive advertising, run corrective advertisements.

7. Third party certification—Products may be examined and/or tested by independent third persons, who certify that they meet certain predetermined standards or make certain guaranties or, in some cases, provide remedies for consumers, who have purchased items which have proven to be inferior or defective.

B. Labeling and packaging.

1. Governed by federal and state statutes.

2. Labels must be accurate when evaluated in terms of the ordinary meanings associated with the words used in labeling, and specify ingredients, name of the manufacturer, quantity, etc.

C. Sales—Certain improper methods of selling are prohibited by state and/or federal legislation covering:

1. Disclosure of terms.

2. Door-to-door sales—"Cooling off" periods are specified, during which purchasers may cancel home sales.

3. Mail order transactions.

4. Referral sales.

D. Warranties. (See Chapters 21 and 50.)

E. Credit.

1. Federal Truth in Lending Act (Consumer Credit Protection Act).

a. Applicable when the debtor is a natural person and the creditor is a lender, seller or provider of services.

b. Credit card holder will not be liable for more than $50 if there was an unauthorized use of the card and notice given to issuer.

c. Disclosure provisions.
1) The purpose of uniform disclosure requirements is to provide consumers with means of comparing the terms and cost of credit.
2) Financing charges, including interest, charges for insurance and loan, finders, credit report, appraisal, financing and service fees, must be stated in an annual percentage rate.

2. Uniform Consumer Credit Code—Adopted by some states but with variations. (See Appendix B.)

   a. Similar to the federal Truth in Lending Act.

   b. Provides maximum credit ceilings and interest rates.

   c. Covers home solicitation and referral sales.

   d. Provisions deal with disclosure and the form and contents of sales agreements.

3. Consumer credit reporting—The Fair Credit Reporting Act requires that, upon request, one, who is refused credit or employment because of a credit bureau report, be supplied with a summary of the information in the report, the sources and recipients of the information and an opportunity to correct errors.

4. Open end credit—Covers a series of credit transactions. Debtor may pay the balance in full or in installments.

5. Rate regulation. See discussion of usury in Chapter 9.

6. Collection and repossession procedures—The federal Fair Debt Collection Practices Act and the Consumer Credit Protection Act, FTC guidelines and state laws prohibit certain debt collection tactics, provide procedures for correcting billing errors, limit amounts of earnings that can be garnished and require notice of repossession to the debtor.

MULTIPLE CHOICE QUESTIONS

1. The federal Consumer Protection Act (Truth in Lending Act):
    a. requires creditors to disclose all finance charges, including interest, in terms of annual percentage rates.
    b. establishes a maximum amount that may be charged by a lender or seller in a loan or credit transaction.
    c. is regarded as the federal usury law.
    d. applies to credit transactions between creditors and debtors without regard to the fact that they are natural persons or corporations.

2. Ordinary expenses incurred by a lender in a loan situation, which will be allowed in addition to the maximum contract rate of interest, are costs of:
    a. examining title to property, which is being given as collateral security.
    b. investigating the financial character of the borrower.
    c. drawing necessary documents.
    d. all of the above.

49

Environmental Law

Increased urbanization, economic growth and advanced methods of production have accentuated the conflict between freedom of contracting and the right to use one's own property, on the one hand, and the needs of society to be protected against harm, caused by pollution to the environment, on the other.

The federal Congress and the state legislatures have responded to the increased awareness of the presence and harmful effects of pollution by enacting statutes aimed at reducing contamination and improving the quality of the air, water and land.

OUTLINE

I.   Private litigation.

    A. Common law remedies, available to one injured by pollution in an action, based on the tort of nuisance, include damages and injunctive relief, but frequently are not successful or the relief granted inadequate.

    B. Some statutes authorize private lawsuits, based upon violations or noncompliance with mandated standards.

II. Federal statutes providing for regulation by administrative agencies.

    A. National Environmental Policy Act (1969) requires the preparation of environmental statements for proposed federal action, affecting the quality of the environment.

    B. Water quality.

1. Water Pollution Control Act, as amended.

2. Marine Protection and Research and Sanctuaries Act of 1972.

3. The Safe Drinking Waters Act of 1974.

4. The Clean Water Act, as amended in 1972 and 1977.

C. Pesticides and toxic substances.

1. Insecticide, Fungicide and Rodenticide Act, as amended by the Environmental Pesticide Control Act of 1972.

2. Toxic Substance Control Act of 1976.

D. Noise—The Noise Control Acts of 1970 and 1972.

E. Radiation—The Resource Conservation Recovery Act of 1976.

F. Air pollution—Clean Air Act of 1963, as amended. The establishment of air quality standards is delegated to the Environmental Protection Agency (EPA).

G. Waste disposal—Federal legislation encourages local and state government participation in setting standards and participating in solving problems of waste disposal.

1. Materials Policy Act of 1970.

2. Resource Conservation and Recovery Act of 1976.

III. Environmental Protection Agency—Primary federal agency for executing environmental regulation.

A. A statement, analyzing the environmental impact of proposed federal action (including legislation), or a statement explaining why an impact statement is not required, must be prepared, indicating the social benefits, risks and costs of the proposed action.

B. Impact statements are prepared by the agency responsible for carrying out a proposed project and include:

1. Identification of the environmental impact of the projected action.

2. Discussion of alternatives.

3. Distinctions between short term and long term impacts.

4. Identification of unavoidable impacts of the proposal.

5. Indication of all irreversible resource uses.

50

Antitrust

Strong public policies in the United States favor the maintenance of competition. For this reason, restraints of trade and other unfair methods of competition have been discouraged and, in some cases, prohibited by judicial decisions and statutes. The Sherman Act was the first major federal legislation adopted to deal with anticompetitive practices and is the subject matter of much of the material in this chapter. It was followed by the Clayton Act, the provisions of which are discussed in this and the following chapter.

THINGS TO KEEP IN MIND

The Sherman Act prohibits contracts, combinations, conspiracies and other joint actions to restrain trade and monopolization or attempts to monopolize trade or commerce. Subsequent legislation has been directed at particular types of business behavior that have the effect of reducing competition.

OUTLINE

I. Antecedents of antitrust statutes.

    A. Common law—General restraints of trade (agreements or promises not to compete) are against public policy and will not be enforced, but reasonable ancillary, partial restraints, which are necessary to protect a property interest (such as goodwill) may be enforced. (See Chapter 9 herein.)

    B. Formation of "trusts" in the late nineteenth century—The trust device was used in order to engage in monopolistic and predatory tactics, the objective being to drive out small competitors in a number of industries.

II. Sherman Antitrust Act (1890)—Deals with unilateral and group attempts or actions to restrain trade or monopolize an area of business.

   A. Section 1 focuses on agreements that are restrictive and have a wrongful purpose.

   B. Section 2 is directed at misuses of monopoly power.

   C. Proscriptive nature of the Sherman Act—Tells people how they should *not* act rather than how they should act (prescriptive or regulatory).

   D. Jurisdiction—Restraints that have significant anticompetitive impact, affecting interstate commerce.

   E. Who has standing or a right to sue?

      1. The Department of Justice.

      2. Private parties, who can show:

         a. Antitrust violation was a substantial factor in an injury incurred, and

         b. The unlawful action of the defendant affected a business activity of the plaintiff that was intended to be protected.

   F. Sanctions and remedies.

      1. Criminal penalties for violations—Fine and/or imprisonment.

      2. Civil remedies.

         a. Obtained by Department of Justice—Injunction, divestiture or seizure of property.

         b. Obtained by a plaintiff in a civil action—Treble damages.

   G. Prohibited conduct.

      1. The rule of reason—Unreasonable general restraints of trade are violations of the Act.

      2. *Per se* violations—As a matter of law, certain conduct violates the Sherman Act, without regard to proof of injury to the public, the reasonableness of the action or the worthiness of motives.

         a. Price fixing—Setting maximum or minimum prices for goods or services.

         b. Horizontal market divisions—Dividing a market or territory among competitors.

         c. Limitations on production so as to control output.

       d. Joint refusals to deal or coercive group boycotts.

III. The Clayton Act (1914)—Prohibits certain monopolistic practices. (See also Chapter 51 in text.)

    A. Section 2 (as amended by the Robinson-Patman Act of 1936)—Price discrimination—It is unlawful for a seller to discriminate in price between different purchasers when the effect would be to lessen competition or tend toward monopoly, except when the difference is due to grade, quality, quantity or cost of transportation or if done, in good faith, to meet competition; nor may a seller perform services for purchasers which are not available on equal terms to all customers. It is also unlawful for any person "knowingly" to induce or receive a discriminatory price.

    B. Section 3—Tying and exclusive dealings contracts—It is unlawful to sell, lease or fix the price of commodities on condition that the purchaser or lessee agrees not to deal in the goods of a competitor of the seller or lessor, when the effect would be to reduce competition or tend to create a monopoly.

    C. Section 7 (as amended by the Celler-Kefauver Act of 1950)—Prohibits acquisitions of stock or assets of another corporation, when the effect might be to substantially lessen competition or tend to create a monopoly in any line of business in any geographic area of the country. The purpose is to preserve competition.

    D. Section 8—Interlocking directorates—Prohibited, if one of the corporations has capital, surplus and undivided profits exceeding one million dollars, when elimination of competition between the two corporations would violate the antitrust laws.

    E. Enforcement of the Clayton Act is carried out by the Federal Trade Commission and the Department of Justice, which has an antitrust division.

IV. Exemptions from the antitrust laws.

    A. Labor unions.

    B. Small businesses.

    C. Agricultural organizations.

    D. Sports.

    E. Insurance and other state and/or federally regulated industries.

    F. Corporations engaging in foreign trade.

FILL-IN QUESTIONS

1. A contract of employment contains a provision to the effect that the employee agrees that, while employed and for ten years thereafter, he will not engage in the same business in competition with his employer anywhere in the U.S. This is a _____ restraint of trade and will not be enforced. If the employee promises not to compete with the employer while employed by him or her and for one year thereafter in a limited geographic area, the provision will be enforced because it is a _____ restraint.

2. A voting trust is a legal arrangement whereby shareholders give the right to vote their shares to a trustee. Under Section 1 of the Sherman Act, it is not illegal to create a voting trust, unless it is a _____.

3. The U.S. (Department of Justice) can bring a _____ action against an individual or corporation, which violates the Sherman Act. An individual or corporation, which has been injured as a result of a violation of the Sherman Act, may recover _____ in a _____ action against the violator.

4. As a matter of law, certain forms of restraints of trade are treated as violations of the Sherman Act, even if they are reasonable and cannot be shown to have been injurious. They are referred to as _____ illegal activities and include _____.

MULTIPLE CHOICE QUESTIONS

1. Strawberry, Coffee and Vanilla are operators of ice cream manufacturing plants in a metropolitan area. They meet informally to compare prices and production and have agreed to divide the market into three equal shares. They have not, however, agreed to sell their comparable ice cream at the same prices.
    a. As they are not fixing prices, this is not illegal *per se*.
    b. The arrangement is an illegal vertical restraint of trade.
    c. The arrangement is an illegal tying agreement under the Clayton Act.
    d. The division of the market is an illegal restraint of trade.

2. A trade association engages in compiling data about an industry and supplying the firms participating in the industry with the collected information. The trade association:
    a. has engaged in an activity that is a *per se* violation of the Sherman Act.
    b. and its members have engaged in an activity that is a *per se* violation of the Sherman Act.
    c. violated the Sherman Act, if its activities go beyond information gathering and supplying and are a facade for price fixing or dividing the market.
    d. does not violate the Sherman Act, if its activities go beyond information gathering and supplying, when the members of the association represent a minority group in the industry.

3. The impact of antitrust legislation is felt directly and most heavily by:
    a. sellers of a commodity in a market in which few firms compete.

b. sellers of a commodity in a market in which many firms compete.
c. consumers, who purchase a commodity, which is produced by only a few manu-
    facturers.
d. the U.S. government to which fines, imposed for violations of the antitrust laws,
    are payable.

4. The following organizations are *not* exempt from the provisions of the antitrust
    laws:
    a. an American firm that engages in exporting goods to foreign countries.
    b. an American manufacturing firm that sells its products in three states.
    c. a labor union which represents workers in three states.
    d. an agricultural cooperative which sells the products of farmers in 20 states.

5. Resale price maintenance is:
    a. a form of vertical price fixing.
    b. a form of horizontal price fixing.
    c. a means of territorial allocation.
    d. never a *per se* violation of the antitrust laws.

The Federal Trade
Commission and Trade
Regulation

Jurisdiction for enforcement of the antitrust laws is conferred upon both the Justice Department and the Federal Trade Commission, which administers other regulatory legislation as well. Much of the material in Chapter 51 deals with the efforts of the FTC to maintain economic competition in a variety of markets.

THINGS TO KEEP IN MIND

Recall from discussions in previous chapters that the FTC also engages in other activities.

Persons, who have been or may be injured because of a violation of the provisions of antitrust laws may seek civil, legal (damages) or equitable (specific performance, injunction or rescission) relief.

OUTLINE

I.   The Federal Trade Commission.

    A. An administrative agency, created by the Federal Trade Commission Act of 1914 (which has since been amended), headed by five commissioners, supported by a large staff, in order to enforce federal statutes aimed at maintaining competition.

    B. The FTC has power to prevent "unfair methods of competition in commerce and unfair or deceptive acts or practices in commerce" (Section 5 as amended by the Magnuson-Moss Act of 1975).

1. Investigatory power relative to alleged antitrust violations.

2. Power to make reports and recommendations to Congress.

3. Power to promulgate interpretative rules, policy statements and regulations defining particular acceptable or unacceptable acts or practices.

4. Enforcement—FTC issues cease and desist orders. Violators may be subject to fines of $10,000 per day.

II. Activities prohibited by the Clayton Act as amended—See Chapter 50 herein.

III. Sanctions and remedies under the antitrust acts.

A. Sherman Act—See Chapter 50 herein.

B. Clayton Act.

1. Criminal sanctions—If a corporation is found guilty of violation of a criminal provision, the officers, directors and agents, who have authorized or committed the unlawful act, are subject to imprisonment and/or fine (Sec. 14).

2. Government initiated civil cases.

a. FTC may issue cease and desist orders.

b. The government may bring actions for divestiture, dissolution or divorcement.

c. The U.S. may recover actual damages for injuries resulting from violations.

3. Private civil remedies.

a. A civil action may be brought in order to recover damages (Sec. 4).

b. Equitable relief may be granted if damages are inadequate and "danger or irreparable loss is immediate" (Sec. 16).

c. A final judgment or decree rendered in a litigated criminal or civil action brought by the U.S. is *prima facie* evidence of violation of the Act (Sec. 5).

IV. Activities regulated and/or investigated by the FTC—Maintaining competition, consumer protection and other economic activities.

A. Energy and the oil industry.

B. Food.

C. Transportation.

D. Health care.

E. Horizontal combinations and restraints of trade, involving competitors in the same market.

   1. Horizontal mergers.

      a. In determining whether or not a merger will tend to result in anticompetitive effects, the FTC relies upon the degree of existing and potential concentration (market shares) of the merging firms, as well as the capital requirements and economies of scale in the industry.

      b. In addition, courts examine the effect of the merger on potential collusion, entry into the market and increases in efficiency, which will result in benefit to consumers.

   2. Horizontal restraints—Practices and conduct restricting competition.

      a. Traditional methods—Price fixing, allocating markets and boycotts.

      b. Hidden methods—Examples include:
        1) Exchange of information.
        2) Dissemination of information by trade association.
        3) Provisions in shopping center leases giving major tenant the right to disapprove prospective tenant.

F. Vertical combinations and restraints of trade involve control over firms in industries at successive stages in production and/or distribution.

   1. Vertical mergers may result in restrictions in supply of resources or inputs to competitors (backward acquisitions) or blocking or foreclosing competitors from part of a market for the product or service.

      a. Such vertical combinations result in barriers to entry into the industry itself or the market and sale of a product.

      b. Factors considered by the FTC and courts include definitions of the relevant product (and the amount of product differentiation), the degree of concentration and the market for the product.

   2. Vertical restraints—Practices and conduct restricting competition.

      a. Long term requirements and output contracts.

      b. Territorial and customer restrictions.

      c. Price fixing.

      d. Tying requirements in contracts.

      e. Reciprocal buying arrangements.

G. Conglomerate mergers which increase the diversification of multi-product or multi-industry firm.

    1. It is often difficult to measure latent changes in market structure, firms' market shares and concentration ratios.

    2. Potential exists for offsetting a loss in one product (caused possibly by price cutting or extensive advertising to drive out competitors) by profitable operations in other products.

H. Industry wide conditions may be investigated by the FTC in order to identify reasons for reduced performance, evidenced by high prices and profits, lack of product innovation or absence of entry by new firms.

FILL-IN QUESTIONS

1. With regard to its authority to enforce the provisions of the antitrust laws, the Federal Trade Commission has power to issue _____ orders. It also has power to _____.

2. The term, monopolize, is not defined in the antitrust laws. Any person, however, who _____ violates Section 2 of the Sherman Act. The Clayton Act prohibits certain monopolistic practices, such as _____ _____ when the effect might be to reduce competition or tend to create a monopoly, and interlocking directorates.

3. A and B Corporations both manufacture the same product and are planning to merge. The merger will be a _____ merger or combination. If the effect of the merger will be _____, it is prohibited by the antitrust laws.

4. C Corporation manufactures a particular product, which is sold by D Corporation in its chain of retail stores. C and D Corporations enter into a contract providing that C will supply all of D's requirements for 20 years and will not sell the product to stores, with which D competes, and D agrees that it will sell the product at a price to be determined by C. This is _____ restraint of trade.

MULTIPLE CHOICE QUESTIONS

1. P Corp., a large national manufacturer of paper products, acquires more than 50% of the outstanding shares of common stock of L Co., a national producer of paper. P Corp. had previously purchased its paper needs from competitors of L Co. but now obtains all of its requirements from L Co. alone.
    a. The acquisition of the stock of L Co. does not violate the Clayton Act because it was not a purchase of the assets of L Co.
    b. Competitors of L Co. have standing to sue P Corp. under the Clayton Act and may recover damages for the actual harm incurred.
    c. Competitors of P Corp. have standing to sue P Corp. under the Clayton Act and may recover treble damages.

d. This is an example of a horizontal combination, which is prohibited by the Clayton Act.

Questions 2, 3 and 4 are based on the following data:

	Alpha Industry				Beta Industry		
Firm	% of sales revenue	Minimum efficient scale as a % of the total market	Capital required for minimum efficient scale, in millions	Firm	% of sales revenue	Minimum efficient scale as a % of the total market	Capital required for minimum efficient scale, in millions
1	40	20	$100	1	15	2.5	$ 2
2	20	5	70	2	15	2.5	2
3	20	5	70	3	15	2.0	3
4	10	2	50	4	15	2.0	3
5	10	2	55	5	10	1.0	2
				6	10	1.0	2
				7	10	1.0	2
				8	10	0.5	2
5	100%	34%	$345	8	100%	12.5%	$18

2. A consolidation is being considered by firms 4 and 5 in Alpha industry.
    a. A consolidation is different than a merger and is not within the purview of the Clayton Act.
    b. Firm 3 cannot bring an action in order to obtain an injunction.
    c. The FTC will issue a cease and desist order because the consolidation will reduce competition in the industry, even though firms 3 and 4 will be forced out of the industry if they do not consolidate.
    d. The FTC may not issue a cease and desist order, even though the consolidation will result in fewer firms in the industry, if it is established that firms 3 and 4 will be forced out of the industry if they do not consolidate.

3. Which of the following statements is *incorrect*?
    a. The opportunity for collusion is greater in Alpha industry than it is in Beta industry.
    b. The degree of concentration is higher in Beta industry than it is in Alpha industry.
    c. A new firm will be more likely to enter Beta industry than Alpha industry.
    d. Firm 1 in Alpha industry has a more dominant position than firms 1 and 2 combined in Beta industry.

4. Assume that there is no evidence of direct agreement among the firms in Beta industry but that they all charge the same price. They are being prosecuted by the U.S. Department of Justice. The prosecution will:
    a. not be successful because there is no evidence of a conspiracy.
    b. be successful because the fact that they all charge a uniform price is sufficient evidence of a conspiracy.

c. be successful because proof of evidence of a conspiracy may be implied from the fact that the firms simultaneously had changed their previously varying prices to the uniform price.

d. none of the above.

5. An agreement between a manufacturer of gidgets and a wholesaler dealer not to sell any parts used to repair the gidgets to a particular retail seller is an illegal:
    a. joint boycott or tying contract.
    b. exclusive dealings and tying contract.
    c. vertical price fixing agreement.
    d. monopolization.

6. An agreement between a manufacturer of photocopy machines and a lessee, to whom the manufacturer leases a machine, whereby the lessee agrees not to purchase its paper from any supplier other than the machine lessor, is an example of:
    a. a joint boycott and price fixing contract.
    b. price fixing and an exclusive dealings contract.
    c. exclusive dealings or tying contract.
    d. a fair trade agreement.

UNIT IX

Protection of Property and Other Interests

The concept of property was introduced in Unit III. As you will recall, property refers to the collection of rights and interests associated with ownership of things. Traditionally, real property (rights and interests relating to land and those things growing on the land or affixed to it or contained above or below it) has been accorded special status by the law. The nature of real property, the various forms of present possessory ownership interests that may exist in such property and the manner of its transfer are discussed in Chapter 52. Topics dealing with present and future non-possessory interests in and restrictions on the use of land are presented in Chapter 53.

Chapter 55 deals with transfers of ownership interests in real and personal property by the creation of trusts and, upon death, by will or in accordance with inheritance statutes.

Owners and others, having interests in real and personal property, will incur financial or economic loss if their property is destroyed or damaged. In such case, in order to provide funds so that their property can be replaced, they may obtain insurance, the subject matter of Chapter 54. Other forms of insurance, such as life insurance, are also covered in Chapter 54.

52

Nature and Ownership of
Real Property

Real property refers to rights associated with ownership or possessory interests in land and things of a permanent nature growing on or affixed to the land or contained above or below the surface. The material in this chapter is concerned with the nature of real property, the types of ownership interest in land and the manner in which they may be acquired or transferred.

THINGS TO KEEP IN MIND

The rights to possession and enjoyment of land are protected by law. Typically, if there is an interference with the use and enjoyment of real property, a tort action may be brought based on trespass. If one has acquired title to real property by conveyance and there is a defect in the title, the transferee may sue the grantor because of a breach of a convenant or a warranty contained in the deed.

OUTLINE

I.   Nature of real property.

   A. The land, or soil itself, waters contained on the land, natural and artificial structures attached to it and plant life and vegetation growing on it.

   B. Subsurface and air rights.

      1. Today one has rights to the air immediately above the land sufficient to have a cause of action, based upon trespass, for a direct interference with the use and enjoyment of the land.

2. A property owner has the exclusive right to minerals, oil and other matter found beneath the surface, but may transfer this right to another.

C. Plant life and vegetation—Includes trees, natural vegetation and crops. (See Chapter 17.)

D. Fixtures—Personal property affixed to real property.

    1. May be agricultural, domestic or trade fixture, which is permanently attached to real property.

    2. Objective intention of the party, who placed the item, determines whether or not the item is a fixture.

    3. Trade fixtures.

        a. Items attached to rented premises by a tenant (who pursues a trade or business) in connection with the business, are treated as personal property of the tenant and usually intended to be removed by the tenant. If their removal causes harm to the premises, the tenant is required to reimburse the landlord.

        b. If fixtures are not trade fixtures, they are usually treated as part of the real property and are not removable by a tenant.

II. Ownership interests in real property—Estates in land.

A. Estates are collections of rights associated with ownership.

B. Freehold estates—Estates for indefinite time (possessory interests in land).

    1. Estates in fee—Transferable during owner's lifetime or as an inheritance.

        a. Fee simple absolute—The owner possesses all the rights one may possess in land, which may be conveyed or inherited.

        b. Fee simple defeasible—A fee that may be divested or terminated upon the happening of some specified event. If the event occurs, the property reverts to the grantor or to a named person.

    2. Life estates—Duration is measured by the life of one or more persons.

        a. May be measured by the life of a person, to whom the estate is given, or the life of another person.

        b. It may not be inherited but may be conveyed during the lifetime of the person by whose life it is measured.

        c. A life tenant has the right to possess, use and convey his or her specific interest in the property, and an obligation to pay taxes, make repairs and not commit waste (cause an impairment to the value of the land).

    d. May be created by voluntary acts of the parties or by operation of law (marital interests). See Chapter 55.

C. Estates less than freehold—Leaseholds that exist for a determinable period of time in accordance with a contract of lease.

  1. Tenancy for a specified term.

    a. Usually a lease is for a specified number of years.

    b. Notice of termination at the end of the term is not necessary.

    c. If the tenant dies, the rights under the lease are treated as part of the decedent's personal property.

    d. Statutes may require that lease be in writing in order to be enforceable.

  2. Tenancy from period to period.

    a. Created by contracting to pay rent periodically without stating the duration of the lease or by tenant holding over after expiration of a lease for a specified term.

    b. Terminated after giving one period's notice or as provided by statute.

  3. Tenancy at will—Terminated upon death or, at common law, the will of either party, or after giving such notice as is required by statute.

  4. Tenancy by sufferance—Wrongful possession of land without the right to so possess.

III. Relationship of landlord and tenant.

A. Landlord's duties and warranties (implied covenants).

  1. Landlord covenants that he or she has the right to possession of the interest he or she is transferring to the tenant.

  2. Landlord covenants that the tenant will have quiet enjoyment.

    a. Landlord will not evict or dispossess tenant from the premises.

    b. Landlord will not interfere with the tenant's right to use and possess premises. If landlord interferes with the tenant's rights, it is a constructive eviction.

  3. Landlord generally has duty to make repairs and necessary improvements, warn tenant of latent defects and pay taxes.

B. Duties owed by the tenant.

      1. Pay agreed rent or, if none is provided for, reasonable rent.

      2. Make normal repairs.

      3. Not use premises so as to injure others.

C. Transfer by tenant of his or her interest by assignment or sublease.

      1. If a tenant makes an assignment of all the remaining rights under the terms of the lease, the assignee assumes the tenant's obligations. If the assignee fails to pay the rent, the original tenant is liable for payment of the rent to the landlord.

      2. If a tenant transfers less than all the remaining rights, the transferee is liable to the tenant and the tenant remains liable to the landlord. This is referred to as a sublease.

      3. A lease may prohibit assignment or subleasing.

D. Termination of a lease and the obligation to pay rent.

      1. Expiration of stated term or in accordance with a provision of the lease.

      2. Actual or constructive eviction.

      3. Destruction of the premises when lease does not cover all of the property.

      4. Surrender of premises by the tenant and acceptance of the surrender by the landlord.

IV. Concurrent ownership—Property may be held by two or more people simultaneously, rather than individually.

A. Tenancy in common—Two or more persons own undivided shares, which may be unequal, in property, transferable during lifetime or by inheritance, without rights of survivorship among the co-tenants.

B. Joint tenancy—Two or more persons own equal undivided shares of an entire estate, which they acquire simultaneously, and have equal rights of enjoyment and rights of survivorship.

      1. The transferor must have clearly indicated an intention to create a joint tenancy.

      2. A joint tenant may sever and transfer his or her interest during his or her lifetime.

C. Tenancy by the entirety—A joint tenancy existing between spouses, which cannot be severed by either without the consent of the other spouse.

D. Condominium ownership—Each owner owns the unit that he or she occupies and is a tenant in common with others with respect to common areas.

V. Transfer of ownership.

A. Conveyance by deed.

1. In order to transfer an interest in land by sale or gift, a conveyance is made by delivery of an instrument called a deed.

   a. Signed by the grantor (the person conveying the real property).

   b. States the names of the grantor (seller or donor) and the grantee (buyer or donee).

   c. Describes the property and the interest conveyed.

   d. Indicates the grantor's intention to make a present transfer of title to real property.

2. Covenants of title that may be included in a deed.

   a. Seizen—Grantor has title and the right to convey the particular estate.

   b. Against encumbrances—The property is not subject to any outstanding rights which would diminish the value of the land.

   c. Quiet enjoyment—No one has a superior title and no one will disturb possession.

3. Types of deeds.

   a. General warranty deed—Includes all covenants.

   b. Special warranty deed—Includes all covenants but warrants only against defects in title arising when the grantor had title.

   c. Quitclaim deed—No covenants are included. Transfer of only that title that the grantor had.

4. Recording the deed—The grantor acknowledges that he signed the deed before a notary public. The deed is then recorded (usually in the county). Recording gives notice to the whole world that the grantee is the owner.

5. Sale of real estate—Usual way in which real property is transferred.

   a. A sale may be accomplished through a broker.

   b. Contract of sale—Required by the statute of frauds to be in writing in order to be enforceable. (See Chapter 11.)

    c. Title examination or search in order to determine if the grantor has a marketable title.

    d. Obtaining a mortgage—Lien given as security to a lender, from whom money is being borrowed in order to purchase property. (A mortgage may also be given as security for a loan of money for other purposes.)

    e. The closing, at which the deed is delivered by the seller and the purchase price paid by the buyer.

B. Will or inheritance. See Chapter 55.

C. Eminent domain—Government takes property for public use and compensates the owner by paying the fair value.

D. Adverse possession—One in actual, open, exclusive, continuous, hostile possession of real property for a statutory period of time acquires title to the property.

FILL-IN QUESTIONS

1. Real property includes rights associated with land and things of a permanent nature _____ .

2. Fixtures are items that are personal property until they are _____ _____ . If such items are affixed to a business premises by a tenant with the understanding that they may be removed, they are referred to as _____ .

3. Ownership interests in land are referred to as _____ , which may be for an indefinite period of time, in which case they are called _____ , or may be for determinable periods, in which case they are _____ .

4. If a tenant makes an assignment of his or her rights under a lease, the assignee pays rent to the _____ ; if the tenant subleases his or her rights, the sublessee pays rent to the _____ . In either event, if the assignee or sublessee fails to pay the rent, the _____ is liable for the unpaid rent to the landlord.

5. If A and B concurrently own equal undivided shares of an entire estate in real property, they will be considered to be _____ only if the grantor clearly indicated an intention to create such a tenancy. Upon A's death, his interest passes to _____ . If A and B are spouses, they will be considered as having a _____ .

6. A _____ is created when two or more persons own undivided shares of an entire estate in real property, which may not be equal, and which may be transferred separately during the lifetimes of the co-tenants and, upon death of a co-tenant, by will or inheritance. A surviving co-tenant has no rights to a deceased co-tenant's interest in the property.

7. Real property may be transferred by the owner during his or her lifetime by _____ _____. If the grantor is transferring merely the interest, which he or she had, the document of conveyance is called a _____ deed. It is used frequently to remove _____ in the title to the property.

MULTIPLE CHOICE QUESTIONS

Unless otherwise indicated, assume that there are no relevant statutes and that common law rules are applicable.

Questions 1 and 2 are based upon the following fact situation: Tennent leased a building under a five year written lease at a monthly rental of $600. The premises were used as a restaurant and Tennent, therefore, installed an air conditioning system, a counter and stools. Six months after the commencement of the lease, the landlord turned off the water and has since refused to reconnect the water pipes. Tennent moved out and wishes to remove the counter and stools without damage to the premises and the air conditioning system, which will inflict considerable damage to the premises.

1. By turning off the water, the landlord has:
   a. violated the implied terms of the year-to-year lease.
   b. actually evicted Tennent by breaching the covenant of possession.
   c. constructively evicted Tennent by breaching the covenant of quiet enjoyment.
   d. not terminated the lease and has a right to receive the monthly rent of $600 from Tennent.

2. The counter, stools and air conditioning system are:
   a. part of the real property and their removal by Tennent is wrongful.
   b. fixtures. They became part of the real property and can be removed only by the owner of the premises.
   c. trade fixtures. Tennent may remove the counter and stools because their removal does not damage the premises but he may not remove the air conditioning system.
   d. trade fixtures. Tennent may remove the counter, stools and air conditioning system but will be required to reimburse the landlord for damage caused by the removal of the air conditioning.

3. In January, Great Records Inc. rented a store in a building from Hamilton Realty Corp. under a three year written lease at a rental of $1,000 per month. Great Records Inc. operated a record store on the premises. In May, the structure was badly damaged, when a helicopter lost one of its rotors and crashed into the building. The record store cannot be used without substantial repairs. If Great Records Inc. leased:
   a. only the store, the lease is terminated and Great Records Inc. need not continue to pay rent.
   b. only the store, the lease is not terminated until the expiration of the three year period.
   c. the entire building, the lease is terminated and Great Records Inc. need not continue to pay rent.

    d. the entire building, Great Records Inc. will be required to make the necessary repairs and Great Records Inc., but not Hamilton Realty Corp., may recover damages from the operator of the helicopter.

4. The greatest ownership interest a person may have in real property is a:
    a. fee simple absolute.
    b. fee simple defeasible.
    c. tenancy by the entirety.
    d. less than freehold estate.

5. Jacob's land was sold to pay his delinquent taxes. The purchaser at the sheriff's sale would acquire title by:
    a. adverse possession.
    b. full warranty deed.
    c. right of eminent domain.
    d. none of the above.

6. Margaret owned real property in fee simple absolute. She made a conveyance to Ann and Betty, with rights of survivorship, as long as the land was used for agricultural purposes.
    a. Ann and Betty are tenants in common of a fee simple absolute.
    b. Ann and Betty are joint tenants of a fee simple defeasible.
    c. If Ann dies, her interest in the property passes in accordance with her will.
    d. If Ann and Betty use the property for industrial purposes, Margaret's remedy is to sue for breach of warranty.

Future Interests,
Nonpossessory Interests,
and Land Use Control

You are now familiar with some of the legal concepts associated with present possessory interests in land. Nonpossessory interests may also be created. For example, the right to possession of real property may be deferred. If so, one may have a future interest in the property—a reversion, possibility of reverter, power of termination, remainder or executory interest—the subject matter of the first section in this chapter. It is also possible to grant nonpossessory interests or rights to other persons in the form of easements, profits and licenses, all of which may restrict the present and future rights of owners of land.

As indicated in the latter section of the chapter, additional limitations on the use of land may be imposed, privately with restrictive covenants (in conveyances) and equitable servitudes (in separate, recorded agreements), and by state zoning statutes or local zoning ordinances.

THINGS TO KEEP IN MIND

The terminology and concepts used and explained in this chapter are probably unfamiliar to most readers. For this reason, it may be necessary to devote considerable time to studying this topic in order to gain understanding of the relevant legal principles. A number of fill-in questions are provided, with which you can test your comprehension of the concepts and terminology used in Chapters 52 and 53.

OUTLINE

I. Future interests—A present, existing right to have possession of real property, after the termination of a preceding estate.

A. Reversionary interests and powers of termination.

   1. Arise when a grantor makes a conveyance of less than all his or her interests without disposing of the residue.

   2. The owner of the reversionary interest may transfer the future interest during his or her lifetime.

   3. Upon the death of the owner of the reversionary interest, the interest vests in his or her heirs or devisees, named in the grantor's will (if it has not been otherwise disposed of during his or her lifetime).

   4. Reversion.

      a. The interest retained by a grantor, who transfers a life estate to another, without making a disposition of the interest remaining after the death of the person, who is the measuring life.

      b. A reversion is a vested future interest.

   5. Possibility of reverter.

      a. The interest retained by a grantor, who has conveyed a fee simple determinable.

      b. It is contingent upon the happening of the event specified in the conveyance, which terminates the grantee's interest automatically.

   6. Power of termination.

      a. The interest retained by a grantor, who has conveyed a fee simple subject to a condition subsequent, which is not automatically terminated upon the happening of the condition.

      b. The grantor (or his or her heirs or devisees) must affirmatively exercise his or her right of entry.

B. Remainders and executory interests.

   1. Created by the same instrument that conveyed a present possessory interest.

   2. May be conveyed and inherited.

   3. Vested remainder—An absolute right to possession, existing at the end of a prior life estate or leasehold.

   4. Contingent remainder—The right to possession depends upon the termination of a preceding estate and the occurrence of a contingency or the existence and identification of some person.

5. Executory interest—The right to possession takes effect either before the natural termination of a preceding estate, upon the happening of some contingency (a shifting executory interest), or after the termination of the preceding estate (a springing executory interest).

C. The rule against perpetuities.

1. Purpose of rule is to prevent remoteness in vesting of interests in property.

2. Any interest in real property, created by deed, will or otherwise, is void unless it must vest within a life (or lives) in being plus 21 years plus the period of gestation.

3. Some modifications of the rule have been made in some states.

II. Nonpossessory interests.

A. Easements and profits.

1. Easement—The limited right to make use of property of another without taking anything from it.

2. Profit—The limited right to go onto the property of another and remove something from it.

3. Easement (or profit) appurtenant—The right to go onto and/or remove something from the land of another (the subservient parcel), which is created for the benefit of the owner of an adjacent parcel of land (the dominant parcel).

   a. If the dominant parcel is sold, the easement may also be transferred.

   b. If the easement is recorded, a subsequent owner of the subservient parcel must recognize the easement or profit.

4. Easement (or profit) in gross—The right to use or remove something from the land of another (which need not be adjacent to the property of the party given the right) for a specific personal or commercial purpose.

5. Creation of an easement or profit.

   a. By deed or will.

   b. By implication, when circumstances surrounding a division of property infer the creation of an easement (or profit) and the use of the property is apparent, necessary and continuous.

   c. By necessity, when circumstances, other than a division of property, are such that it is clearly necessary that one person use another's property.

d. By prescription, when one person, without permission, openly, adversely, notoriously and continually uses or takes something from the land of another for the period of time provided by statute.

6. Termination of easement (or profit) may be by:

   a. Deed, expiration of agreed duration or fulfillment of the purpose for which the easement (or profit) was created.

   b. Intentional abandonment.

   c. Merger of the dominant and subservient parcels.

   d. Destruction of the subservient property.

   e. Prescription, when the owner of the subservient property prevents the use of the easement (or profit) for a statutory period.

B. License—Revocable, nontransferable right to use property of another with consent, created by contract.

III. Land use control—Limitations placed upon property owners' rights to use or convey property.

A. Private agreements.

1. Restrictive covenant running with the land—An agreement made by an owner of land which binds subsequent owners of the land to a restriction or limitation on some ownership right. Requisites:

   a. Written agreement, usually contained in a conveyance.

   b. Clear intention that the covenant is to bind subsequent owners. Use of words, "successors, heirs and assigns" is usually sufficient.

   c. The subject matter of the covenant has some connection with the land.

   d. The original parties were in privity of estate at the time the covenant was created.

2. Equitable servitude.

   a. A restriction on some ownership right, created by a written instrument, other than a conveyance.

   b. Constructive notice of the restriction is given by recording.

3. Restrictive covenants and equitable servitudes, which provide for discrimination, are unconstitutional and prohibited by statute, and will not be enforced.

B. Zoning.

1. State and local control of land use may be effected by exercises of the power of eminent domain (requiring payment of compensation for the taking of property) or the police power, in order to protect the public health, safety, morals and general welfare (without payment of compensation).

2. Limitations on the power of the states to restrict land use.

   a. If regulation is confiscatory, compensation must be paid to the owner.

   b. If a restriction is arbitrary, unreasonable, discriminatory or without a rational basis, it will be deemed to be a taking of property without due process or a denial of the equal protections of the laws, which are prohibited by the Fourteenth Amendment.

3. Existing nonconforming uses will be permitted for a reasonable period of time.

4. Floating zones—The amount of land designated for a particular purpose is determined initially but none of the land is preassigned.

5. Variances.

   a. Obtained by owner, whose use of land is limited by existing zoning regulation, in order to use it for an alternative purpose.

   b. Granted upon showing:
      1) As zoned, the land will not produce a reasonable return.
      2) Adverse effect of zoning is peculiar to the applicant rather than all land owners in the zone.
      3) Variance will not substantially alter the essential character of the zoned area.

FILL-IN QUESTIONS

1. A future interest is not created if a grantor makes a conveyance in fee _____ _____.

2. If a grantor conveys a fee simple determinable, the estate terminates automatically upon the happening of some event and possession of the property will revert to the grantor, who has retained a _____ or pass to another person, to whom the grantor gave a _____.

3. A _____ is created in the same instrument by which a grantor conveys a fee simple determinable.

4. If a grantor conveys a fee simple determinable, without naming a remainderman, the grantor may subsequently transfer his or her future interest to another person.

The transferee will then be the owner of the _____. If the grantor does not transfer the future interest during his or her lifetime, it passes to the grantor's heirs or devisees, who will then be the owners of the _____.

5. A possibility of reverter and _____ may never vest, if the conditioning event, which terminates the fee simple determinable, does not occur.

6. Upon the death of the person, whose life determines or measures a life estate, the possessory interest reverts to the grantor, who has a vested interest, which is referred to as a _____, or passes to another person, to whom the grantor gave a _____ when he or she conveyed the life estate.

7. If a grantor conveys a life estate, without naming a remainderman, the grantor may subsequently transfer his or her future reversionary interest to another person. The transferee will then be the owner of _____. If a grantor does not transfer his or her reversionary interest during his or her lifetime, it passes to the grantor's heirs or devisees, who will then be the owners of the _____.

8. A _____ is created in the same instrument by which a grantor conveys a life estate.

9. A conveyance of a fee simple, subject to a condition subsequent, does not terminate automatically upon the happening of the conditioning event. The grantor of such an estate retains a _____, which he or she must affirmatively exercise, or the person, to whom the grantor has given _____ must exercise his or her right to possession.

10. The right to use property of another in a specified manner, without removing anything from it, is referred to as _____. The right to go onto the property of another and remove something from it is called _____. These rights are _____ interests in land and may be given to owners of adjacent property, in which case they are called _____.

11. A grantor may restrict the right to use or further transfer land by making a conveyance containing _____. The use or right to make future transfers of land may also be restricted by recording a separate instrument. This is referred to as _____.

MULTIPLE CHOICE QUESTIONS

Questions 1 and 2 are based on the following fact situation: Teasdale had no living relatives but died leaving a will, by which he granted a life estate to certain real property to McCormick, with remainder to Nesbett and Owens, as joint tenants with right of survivorship.

1. The following statement is true:
    a. McCormick has a present possessory freehold interest.
    b. McCormick may neither transfer his interest during his lifetime nor, upon his death, by will.

   c. The gift to McCormick will fail because the devise to McCormick violates the rule against perpetuities. ·
   d. As a life tenant, McCormick has the right to remove improvements and mineral deposits from the land.

2. With regard to Nesbett and Owens:
   a. during the lifetime of McCormick, their interests are not subject to being inherited.
   b. during the lifetime of McCormick, their interests may not be transferred.
   c. they have vested remainders.
   d. they are tenants in common.

3. Abrams owned 100 acres of land, only ten of which bordered on a road. Abrams sold and conveyed 25 acres to Bennett and, because the 25 acres did not border on any road, granted the right to Bennett, in his deed, to go over a described strip of his (Abrams') land in order to reach Bennett's land.
   a. Bennett has an easement by prescription.
   b. If Bennett later conveys the land to Calahan, Calahan does not have the right to go over Abrams' land.
   c. Bennett has an easement in gross.
   d. Bennett has an appurtenant easement.

4. A municipal ordinance requiring that pet animals be restrained from leaving their owners' property is:
   a. unconstitutional because it interferes with an owner's rights with respect to his real property.
   b. not a valid exercise of governmental power because an owner of property has an absolute right to use his own property.
   c. a valid interference with owners' rights with respect to property.
   d. an invalid interference with the use of both personal and real property.

Insurance

The objective of insurance is to transfer and allocate risk—an existing contingency, over which one has little control, but which will result in an economic loss. In order to obtain insurance, one enters into a particular kind of contract, called an insurance policy. For it to be valid and enforceable, all the requisites of a contract must be present and, in addition, the person obtaining the insurance must have an insurable interest in the subject matter (life, health or property) which is insured.

The first part of the chapter is devoted to general principles of insurance law. Characteristics of particular types of insurance are discussed in the last segment of the material.

THINGS TO KEEP IN MIND

Insurance companies, insurance agents and brokers, the contents of insurance policies, the rates charged as premiums, etc., are subject to regulation by the several states.

OUTLINE

I. The nature of insurance.

    A. Terminology.

        1. Policy—Instrument by which a contract of insurance is made.

        2. Parties.

            a. Insurer—Insurance company which issues a policy.

    b. Insured—The person obtaining property insurance or the person, whose life is insured under the terms of a life insurance policy.

    c. Insurance agent—Employed by the insurer, for which he or she is an agent. (See Chapters 33 through 35.)

    d. Insurance broker—An independent contractor, who is treated as an agent for the person for whom he or she is obtaining insurance, except when otherwise provided by state statute.

3. Premium—The consideration paid to the insurer by the party obtaining insurance.

4. Insurable interest—A legal or equitable interest in the subject matter of insurance (a life or property), such that one will benefit from its preservation or incur a direct, pecuniary or monetary loss if it is destroyed or damaged.

    a. Property (real or personal) insurance.
      1) An insurable interest must exist at the time of the loss insured against.
      2) The following people have insurable interests in property—owners, including life tenants, joint tenants, tenants in common and remaindermen, lessees, mortgagees, bailees, pledgees, trustees and buyers and sellers, who have made executory contracts for the sale of property.

    b. Life insurance.
      1) An insurable interest must exist at the time the policy is obtained.
      2) Every person has an insurable interest in his or her own life.
      3) A spouse, child or parent has an insurable interest in the life of his or her spouse, parent or child.
      4) A creditor has an insurable interest in the life of a debtor.
      5) Partners have insurable interests in the lives of co-partners.
      6) Business units have insurable interests in the lives of "key" personnel.
      7) A beneficiary or assignee need not have an insurable interest in the life of the person whose life is insured.

B. The insurance contract.

1. General principles of contract law are applicable.

2. When an insurance policy is effective.

    a. Application made to an insurance broker—Customer is not insured until the broker procures a policy.

    b. Application made to an agent of an insurer.
      1) Life insurance—Insurance is effective after application is accepted

and premium is paid. A binder may result in earlier coverage upon payment of a premium.

    2) Property insurance is effective when agreement is reached as to coverage. A binder may be given.

3. Interpretation of provisions when terms of policy are ambiguous.

    a. Words are given their ordinary meaning unless it is clear that a technical or unusual meaning has been intended.

    b. Provisions are interpreted most strongly against the insurer which prepared the contract.

C. Insurance contract clauses.

    1. Subrogation.

        a. If an insurer of property pays an insured for a loss, caused by another's intentional or negligent act, it is subrogated to (or "stands in the shoes" of) the insured.

        b. An insurer has no right of subrogation against a third person, who caused the death of one covered by life insurance.

    2. Multiple insurance coverage ("other insurance," "*pro rata*," etc., clauses)—If there are multiple policies covering the same property or health risk, the loss is apportioned among the several insurers.

D. Cancellation of insurance policies—Written notice must be given.

    1. Property insurance may be cancelled by either party upon giving required notice.

    2. Life insurance.

        a. Most policies contain provisions for grace periods, during which delinquent payments can be made in order to prevent lapse of insurance coverage.

        b. Statutes often require that a smaller paid up policy be issued or extended insurance coverage be given or the cash surrender value be paid to the owner of the policy.

E. Payment by an insurer may be denied or a policy rescinded.

    1. Failure to comply with reasonable requirements as to notice and proof of loss.

    2. Acts that are illegal or against public policy.

    3. Lack of insurable interest.

4. Policy procured through use of fraud, misrepresentation, etc.

5. An insurance company may not contest or refuse payment, after a stated period of time, if the insurance policy contained an incontestability clause.

II. Types of insurance.

A. Life insurance.

1. Term insurance—Provides temporary coverage during a stated period, but may be renewable after the period or convertible into whole life insurance. Does not have savings features.

a. Level term insurance.

b. Decreasing term insurance.

c. Mortgage term insurance.

2. Whole (straight) life insurance—Stated premiums are paid during lifetime of the insured.

a. Investment feature—Cash value increases over time and may be borrowed.

b. May provide for retirement income (annuity or living benefit program).

3. Death benefits—Distribution of proceeds options.

4. Other types of life insurance.

a. Limited payment whole life insurance.

b. Endowment policies.

B. Home, property and liability insurance.

1. Standard fire insurance policy.

2. Homeowner's policy with property and liability coverage.

3. Floater policies.

4. Coinsurance clauses—The insured is required to insure property at a stated percent of its full replacement value in order to recover the face amount of the policy or the replacement cost when there has been a partial loss.

$$\text{Loss} \times \frac{\text{Amount of insurance carried}}{\substack{\text{Amount of insurance required} \\ (\% \times \text{replacement value})}} = \text{Amount of recovery}$$

C. Automobile insurance.

1. Insurance to cover liability for property damage and bodily injury to others.

2. Collision insurance covers damage to the insured's auto.

3. Comprehensive insurance covers loss, damage and destruction caused by fire, hurricane, hail and vandalism.

4. Other forms of coverage.

    a. Uninsured motorists.

    b. Accidental death benefits.

    c. Medical payments.

    d. No-fault auto insurance.

D. Accident and health insurance.

1. Hospital expenses.

2. Surgical expenses.

3. Regular medical protection.

4. Major medical insurance.

5. Dental insurance.

6. Disability for income earners and/or homemakers.

7. Workmen's compensation insurance.

FILL-IN QUESTIONS

1. In general, wagering bargains are illegal, because they are agreements based upon _____ risks, and are distinguishable from contracts of insurance, which provide for _____ existing risks.

2. With regard to property insurance, any person, who has a legal or equitable interest in real or personal property, is treated as having an _____ interest because he or she will benefit if the property is not damaged or destroyed or will _____.

3. In order to recover under a policy providing for property insurance, the insured must have an _____ interest at the time that _____.

4. With regard to life insurance, the owner of a life insurance policy must have an _____ interest in the life of the person whose life is insured. One can

obtain a life insurance policy covering his or her own life or the life of another if he or she will benefit economically from the continued life of the person whose life is insured or will _____ .

5.   In order to recover under a life insurance policy, the owner of the policy must have had an _____ interest at the time _____ .

MULTIPLE CHOICE QUESTIONS

1.   John, an insured, is fifty years of age. In applying for life insurance, he misstated his age as being 47. The amount of insurance on his life will be adjusted to the sum that the premiums paid by John would have purchased:
      a. at age 47.
      b. at age 50.
      c. at a reasonable age.
      d. at no age because the policy is unenforceable.

2.   Carol and Nan were business partners. They agreed that each would insure the life of the other for her own benefit. On the application for insurance, Nan stated that she had never had any heart trouble. She had, in fact, suffered a heart attack three years before. Carol's policy on Nan's life contained the usual two year incontestability clause. Four years later, after the dissolution of the partnership but while the policy on her life was still in force, Nan was killed when struck by a car driven by Marcia.
      a. Carol cannot recover from the insurer because of the misrepresentation in the application.
      b. Carol cannot recover because the partnership has been dissolved and she, therefore, lacks an insurable interest.
      c. Carol can recover if the insurance company refuses to pay the proceeds of the life insurance on Nan's life to her.
      d. If the insurance company has to pay Nan the proceeds of the life insurance on Nan's life to Carol, it will be subrogated to Nan's rights against Marcia.

3.   An insurance company paid Zandarski for a loss due to fire. The insurance company has a right to recover from Frazer, who caused the fire. Such right is known as:
      a. insurable interest.
      b. subrogation.
      c. subordination.
      d. contribution.

4.   The Smart Corp. obtained a fire insurance policy on its factory from the ABC Insurance Company. The policy was for $500,000 which was the value of the property insured. The policy was the standard fire insurance policy sold in the United States. A fire occurred and resulted in a $100,000 loss. Which of the following will prevent Smart Corp. from recovering the full amount of its loss from the insurance company?
      a. The coinsurance clause.
      b. Smart Corp. had a similar policy with another company for $300,000.

c. $200,000 worth of the loss was caused by smoke and water damage.

d. Smart Corp. did not notify ABC Insurance Company of the fire until the day after the fire.

Questions 5 and 6 are based on the following fact situation: Young was the owner of a warehouse that was insured by the Ivy Fire Insurance Co. The face value of the fire insurance policy was $600,000. The policy covered the warehouse itself and the contents and contained a 90% coinsurance clause. Careless, an employee of Young, negligently dropped a lighted cigarette on some packing material which caught fire.

5. Assume that the fire totally destroyed the warehouse and the goods stored therein and that the loss was subsequently appraised at $1 million. Young is entitled to a payment of:

   a. $600,000, the face amount of the policy, from Ivy Fire Insurance Co. because there was a total loss.

   b. $900,000 from Ivy Fire Insurance Co. because of the coinsurance clause.

   c. $540,000 from Ivy Fire Insurance Co. because of the coinsurance clause.

   d. Nothing because the fire was caused by the negligence of an employee of Young's.

6. Assume that the fire damaged the warehouse and destroyed goods, valued at $100,000. Repairs to the warehouse will cost $80,000. At the time of the fire loss, the replacement value of the warehouse was $900,000.

   a. Young is entitled to a payment of $120,000 because of the coinsurance clause.

   b. Young is entitled to a payment of $162,000 because of the coinsurance clause.

   c. Young is entitled to a payment of $20,000 and the insurance company will be required to pay $100,000 to the people who had stored the goods that were destroyed in the fire.

   d. Young is entitled to a payment of $72,000 from the insurance company. The owners of the goods stored (and destroyed) in the warehouse are entitled to a payment of $90,000 from the insurance company and $10,000 from Young.

Wills, Trust and Estates

As indicated in Chapters 15, 17 and 52, a person may transfer ownership rights with respect to personal and real property by sale or gift during his or her lifetime. A person may also provide for the disposition of his or her property upon his or her death. Compliance with certain formalities, however, is required. All states have inheritance statutes regulating the disposition of decedents' estates by will, by descent and distribution and by establishment of trusts. Some states have adopted the Uniform Probate Act. These topics, as well as the taxation of inheritances and estates, are discussed in this chapter.

THINGS TO KEEP IN MIND

Although the purposes of inheritance laws are similar among the states, the manner in which these objectives are achieved varies. Some states have recently revised their statutes and the legislatures in other jurisdictions are considering revisions.

OUTLINE

I. Wills—Final, formal declaration by persons concerning the manner in which their property is to be disposed of after their death; during one's lifetime, one may change and/or revoke his or her will.

    A. Terminology.

        1. Testator (male) or testatrix (female)—Person who has made a will.

        2. Probate court—Court which administers the law relating to wills and estates of decedents.

3. Executor (male) or executrix (female)—Personal representative, named in a will, to settle the affairs of a decedent.

4. Administrator or administratrix—Personal representative, appointed by a court to settle the affairs of a decedent, who did not leave a will or who left a will but failed to name an executor or named an executor, who is unable or unwilling to serve.

5. Devise—Gift of real property by will. Title vests in devisee.

6. Bequest (legacy)—Gift of personal property by will. Title vests initially in personal representative.

7. Specific devise or bequest—Gift of identified, particular, described property.

8. General devise or bequest—Gift of a quantity of real property or personal property (usually a sum of money) without a specific identification or description of it.

9. Residuary clause—Provision for a disposition of remaining property, not otherwise effectively disposed of by devise and bequest, after payment of decedent's obligations.

B. Testamentary capacity.

1. Age—In most states, 18 is the minimum age for executing a will.

2. "Being of sound mind."

    a. Able to formulate and comprehend a personal plan for the disposition of one's property.

    b. Document intended to be a will.

    c. Not necessarily the same as contractual capacity.

3. Capacity may not exist if will was executed because of fraud (in the inducement or execution), duress, undue influence or mistake.

C. Formal requirements.

1. A will must be in writing.

    a. Holographic will—Handwritten, dated and signed by testator. Some statutes do not require witnessing and publication.

    b. Nuncupative will—A few states permit oral wills under special circumstances.

2. A will must be signed by the testator.

3. A will must be attested by two or more witnesses. Some statutes require that they be disinterested (not benefit from the will), witness the signing of the will by the testator and/or sign in each other's presence.

4. Testator is required to orally declare that the will is his last will and testament in some states (publication).

D. Revocation by act of the testator.

1. Intentional, deliberate burning, tearing, cancellation, obliteration or destruction by the testator or another person, in the presence of and at the direction of the testator, in compliance with statute.

2. Codicil—Separate writing which revokes, amends or supplements a prior will.

   a. Executed with same formality as a will.

   b. Refers to testator's will.

   c. If a codicil, or a later will, does not expressly revoke a prior will, the codicil or later will controls when it is inconsistent with a provision in an earlier will.

E. Revocation by operation of law (varies from state to state)—Subsequent marriage, divorce, annulment, birth or adoption of children.

F. Renunciation of rights under a will.

1. A surviving spouse often has a right to take a statutory marital intestate ("forced") share, rather than take under will of deceased spouse.

2. A beneficiary may renounce a devise or legacy.

II. Statutes of descent and distribution.

A. Provide for inheritance of property by intestate succession if a decedent failed to execute a valid will or omitted a provision for the disposition of some property.

B. Statutory rules vary from state to state.

C. Descent—Real property vests in heirs upon the death of the owner of land.

D. Title to personal property vests in the personal representative of a decedent, who makes distributions in accordance with statute, after paying obligations of the decedent and the estate.

E. General statutory pattern for distribution of decedent's property, if decedent is survived by:

   1. Spouse and no descendants (children, grandchildren, etc.)—Spouse inherits entire estate.

   2. Spouse and one or more descendants—Spouse takes one-third (elective, marital share) and children share remaining two-thirds equally.

      a. In some states, if there is only one child, the spouse takes one-half and the child one-half.

      b. If a child predeceased the decedent, his or her children share equally the share his or her parent would have taken (*per stirpes*).

      c. A statute may also provide that a spouse is entitled to homestead, household and other allowances.

   3. Surviving children or descendants, but no surviving spouse—Children share equally and descendants of children, who died before the decedent, share *per stirpes*.

   4. No spouse or lineal descendants.

      a. Parents and/or siblings (and lineal descendants of deceased brothers and sisters *per stirpes*).

      b. Grandparents.

      c. Collateral heirs, such as aunts, uncles, nieces and nephews.

   5. If no relatives survive decedent, property escheats to the state or county.

III. Trusts.

   A. A trust is created when one person (the settlor) transfers legal title to property to another (the trustee) to administer the property (the *res* or *corpus*) for the benefit of another person or persons (the beneficiaries).

      1. The settlor must have an interest in the property that becomes the trust *corpus* and an intention to create a trust.

      2. The beneficiary must be an identified, existing natural person or entity.

      3. The trustee owes fiduciary duties to the beneficiaries.

   B. Express trust—Intentionally created by the settlor.

      1. *Inter vivos* trust.

      a. Comes into existence during the lifetime of the settlor.

      b. May be orally created unless subject to a provision of the statute of frauds.

  2. Testamentary trust.

      a. Comes into existence upon the death of the settlor.

      b. Formalities required for execution of a will must be complied with.

C. Implied trusts created by operation of law.

  1. Resulting trust—The intention of the settlor to create a trust is presumed.

  2. Constructive trust may be imposed as a remedy, without regard to the intention of the parties, in order to prevent unjust enrichment.

IV. Estate administration.

A. The personal representative (the executor or appointed administrator) is supervised by the court (usually a probate court).

  1. Collects and preserves the decedent's property.

  2. Receives and pays valid claims of creditors and taxes.

  3. Required to post a bond to insure the honest and faithful performance of his or her duties.

  4. Distributes the estate pursuant to court order.

B. Some statutes may permit distribution of assets of a decedent without probate proceedings, and/or in accordance with family settlement agreements.

V. Federal and state taxation of estates and inheritances.

FILL-IN QUESTIONS

1. A personal representative of a decedent is referred to as an _____ if he or she has been named by the decedent in a properly executed and witnessed _____. If a personal representative is appointed by a _____ court to settle the affairs of a decedent, he or she is referred to as an _____ _____.

2. In general, in order to be effective, a will, executed by one having _____ capacity, must be _____ _____.

3. Statutes of descent and distribution provide for inheritance of property if a decedent _____ .
    Such statutes usually provide that, if a decedent died leaving a spouse and children, the _____ may take an elective one-third share and the remaining share is divided _____ . Grandchildren, whose parents died before the decedent, divide _____ .

4. An express trust is created when a person (_____) transfers title to real property or personal property to another person (_____) for the benefit of _____ .

5. An *inter vivos* trust is a trust that comes into existence _____ _____ ; a testamentary trust is one that comes into existence _____ _____ of the settlor and will be effective if the settlor has complied with statutes _____ .

MULTIPLE CHOICE QUESTIONS

Questions 1 and 2 are based on the following fact situation: At the time of his death, John Doe, a widower, was the owner of a farm, $20,000 worth of General Motors Corporation stock and $30,000 worth of miscellaneous personal property. His properly executed and witnessed will provided that the farm be left to his only son, the stock in General Motors to his only daughter, and, after payment of taxes and debts, the remaining personal property be divided equally between the son and daughter.

1. Upon John Doe's death:
    a. title to the farm vested in John Doe's son.
    b. title to the stock vested in John Doe's daughter.
    c. title to the miscellaneous personal property vested in an executor appointed by a court to administer the estate, if none was named in the will by John Doe.
    d. title to the miscellaneous personal property vested in the testator, named in the will by John Doe, to administer the estate.

2. The gift:
    a. of the farm to the son was a general bequest.
    b. of the stock to the daughter was a general bequest.
    c. of the stock to the daughter was a specific devise.
    d. of the miscellaneous personal property was a general bequest.

Questions 3 and 4 are based on the following fact situation: In 1970 Mary executed a will which provided that, upon her death, her estate was to be equally divided among her children, August, April and May. Mary died in 1980.

3. If Mary:
    a. was declared judicially insane in 1975, the will was revoked by operation of law.
    b. was divorced from her husband in 1976, the will was revoked by operation of law.
    c. crossed out May's name in the will in 1978, Mary has effectively amended the will.

    d. signed a writing in 1975, stating that her daughter, June, was to share in her estate with her other children, in the presence of two neighbors, who witnessed the writing, Mary has made an effective codicil.

4. Mary's husband:
    a. is not entitled to any share in her estate if he married Mary in 1977.
    b. is not entitled to any share in her estate if they were separated in 1978.
    c. is entitled to take his statutory intestate share.
    d. is entitled to share equally with the named children.

Questions 5, 6 and 7 are based on the following fact situation: H, the husband of W, and father of A and B, died without leaving a will. Before the death of H, H's son, S, who had two children, and H's daughter, D, who had four children, died.

5. Under the statutes of descent and distribution in most states:
    a. W inherits the entire estate.
    b. W takes a life estate in all of H's property.
    c. W, A and B share the entire estate equally.
    d. W may renounce her right to take any share in H's estate.

6. After W has taken her elective share, the rest of the estate is divided:
    a. equally among A and B.
    b. A takes a one-quarter share, B takes a one-quarter share, D's four children and S's two children share equally in the remaining one-half.
    c. A takes a one-quarter share, B takes a one-quarter share, D's children share D's one-quarter share equally and S's children share S's one-quarter share equally.
    d. equally among A, B and the six grandchildren.

7. Assume that H left $18,000 worth of property that has all been reduced to cash. The distribution will be as follows:
    a. W receives $6,000; A receives $3,000; B receives $3,000; S's two children each receive $1,500; D's children each receive $750.
    b. W receives $6,000; A receives $3,000; B receives $3,000; S's children each receive $1,000; D's children each receive $1,000.
    c. W receives $6,000 and A, B, each of S's children and each of D's children receive $1,500.
    d. W, A, B, S's children and D's children each receive $2,000.

8. In her will, Settling conveyed real property to the Orphans' Foundation, a charitable organization, for use in benefiting orphans.
    a. If the Orphans' Foundation has ceased to exist but other similar organizations exist, the property will pass to Settling's heirs.
    b. The Orphans' Foundation holds legal and equitable title to the property.
    c. A resulting trust arises for the benefit of orphans.
    d. The Orphans' Foundation is a fiduciary and has power to sell the property in order to carry out the purposes of the trust.

9. A person has acquired property under circumstances which make it unjust for him to retain it.
    a. An implied resulting trust will arise by operati: of law.
    b. A constructive trust may be imposed by a court.
    c. The rule against perpetuities will be applied by a court.
    d. A probate court will administer the trust.

ANSWER SECTION

CHAPTER 1

Fill-In Questions

1. judges in deciding cases based on general principles of law established in previously decided cases.
2. private law; public law.
3. the federal and state constitutions, statutes enacted by the United States Congress, state legislative bodies, local ordinances, administrative agency rules and case law.

Multiple Choice Questions

1. c
2. b
3. d
4. e
5. d
6. b
7. b
8. a

CHAPTER 2

Fill-In Questions

1. jurisdiction.
2. general; United States District Court; United States Supreme Court or Patent Court or Court of Claims or Bankruptcy Court or Customs Court, etc.; special.
3. appellate; the Supreme Court or the Circuit Court of Appeals; District Court.
4. plaintiff; filing a complaint with the clerk of the court and serving a copy with the summons on the defendant.
5. to dismiss; a deposition be taken.

Multiple Choice Questions

1. d
2. d
3. c
4. b
5. d
6. a

CHAPTER 3

Fill-In Questions

1. defendant breached a duty, that was owed, which breach of duty was the proximate cause of the injury incurred by the plaintiff.
2. person; property.
3. that the defendant has published false statements concerning the product or business of the plaintiff; malicious injury to business or combination to divert trade.
4. supervening or intervening, unforeseen force, assumption of the risk, contributory or comparative negligence. (Do you know whether or not the legislature or courts of the state in which you reside have adopted the doctrine of comparative negligence?)

Multiple Choice Questions

1. d
2. a
3. b
4. a
5. c
6. a
7. b

CHAPTER 4

Fill-In Questions

1. wrong; the state.
2. committed a specified wrongful act (or, in some cases, failed to perform a required act); purpose, knowledge and awareness, recklessness or negligence or implied.
3. defense.
4. unreasonable searches and seizures; cruel and unusual punishment and excessive bail or fine.
5. self incrimination and double jeopardy.
6. a speedy, public trial by jury and the right to be informed of the charges against him or her, to be confronted with the person accusing him or her of committing a crime, to subpoena witnesses and to the assistance of an attorney.

Multiple Choice Questions

1. b
2. b
3. c
4. a
5. c
6. d

CHAPTER 5

Fill-In Questions

1. two or more.
2. an agreement by two or more competent parties, whose apparent assent to the same terms is real and genuine, supported by valid, legal consideration, in the form required by law (if one is required) and having a legal purpose and subject matter.
3. an express; an implied-in-fact.
4. bilateral; performance of or forbearance from an act.
5. formal; informal; informal contracts.

Multiple Choice Questions

1.	c	6.	d
2.	c	7.	b
3.	c	8.	d
4.	a	9.	c
5.	b	10.	b

CHAPTER 6

Fill-In Questions

1. an offer; accepts.
2. identification of parties, the sum of money being borrowed, personal services to be performed or real or personal property being sold. (Note—Under certain circumstances the price and quantity need not be specified with certainty if a method is provided by which they can be made certain.)
3. revocation.
4. rejection or counteroffer.
5. one of the parties has died or been adjudicated incompetent, the subject matter has been destroyed, a statute has been enacted which makes performance of the contract illegal or lapse of time.

Multiple Choice Questions

1.	a	6.	b
2.	c	7.	b
3.	c	8.	d
4.	c	9.	b
5.	a	10.	d

CHAPTER 7

Fill-In Questions

1. benefit; detriment.
2. mature, liquidated, undisputed
3. illusory; consideration; consideration; requirements.
4. modifications of existing contracts under Sec. 2-209 of the U.C.C.; a signed writing which complies with the Model Written Obligations Act or other state statute; a new promise to pay a debt barred by the statute of limitations or a debt discharged in bankruptcy.

Multiple Choice Questions

1.	a	7.	a
2.	c	8.	c
3.	d	9.	b
4.	b	10.	c
5.	c	11.	d
6.	d	12.	a

CHAPTER 8

Fill-In Questions

1. voidable; disaffirm, avoid or rescind.
2. disaffirm, avoid or rescind.
3. food, shelter, clothing, necessary medical or dental care; the reasonable value.
4. majority.
5. he or she cannot appreciate, understand or comprehend the nature and effect of a particular transaction; void.

Multiple Choice Questions

1.	c	6.	c
2.	a	7.	d
3.	c	8.	d
4.	d	9.	a
5.	b	10.	b

CHAPTER 9

Fill-In Questions

1. statutes; public policy.
2. Usury.
3. $0 in those states which treat the entire transaction as tainted with illegality because of the usurious interest. $100 in those states which treat only the interest as being illegal because of usury. $110 in those states which treat only the excess interest as being usurious.
4. wagering or gambling; transferring or shifting.
5. restraint of trade; reasonable.

Multiple Choice Questions

1. a
2. a
3. d
4. d
5. b
6. c
7. a
8. c

CHAPTER 10

Fill-In Questions

1. disaffirm or avoid; voidable.
2. execution; inducement.
3. mutual or bilateral; unilateral.
4. undue influence.

Multiple Choice Questions

1.	b	7.	d
2.	c	8.	c
3.	b	9.	b
4.	a	10.	a
5.	d	11.	a
6.	a		

CHAPTER 11

Fill-In Questions

1. not performable within one year; to answer for the debt, default or miscarriage of another; for the sale of an interest in real property; for the sale of goods when the price is $500 or more; for the sale of securities; for the sale of miscellaneous personal property when the price is greater than $5000; in consideration of marriage; of an administrator or executor to pay a debt of the estate out of his own property.
2. to pay the debt or answer for the miscarriage or obligation of another; the leading object or main purpose was to benefit the promisor.
3. 500.
4. inadmissible.
5. void; voidable.
6. the meaning of ambiguous or vague terms; a modification; that the contract was void or voidable or otherwise terminated; that the writing was incomplete; gross errors contained in the writing.

Multiple Choice Questions

1.	c	6.	c
2.	d	7.	c
3.	c	8.	b
4.	a	9.	a
5.	a		

CHAPTER 12

Fill-In Questions

1. donee; creditor; incidental.
2. assignment; assignor; assignee.
3. delegated.

Multiple Choice Questions

1. d
2. b
3. a
4. c
5. c
6. c
7. a
8. c
9. c

CHAPTER 13

Fill-In Questions

1. precedent; subsequent.
2. full, complete performance.
3. mutual rescission, substituted agreement; novation.
4. the statute of limitations has run or a decree in bankruptcy has been issued.
5. impossibility.

Multiple Choice Questions

1. c
2. d
3. d
4. a
5. c
6. b
7. a
8. d

CHAPTER 14

Fill-In Questions

1. compensatory money.
2. the contract price; the market price.
3. liquidated damages; is not excessive but bears a reasonable relationship to the foreseeable, expected damages that would be incurred if the contract were breached.
4. Rescission and restitution.
5. rescission and restitution, specific performance, injunction, reformation and quasi contract; inadequate.

Multiple Choice Questions

1. b   6. b
2. c   7. d
3. a   8. c
4. c   9. d
5. a

CHAPTER 15

Fill-In Questions

1. rights and interests; capable of being possessed.
2. occupation, gift, accession, confusion, inheritance and creation.
3. donative intent, delivery by donor; acceptance by donee.
4. inadvertently left or misplaced it; accidentally and involuntarily left it.

Multiple Choice Questions

1. a
2. a
3. a
4. c
5. d
6. d
7. a
8. c
9. c

CHAPTER 16

Fill-In Questions

1. bailor; personal; bailee; return.
2. constructively; constructive.
3. great; slight; bailments for mutual benefit; ordinary.

Multiple Choice Questions

1. c
2. d
3. a
4. b
5. b
6. c
7. b
8. a
9. a
10. c

CHAPTER 17

Fill-In Questions

1. transfer; goods or tangible personal property; price.
2. merchants; deal in goods of the kind involved in the sales transaction.
3. price; quantity.
4. new consideration; the contract, as modified, provided for the sale of goods for a price of $500 or more.

Multiple Choice Questions

1. b
2. d
3. d
4. d
5. c
6. a
7. a
8. b
9. d

CHAPTER 18

Fill-In Questions

1. a contract to sell goods in the future.
2. the sales contract is formed; marked, shipped.
3. on approval; or return.
4. of contracting; the buyer receives the goods from the merchant.
5. shipment; delivered to the carrier; an insurable interest.

Multiple Choice Questions

1. c
2. b
3. a
4. b
5. a

CHAPTER 19

Fill-In Questions

1. that conform to the contract; pay for; concurrent.
2. put the goods into the possession of the carrier.
3. delivered to the dock "alongside" of the ship; unloaded.
4. insurance during transit; transportation charges or freight charges; cost of the goods and transportation charges or freight charges; buyer or purchaser or consignee.
5. accept all of the goods; reject all of the goods; accept some of the goods and reject others that do not conform to the contract.
6. received by the buyer; any other commercially acceptable method.

Multiple Choice Questions

1. d
2. b
3. c
4. b
5. a
6. c
7. b
8. a

CHAPTER 20

Fill-In Questions

1. free from any liens, security interests or other encumbrances; free from adverse claims based on patents, trademark, trade name, copyright, etc., infringement.
2. express; factual.
3. merchantable; fit for the particular purpose intended.
4. reasonably fit for the normal or ordinary purpose for which such goods are usually used; of average or usual quality existing in the market; merchantability.
5. fitness for a particular purpose; express; express; implied warranty of merchantability or title.

Multiple Choice Questions

1.	c	6.	c
2.	b	7.	d
3.	b	8.	a
4.	b	9.	c
5.	a		

CHAPTER 21

Fill-In Questions

1. warranty; negligent.
2. express warranty; reasonably relied upon the representation; injured.
3. privity of contract; negligence; failed to exercise reasonable care.
4. third party beneficiary; use, consume or be affected.
5. the defect resulted in the product being unreasonably dangerous, while in ordinary use, and that the defect was the proximate cause of his or her injury.

Multiple Choice Questions

1. a
2. d
3. c
4. c
5. b
6. b
7. d

CHAPTER 22

Fill-In Questions

1. withhold delivery of the goods; stop delivery of the goods in the possession of a bailee.
2. recover the purchase price; sue for damages; identify the goods to the contract; resell goods, of which he or she rightfully has possession; cancel the contract.
3. reclaim the goods from the buyer.
4. recover identified goods, if the seller becomes insolvent (within ten days after receiving first payment); effect cover by contracting for the purchase of substitute goods; replevin the goods; obtain an order for specific performance; sue for damages; cancel the contract; resell properly rejected goods in his or her possession, if he or she had a security interest in the goods.

Multiple Choice Questions

1. a
2. c
3. d
4. a
5. b

CHAPTER 23

Fill-In Questions

1. note; maker; John Jones; demand or sight.
2. draft; David Duke; Ben Beier; bearer; time.

Multiple Choice Questions

1. d
2. c
3. c
4. a
5. a

CHAPTER 24

Fill-In Questions

1. It is in writing, signed by the drawer of the draft, contains an unconditional order to pay a sum certain in money on demand; it is not payable to the order of a named payee or bearer.
2. It is in writing, signed by the maker of the note, to pay a sum certain in money at a definite fixed future time, to the order of a named payee; single, unconditional promise to pay, because payment will depend on the existence and sufficiency of a particular source of funds.
3. It is in writing, signed by the maker, containing a single, absolute promise to pay a sum certain in money, to a named payee, and payable to the order of the payee; it is not payable on demand or at a definite fixed or determinable future time.

Multiple Choice Questions

1. a
2. d
3. a
4. d
5. c
6. b
7. d
8. a
9. b
10. b

CHAPTER 25

Fill-In Questions

1. s/s Howard How, Pay to the order of Tom Trustee for the benefit of Benny Fishiary.
2. s/s Tom Trustee, as trustee for Benny Fishiary.
3. s/s Henry Hunt, for deposit only (or for collection).

Multiple Choice Questions

1. b   6. b
2. d   7. b
3. c   8. a
4. c   9. a
5. b   10. a

CHAPTER 26

Fill-In Questions

1. bearer; in blank.
2. in good faith, for value; overdue; dishonored; any defenses against it.
3. actually given or performed; performance of services, delivery or sale of property or payment of money; under legal process; not in the ordinary course of business.
4. holder; there are defenses against the instrument or that there are claims to it.

Multiple Choice Questions

1. d
2. b
3. a
4. b
5. a
6. c

CHAPTER 27

Fill-In Questions

1. signature; the contract that is implied in the negotiable instrument.
2. the maker of a note and the acceptor of a draft; the drawer of a draft, unqualified indorsers and accommodation parties.
3. notice of dishonor.
4. good title; no knowledge that the signature of the maker or drawer is not authorized; the instrument has not been materially altered.
5. breach of contract, lack or failure of consideration, lack of real, genuine assent (fraud in the inducement, misrepresentation, mistake, undue influence, duress that is not extreme), illegality or incapacity, which renders a contract voidable (rather than void), discharge by payment or other satisfaction or discharge by cancellation or renunciation when the instrument is not removed from circulation or some evidence of the discharge indicated on the instrument itself; unauthorized completion of an incomplete instrument, conditional delivery or nondelivery; any holder, including a holder in due course.

Multiple Choice Questions

1. a
2. d
3. b
4. a
5. c
6. c
7. d
8. b
9. b

CHAPTER 28

Fill-In Questions

1. customer; payor.
2. cashier's check; certified check.
3. the drawer; a holder; prior indorsers.
4. (2) a stale check (an uncertified check dated more than six months before); (3) the depositor has died or become otherwise incompetent; (4) the depositor has given the bank a stop payment order; (5) there is a forgery, alteration or irregularity on the instrument.

Multiple Choice Questions

1. b
2. a
3. c
4. b
5. a
6. d

CHAPTER 29

Fill-In Questions

1. security interest; secured party.
2. collateral.
3. consumer goods; inventory.
4. attached; perfected.
5. rights in the collateral; given value.

Multiple Choice Questions

1. b
2. a
3. c
4. d
5. c
6. d

CHAPTER 30

Fill-In Questions

1. after acquired property of the debtor; future advances to be given by the secured party.
2. persons who have perfected their security interests in the same collateral or who have become lien creditors or who have purchased the collateral from the debtor in the ordinary course of business.
3. in the ordinary course of business. (See Chapter 31 for information dealing with possessory liens.)
4. whose security interest attached first or the one who perfected first.
5. dispose of it by sale or other commercially reasonable means and apply the proceeds to the satisfaction of the underlying obligation.

Multiple Choice Questions

1. c
2. b
3. d
4. d
5. b
6. a

CHAPTER 31

Fill-In Questions

1. surety; guarantor.
2. mechanic's.
3. artisan's.
4. directing the sheriff to seize specified property of the debtor, sell it and deliver the proceeds to the judgment creditor.
5. Garnishment.
6. mortgagor/debtor.
7. the family home and furniture or household furnishings; pensions on account of military service and a proportion of disposable income paid as wages.

Multiple Choice Questions

1. d   5. d
2. b   6. a
3. c   7. d
4. a

CHAPTER 32

Fill-In Questions

1. bankruptcy; equity.
2. firm, association, partnership or corporation; $5,000; involuntary liquidation.
3. the bankruptcy court; six months.
4. the debtor.
5. that creditor being favored over other creditors; the trustee of the debtor's estate.
6. reorganization; an adjustment of debts.

Multiple Choice Questions

1. c
2. d
3. a
4. a
5. d

CHAPTER 33

Fill-In Questions

1. employee or servant; agent.
2. independent contractor.
3. ratification, estoppel or operation of law.
4. coupled with an interest.
5. revoking; the agency was an agency at will (not created for a stated period of time or purpose) or for cause.
6. the bankruptcy of the principal, impossibility (destruction of the subject matter, outbreak of war, change in law making the agency illegal or unforeseen circumstances).

Multiple Choice Questions

1. c
2. d
3. a
4. c
5. b
6. b
7. c
8. d
9. c
10. d

CHAPTER 34

Fill-In Questions

1. follow lawful instructions without deviation, use reasonable skills and diligence in acting on behalf of his principal and use special skills which he or she possesses, relating to the agency.
2. loyally, in good faith in furthering the interests of his or her principal, without benefiting himself or herself or a third person in conflict with the interests of his or her principal; voidable.
3. reasonable compensation for his or her services.
4. indemnification; indemnification.

Multiple Choice Questions

1. a
2. b
3. d
4. c
5. b
6. b

CHAPTER 35

Fill-In Questions

1. scope of authority.
2. express; generally known custom or usage or an emergency situation.
3. ratified; not; breach of an implied warranty of authority.
4. torts; the scope of their authority or employment in furtherance of the business of the superior.

Multiple Choice Questions

1. d
2. c
3. c
4. a
5. a
6. a
7. b
8. c
9. a
10. b

CHAPTER 37

Fill-In Questions

1. an entity; an aggregate of its individual members or partners.
2. express agreement; contribute capital or make joint investments, are co-owners of property that is used for partnership purposes and share profits of the business.
3. possess partnership property for partnership purposes.
4. a tenant in partnership.
5. act of the parties or partners.
6. death of a partner, its bankruptcy or that of a partner or illegality.
7. its winding up by the partners (or liquidation by distribution of partnership property in accordance with law).

Multiple Choice Questions

1. a
2. b
3. a
4. c
5. a
6. a
7. d
8. a
9. c
10. a

Solutions for 4, 5 and 6:

4. The amount that is due = $145,000 owed to creditors + $10,000, return of capital to P + $5,000, return of capital to Q = $160,000.

5. The outside creditors get paid in full. $100,000 is available from the partnership assets and the deficiency of $60,000 is theoretically met by equal contributions from P and Q. Of this, $45,000 is paid to creditors and the balance to P and Q.

6. Each partner's share of the total firm deficiency of $60,000 is half, or $30,000. Q, however, only has $5,000 of personal assets that can be reached by creditors of the partnership under the principle of marshalling of assets. The creditors can reach up to $50,000 of P's personal assets but only need $40,000 to satisfy claims of the $45,000 deficiency.

CHAPTER 38

Fill-In Questions

1. manage the affairs of the partnership.
2. change the scope or nature of the partnership business; alter the capital structure; admit new partners; assign partnership property for the benefit of creditors; dispose of the partnership goodwill; confess judgment; submit a dispute, involving the partnership, to arbitration; or undertake any act that would make the further conduct of the partnership business impossible.
3. his or her actual or apparent authority or the co-partners ratified the contract.
4. buy and sell goods of the kind in which the partnership regularly deals, give warranties, borrow money and issue and negotiate commercial paper on behalf of the other partners.
5. jointly; jointly and severally.

Multiple Choice Questions

1.	b	4.	b
2.	d	5.	a
3.	c	6.	b

CHAPTER 39

Fill-In Questions

1. the partnership name, its duration, the nature of its business, the location of its place of business, the names and addresses of members, the capital contribution of limited partners and their share of profits and other compensation, methods for changes in membership and subsequent continuation of the business; signed by the members of the partnership; filed.
2. his or her capital contribution.
3. the limited partner participated in management or his or her surname is used in the name of the firm.
4. dies, retires, withdraws or is expelled for cause, becomes insane or bankrupt, unless otherwise provided in its certificate or unless the other members consent to its continuation; The death, retirement or bankruptcy (unless it results in the bankruptcy of the firm).

Multiple Choice Questions

1.	c	4.	a
2.	c	5.	a
3.	b		

CHAPTER 40

Fill-In Questions

1. does not limit the application of the statutory provision to natural persons.
2. shareholders are not personally liable for obligations of the corporation; shareholders do not have the right to possess corporate property (they are not tenants in partnership, tenants in common or joint tenants with other shareholders with respect to corporate property); death of a shareholder does not dissolve the corporation; shareholders are not representatives of the corporation nor agents for other shareholders nor fiduciaries of the corporation or the other shareholders.
3. public; private.
4. *de jure; de facto;* the state.

Multiple Choice Questions

1. c
2. d
3. a
4. d
5. a
6. d

CHAPTER 41

Fill-In Questions

1. Statutory, general; the power to have and use a corporate seal; to have perpetual existence; to enter into contracts; to sue and be sued; to issue shares of stock; to borrow and lend money; to acquire by purchase or otherwise real and personal property; to dispose of by sale or otherwise real or personal property; to conduct its business and carry on its operations; to elect or appoint officers and agents and define their duties and fix their compensation; to make and alter by-laws, not inconsistent with its charter (articles or certificate of incorporation) or the laws of the state of incorporation; to transact lawful business.
2. *ultra vires;* cannot assert or raise.
3. legal; equitable.
4. Shareholders; directors.
5. corporation (not the shareholders).

Multiple Choice Questions

1. a
2. b
3. c
4. c
5. c
6. a

CHAPTER 42

Fill-In Questions

1. a certificate or license to do business; registered office and registered agent.
2. certificate or license to do business as a foreign corporation.

Multiple Choice Questions

1. c
2. b

CHAPTER 43

Fill-In Questions

1. shares of stock; bonds and debentures; dividends.
2. bonds; debentures.
3. rights to dividends; liquidation rights.
4. Blue Sky Laws; Securities Act of 1933; Securities Exchange Act of 1934; Securities and Exchange Commission (SEC); interstate commerce; mails.

Multiple Choice Questions

1. b
2. c
3. a
4. d
5. c
6. d

CHAPTER 44

Fill-In Questions

1. inspect the books and records of the corporation (and to receive notice of special meetings of the board of directors); the directors convened as a board.
2. his or her dissent is entered in the minutes of the meeting of the board of directors or a written dissent filed with the minutes; poor business judgment; relating to the corporation, not brought by or on behalf of the corporation.
3. unpaid stock subscriptions; improperly or illegally declared dividends, when they had knowledge thereof; deficiencies caused by failure to pay satisfactory consideration for shares of stock issued by the corporation.
4. property; services actually performed.
5. preemptive rights.

Multiple Choice Questions

1.	d	5.	c
2.	a	6.	d
3.	c	7.	b
4.	a		

CHAPTER 45

Fill-In Questions

1. cease to exist and disappear; the assets of A and B Corporations; the liabilities, debts and obligations of A and B Corporations; shares of C Corporation stock.
2. cease to exist and disappear; a new corporation, which comes into existence because of the consolidation.
3. shareholder approval; not cease; the character of the corporation's assets and business.
4. shareholders and creditors of the corporation; cannot.
5. the fair market value of his or her shares; an appraisal of the fair market value of his or her shares. (The court may appoint appraisers "to receive evidence and recommend a decision on the question of fair market value." MBCA Sec. 81.)

Multiple Choice Questions

1. b
2. c
3. a
4. c
5. c
6. d

CHAPTER 47

Fill-In Questions

1. judicial interpretation of statutory regulations.
2. arbitrary, capricious, not supported by the record or contrary to law.
3. ministerial; investigatory; rule making.
4. profits, advertising, quotas, licensing, allocation rights, standards and disclosures; use of certain materials and processes in production.
5. consumer products, working conditions and employment.
6. utilities, some carriers, those engaged in communications, inventors and authors.

Multiple Choice Questions

1.	d	3.	a
2.	d	4.	c

CHAPTER 48

Multiple Choice Questions

1. a
2. d

CHAPTER 50

Fill-In Questions

1. unreasonable, general; reasonable, partial, ancillary.
2. restraint of interstate or foreign trade or commerce.
3. criminal or civil (equitable); treble damages; civil.
4. *per se*; price fixing (setting minimum or maximum prices), horizontal market division (dividing a market among competitors), agreements limiting production or establishing quotas, joint refusals to deal or coercive group boycotts.

Multiple Choice Questions

1.	d	4.	b
2.	c	5.	a
3.	a		

CHAPTER 51

Fill-In Questions

1. cease and desist; initiate investigations and promulgate interpretative rules, policy statements and regulations.
2. monopolizes or attempts to monopolize interstate commerce; price discrimination, exclusive dealings and tying contracts and acquisition of stock or assets of another corporation.
3. horizontal; anticompetitive (or to lessen competition or tend to create a monopoly).
4. a vertical, illegal.

Multiple Choice Questions

1. b
2. d
3. b
4. c
5. a
6. c

CHAPTER 52

Fill-In Questions

1. growing on or affixed to the land or contained above or below the surface of the land.
2. affixed to the real property; trade fixtures.
3. estates; estates in fee or life estates (or freehold estates); estates less than freehold or leaseholds.
4. landlord; tenant, from whom the sublease was obtained; original tenant (or lessee).
5. joint tenants; B, the surviving joint tenant; tenancy by the entirety.
6. tenancy in common.
7. delivery of a deed of conveyance; quitclaim; clouds or defects.

Multiple Choice Questions

1. c
2. d
3. a
4. a
5. d
6. b

CHAPTER 53

Fill-In Questions

1. simple absolute.
2. possibility of reverter; contingent remainder.
3. contingent remainder.
4. possibility of reverter; possibility of reverter.
5. contingent remainder.
6. reversion; vested remainder.
7. reversion; reversion.
8. vested remainder.
9. power of termination or entry; executory interest.
10. an easement; profit; nonpossessory; easements or profits appurtenant.
11. a restrictive convenant running with the land; equitable servitude.

Multiple Choice Questions

1. a   3. d
2. c   4. c

CHAPTER 54

Fill-In Questions

1. creating; transferring and allocating.
2. insurable; incur a financial or pecuniary loss if the property is damaged or destroyed.
3. insurable; the loss is incurred.
4. insurable; incur a pecuniary of financial detriment or loss if that person dies.
5. insurable; the insurance policy was obtained.

Multiple Choice Questions

1. b   4. b
2. c   5. a
3. b   6. a
        Solution:

$$\text{Loss} \times \frac{\text{Amount of Insurance Carried}}{\text{Amount of Insurance Required}} = \text{Amount of Recovery}$$

$$\$80,000 + \$100,000 \times \frac{\$600,000}{90\%(\$900,000 + \$100,000)}$$

$$\$180,000 \times \frac{2}{3} = \$120,000.$$

CHAPTER 55

Fill-In Questions

1.   executor or executrix; will; probate; administrator or administratrix.
2.   testamentary; in writing, signed by the testator or testatrix, attested by two or more witnesses (who may be required to be disinterested, to witness the signing of the will by the testator and to sign in the presence of each other) and, in some states, published and declared by the testator to be his or her last will and testament.
3.   failed to execute a valid will or to provide for the disposition of some property in his or her will; spouse; equally among the children; equally the share their parent would have received (*per stirpes*).
4.   the settlor; the trustee; another person, a beneficiary, or other persons, beneficiaries.
5.   during the lifetime of the settlor; upon the death; prescribing formalities for the execution of wills.

Multiple Choice Questions

1.   a
2.   d
3.   d
4.   c
5.   d
6.   c
7.   a
8.   d
9.   b